An Introduction to Object Relations

Lavinia Gomez

FREE ASSOCIATION BOOKS/LONDON

First published in 1997 by
FREE ASSOCIATION BOOKS
57 Warren Street, London W1P 5PA

Reprinted 1998

A CIP catalogue record for this book is available
from the British Library

ISBN 1 85342 347 0 pbk

Produced for Free Association Books Ltd by
Chase Production Services, Chadlington, OX7 3LN
Printed in the EC by J.W. Arrowsmith Ltd, Bristol

AN INTRODUCTION TO OBJECT RELATIONS

FOR MADDIE AND NICK, JOSH AND JOE

CONTENTS

ACKNOWLEDGEMENTS

Very many people have given help and encouragement during the writing of this book. I would first of all like to thank Gill Davies, of Free Association Books, whose patient and clear guidance and personal interest and encouragement made the whole process far less daunting and much more enjoyable. Tim Bartlett, of New York University Press, has also been consistently helpful and constructive.

Like all teachers, I have learned a great deal from the students of psychotherapy and counselling with whom I have worked. Their lively and challenging questions and arguments have helped me clarify my thinking as nothing else could. So also, in a different way, have all those who have shared their worlds with me in therapy and supervision, where the roots of understanding grow in mutual experience. Those people whose personal experience is used as illustrative material have made a special contribution. All such material is used with permission, apart from the brief vignettes which are based on amalgamations rather than single individuals. Identifying details have been changed.

David Dyke, Catherine Leder, Kristiane Preisinger and Adella Shapiro all offered useful comments on the text, and Professor John Balint and Professor André Haynal made specific contributions to the chapter on Michael Balint. I am especially appreciative of the careful and critical reading of the whole text carried out by Anthea Gomez. While all shortcomings remain my responsibility, her detailed comments led to substantial improvement and her continued enthusiasm was always heartening.

Thanks, finally, to Cathy and Chris Gomez, who make sure I remember always that things other than work are important; and to David Smart, whose lucid mind, warm encouragement and reliable cooking all helped the writing process along.

INTRODUCTION

The purpose of this book is to introduce the world of Object Relations to students of psychotherapy and counselling of all theoretical approaches, as well as to other interested people. It is divided into two parts: theory and application. The first part opens with a summary of Freudian theory, the base from which Object Relations grew. It goes on to chart the historical development of Object Relations through the varying perspectives of its major founding contributors. The second part discusses practical and theoretical questions which arise in the application of an Object Relations approach. A chapter on practice explores the use of Object Relations ideas and attitudes in psychotherapy and counselling of all orientations, and more broadly in the helping professions and beyond. The next chapter, 'Working with Difference and Diversity', considers the limitations of Object Relations' classic texts and asks what Object Relations has to offer in the political and cultural context of today. The final chapter looks beneath the surface of Object Relations theories to question the assumptions on which they are built.

What is Object Relations?

Object Relations was originally a British development of Freudian psychoanalytic theory. Rather than seeing the human being as a system of biological drives, Object Relations places relationship at the heart of what it is to be human.

The term 'object' does not refer to an inanimate thing, but is a carry-over from the Freudian idea of the target, or object, of the instinct. In Object Relations terms it is used in the philosophical sense of the distinction between subject and object. Our need for others is the need of an experiencing 'I' for another experiencing 'I' to make contact with. 'Part-object' means a part or aspect of a person. We may relate to a body part rather than a complete person: the infant to the mother's breast, the pornographer to genitals; or to a person as a function rather than a complete human being such as dentist, waiter or tax inspector; or to an aspect of the person, seeing them solely as the clever or the irritating person, or the one who might lend me money. 'Object' can also include, though secondarily, a non-human thing or idea which is subjectively important through its human associations, such as home, art, politics.

Object Relations sees the self as a personal sphere which develops and exists within a context of relationship, and is itself made up of internal relationships between different aspects of the person. Object Relations theories rest on the belief that the human being is essentially social: our need for contact with others is primary, and cannot be explained in terms of other needs or reduced to something more basic.

An Object Relations framework places the human being in a dual world of external and internal relationship. Each of these worlds affects the other. Our inner world is a changing dynamic process, with some more fixed and some more fluid patterns, both conscious and unconscious. These dynamics influence how we experience external reality and are also themselves influenced by our experience of external reality. We are thus fairly stable beings, with enduring structures and personality styles; but these can be modified or changed to some extent through our experience of life, particularly our experiences in relationship.

Object Relations does not have a significant transpersonal or spiritual element, reflecting its emergence from Freudian rather than Jungian roots. Like Freudian theory, it sees life as an inherently mixed experience, with distress and inner conflict being to some extent inevitable. Anxiety may be modified, mitigated or managed, but not eradicated.

OBJECT RELATIONS THEORISTS

The Object Relations tradition is not a systematic, sequential theoretical development, but rather a loose school of diverse and often conflicting perspectives which hold in common the basic premises of Object Relations: that the need for relationship is primary, and that the self is made up of internal relationships at both conscious and unconscious levels.

Object Relations began with Freud's own moves beyond his basic theoretical premises, moves which gathered momentum towards the end of his life. The title of Frank Sulloway's comprehensive study, *Freud: Biologist of the Mind* (1979), expresses Freud's starting point. His early psychology presents the mind as concrete, measurable and ultimately physiological. His later work, however, includes a more subjective view of the mind as the focus of experience, highlighting the importance of relationships with other people and also the internal relationships that make up the complexity of the person. Concepts such as the Oedipus Complex with its interpersonal structure, and the super-ego as an internalisation of the parent, demonstrate the addition of a relational perspective to his earlier view that emotional development was based on endogenous processes.

Klein was not a scientist and therefore easily discarded the biological approach she inherited from Freud. She used the same terms as Freud but with a different emphasis and meaning. Kleinian theory stems from a subjective base, in contrast to the physical scientific base of Freud's earlier work, and takes further the interpretative strand developed in his later concepts. She opened up the idea of an inner world in which each of us lives, interacting with and influencing the external world and our perception of it. She never appeared to appreciate the gulf she had opened up between her conception of psychoanalysis and Freud's: she certainly never made the breach between their viewpoints explicit, presenting her work as an unfolding of Freud's thought rather than a challenge to it.

Fairbairn, working at about the same time as Klein, did make his differences with Freud explicit. He argued that Freudian premises were out of tune with current scientific thinking. Redefining the purpose of life as relationship rather than the gratification of instincts, he proposed a model of the mind which did away entirely with Freud's biological foundations. His forthright disagreement with Freud's theoretical premises was one reason for his relative neglect in psychoanalytic circles.

Winnicott did less to change theory but more to communicate it. He is a poetic discursor on the mother–infant relationship, the treatment of psychosis, and the intersubjective experience of the self. A natural experimenter, he brought psychoanalytic concepts and attitudes to paediatrics, his other strand of work, creating his own ways of intervening therapeutically in all kinds of doctor–patient situations. Winnicott's work has a wide resonance because his professional world was so much more extensive than the confines of the psychoanalytic consulting room.

Balint also brought psychoanalysis to the medical world, underlining the importance of the doctor–patient relationship alongside the technology of medical treatment. In addition, his attention to the therapeutic relationship enabled him to develop an original perspective on early emotional development. His articulation of the problems inherent in working with more disturbed people offers insight and guidance to practitioners of all orientations today, as do his cautionary comments on the limitations of any psychological theory.

Guntrip did more than anyone to communicate Fairbairn's ideas, though at one remove. His compassionate evocations of the schizoid states, and the therapeutic process needed to address them, engender sympathy rather than judgement for the emotionally disturbed person. He hoped to bring together Fairbairn's theoretical rigour and Winnicott's empathic practice to create an integrated Object Relations psychotherapy.

Bowlby brought a modern scientific attitude and approach to Object Relations – which, incidentally, was far from welcomed by his colleagues. Turning to the new sciences of ethology and systems theory, he proposed his own synthesis of Freudian and Object Relations premises in the idea of inbuilt attachment behaviour. He devoted the major part of his professional life to research into attachment and loss rather than working directly with patients. None who have seen the films made by his colleagues, James and Joyce Robertson, can fail to be moved. *A Two-Year-Old goes to Hospital* (Robertson 1952) and *John, aged 17 Months* (Robertson and Robertson 1976) provide chilling evidence of the young child's absolute need for stable relationship. Bowlby's influence on social policy was direct and far-reaching. His Attachment Theory is a subsection within Object Relations with particular links to social arrangements.

OBJECT RELATIONS IN THE HELPING PROFESSIONS

Object Relations is a loosely integrated theory rather than a set approach. It offers a flexible and non-prescriptive framework for understanding and working with people, and has been brought together with widely differing therapeutic models and approaches. The American schools of Ego Psychology and Self Psychology are now becoming linked with Object Relations. Some Jungian approaches include Object Relations in their training and their thinking. The humanistic psychotherapies and the world of counselling have found in the Object Relations tradition enriching conceptual frameworks which deepen their understanding of what it is to be a person and what psychotherapy and counselling mean; and even the Behavioural school now acknowledges the importance of the therapeutic relationship.

Because relationship is at its centre, an Object Relations framework can only be used authentically. Its tools are openness and attention to one's own and others' feelings, thoughts, sensations, attitudes and hunches. Through its detailed focus on internal and interpersonal unconscious processes, Object Relations can help counsellors, psycho-therapists, teachers, social workers and others in the caring professions to understand and work with people who may otherwise seem unpredictable and baffling.

Freudian theory and Object Relations developed in the cultural context of Europe in the late nineteenth and twentieth centuries. Their ideas are therefore culture-bound both in their philosophical foundations and through their origins in the experience of white, mostly male, middle-class people. Ideas which resonate with a certain cultural group cannot automatically be applied universally, and there is an urgent need for wider influences to be brought to current theory and practice. Through working across cultural groupings, all practitioners may foster their awareness of difference and contribute to the modification and expansion of psychological theory.

OBJECT RELATIONS AND SOCIETY

Object Relations has had a revolutionary effect on Western societies in general, as well as in the small world of psychotherapy. Since the crucial importance of close and continuous relationship has been recognised, social policy has been transformed. Far greater efforts are now made to prevent the separation of young children from their parents. Hospitals are more likely to encourage than forbid parents to stay with their young children, and children in care are placed with foster families in preference to impersonal institutions. Refugee children remain with a parent whenever possible, rather than being 'rescued' and brought up in foreign institutions as happened in previous times. The closure of psychiatric hospitals has involved a partial recognition of the shortcomings of impersonal institutional care for vulnerable adults, and the key-worker system with its nurturance of relationship has spread throughout welfare work. We now see close relationship as a necessary context for human development, and an essential part of a satisfying life.

Part I

Theory

1

SIGMUND FREUD: THE BEGINNING OF PSYCHOANALYSIS

INTRODUCTION

Attitudes and ideas deriving from Freud's psychoanalysis permeate Western culture. Twentieth-century art, drama and film reflect his conflicted sense of the human condition, giving dramatic substance to his proclamation that we are driven by forces we know little about. The advertising industry exploits the powerful unconscious roots of sexuality and aggression as the tools of its trade. Freud's view that the personality evolves from intensely formative childhood experiences is the cornerstone of social and educational policies, with their focus on the family as the context for emotional development and the mediator of social mores.

Commonly used terms such as 'Freudian slip' demonstrate the extent to which his ideas have become incorporated into everyday life. Yet he is still a controversial figure, evoking responses from adulation to abhorrence with more balanced views comparatively thin on the ground. These strong opposing reactions appear to arise from his personality and style as well as from the unsettling nature of his subject.

It is not feasible in a single chapter to do more than sketch an outline of Freud's main ideas. This is therefore a brief introduction rather than a detailed study, with the main purpose of clarifying the base from which Object Relations developed. Readers may be interested to explore some of the historical, biographical and theoretical studies of Freud and nineteenth-century Vienna, and especially to read his own wide-ranging and influential writing for themselves.

Who then was this person who has had such far-reaching effects on the Western world?

FREUD'S LIFE

Sigismund Schlomo Freud was born in Austria in 1856 into a middle-class, non-religious Jewish family. His father Jacob was considerably older than his mother and had adult children from a previous marriage. Freud was the eldest of the eight children of this marriage and, with his intellectual brilliance and stalwart confidence, became the focus of the family's hopes of success and recognition in the gentile society in which they lived. He decided in adolescence that 'Sigmund' was preferable to his given names, and this was the name he used in adulthood.

Austria was embroiled in political and cultural turmoil, and Vienna, where Freud grew up, was at its epicentre (Taylor 1948; Schorske 1961). Social unrest was fuelled by economic disaster with a stock market crash in 1873. The Habsburgs, the longest-ruling royal family in Europe, were in the throes of self-destruction: Europe was rocked by the double suicide of Crown Prince Rudolf and his teenage mistress in 1889, and the Austro-Hungarian Empire disintegrated at the end of the First World War. Schnitzler and Schoenberg, Klimt and Kokoschka, Wittgenstein and Hitler all emerged from nineteenth-century Vienna. It is in this cauldron of revolution and transformation that we should locate Freud and his ideas.

Freud studied medicine, and an early example of his reckless creativity was his promotion of cocaine. He was dismayed by the addictive potential it proved to have after he had exacerbated the suffering of a dying friend by prescribing him cocaine in an attempt to cure his addiction to morphine. He moved away from research and into psychiatry so that he could support a family, marrying Martha Bernays in 1886 after a prolonged engagement. He chose the names of all six of their children after friends and historical figures he admired. He seems to have been an affectionate father; he found the death of his favourite daughter Sophie in 1920 desperately hard to encompass. The household included Martha's sister Minna, who with Martha and their daughter Anna encircled him to the end of his life.

Anti-Semitism was an increasingly virulent force in Freud's life. He tells of his childhood disappointment in his father's failure to stand up to a bullying Christian who threw his cap into the gutter (Gay 1988: 11–12). He vowed that he would not become a 'humble Jew', and he never went back on this decision. As an old man, suffering from cancer, his work banned and his books burned under the Nazi régime, he and his immediate family were allowed to leave Austria after eminent French and English friends had appealed on their behalf and paid a large sum of money. It proved impossible to bring his four elderly sisters out with the rest of the family, and they died in concentration camps. A condition for the Freuds' emigration was that Freud should sign a statement to the effect that he had been treated well and his scientific work respected. He agreed, with the stipulation that he could add his own endorsement. This read, with heavy irony: 'I can most highly recommend the Gestapo to everyone' (Gay 1988: 628).

Freud arrived in London in 1938, where he died a year later. The house in Hampstead where he and his family lived is now the Freud Museum. It offers a fascinating insight into the extensive Freud family and the formative years of psychoanalysis.

Perhaps we may assume that Freud's paradoxical beginnings deeply conditioned his life and his work. He was a member of an increasingly persecuted minority and also the centre of attention in his family. This dual position was repeated in his later life when he was buffered from hostile reactions to his ideas by the group of loyal colleagues surrounding him. They were expected to take their places as followers with himself as their head, an expectation which led inevitably to what Freud experienced as the defection of those in whom he had held the highest hopes. Talented and original thinkers such as Alfred Adler, Carl Jung and Wilhelm Reich left the Freud circle to develop their ideas with more independence than was possible from within it. Freud felt repeatedly betrayed by those in whom he had placed most trust, yet there were always more ready to take their place; and to the end of his life Freud maintained a dominance within psychoanalysis that was never successfully challenged.

Reading his work reveals, on the one hand, his scientific devotion to truth, with the insistence that his ideas are just a beginning, and, on the other, his arrogant assertions that only those who have been psychoanalysed have the right to criticise his work. The subjects he addressed were bound to lead to fear and revulsion. He studied perversion, neurosis and dreams; initially proposed that neurosis was caused by child sexual abuse; and suggested disquietingly that sexual life began in the cradle. The paradoxes and contradictions of Freud's life are embodied in his theories.

FREUD'S THEORIES

Overview

Most of the concepts that make up Freud's psychoanalysis were already present in his cultural milieu: they were not the original creations that he and his followers often made them out to be.

Infantile sexuality, bisexuality, the unconscious, the id, were all current ideas. Freud's achievement was not in their invention, but rather in treating seriously the unpopular and unprestigious subject of mental disturbance. He had the then revolutionary idea that the individual was not in total charge of the whole self.

Freudian psychoanalytic theory, developed as a totally new subject, is based on several assumptions:

- that mental life can be explained, thus challenging significantly the notion of free will;
- that the mind has a specific structure and follows intrinsic laws;
- that mental life is evolutionary and developmental. Following Darwin, Freud maintained that the adult mind can only be understood in terms of the formative experiences of the child;
- that the mind holds unconscious forces of tremendous intensity and power which, though not experienced directly, nevertheless have a far greater influence over human beings than they can recognise. Although the unconscious was not a new concept, Freud made it a cornerstone of psychoanalysis;
- that the mind is an aspect of the body. The biological facts of procreation and death comprise the basis of our mental as well as our physical life. Sexuality is the paradigm for all desire; infantile sexuality is primitive desire, rooted in the body.

Early Freudian theory is materialist, treating psychology as at root a physical matter. His earlier works treat the mind as though it were made up of concrete fixtures which can only be moved by force: Newtonian physics with a vengeance. Freud's formulations have a solidity reminiscent of heavy Victorian furniture: oak tables and mahogany sideboards, built to last, and movable only with effort and deliberation.

Freud was a dualist. His concepts typically come in pairs: ego and id, conscious and unconscious, Eros and the death instinct. It is a mode of experience which as individuals we either resonate with or do not comprehend. Freud himself recognised that some of his ideas stemmed from an emotional base. In *Civilisation and its Discontents*, he acknowledged the controversy provoked by his concept of a death instinct, 'but in the course of time', he wrote, '[these ideas] have gained such a hold upon me that I can no longer think in any other way' (Freud 1930, S.E. 21: 119).

Freud's pessimism arose from the conflict that his dualism implies. His view of life was uncompromising: that the good person and the worthwhile life result from the managing of conflict. We are divided beings, without underlying unity, bliss or harmony. The most we can do individually is to take responsibility for our destructiveness and minimise the damage that arises from it. Society is in inevitable opposition to the individual, who nevertheless depends on the group. Western civilisation in Freud's view demanded too high a price in repression, leading to neurosis in its members. He saw religion as self-delusion based on unrecognised infantile need. The purpose of psychoanalysis, he wrote to an imaginary patient, is not to promote happiness, 'but much will be gained if we succeed in transforming your hysterical misery into ordinary unhappiness' (Breuer and Freud 1895, S.E. 2: 305).

Although Freud hoped that psychoanalysis would be accepted as a science, its concepts were not derived from the natural scientific methods of experiment and verification. Instead, they arose from introspection and retrospection, in large part Freud's own. The Freudian picture of the infant and child was reconstructed primarily through the self-analysis to which Freud gave the last half-hour of his day, and only secondarily through his interpretations of his adult patients' experiences and memories. His theories are therefore subjectively rather than objectively based and illustrate how the mind experiences and understands itself, mediated by nineteenth-century Western scientific and social thought. This subjective base meant that Freud was continually developing and changing his ideas – sometimes within the space of a single paper.

Without the provisional acceptance of Freud's materialist, evolutionary, dualistic base, we shall not be in a position to understand or think about his theories. With these attitudes and perspectives in mind, we may proceed to a brief survey of the most important of Freud's ideas, as he formulated them towards the end of his life (Freud 1938a, S.E. 23).

In his later theories, Freud came to divide mental life in several ways. Structurally, he saw the mind as three entities: id, ego and super-ego. Dynamically, he saw mental life as proceeding on conscious and unconscious levels. The power driving mental life derived from two major instinct groups: Eros, or the life instinct, and Thanatos, usually known as the death instinct. Mental and emotional maturity is gained slowly, through developmental stages termed primary narcissism, auto-erotic, oral, anal, phallic and genital. The climax of early development arrives between the ages of about three and seven, in the drama of the Oedipus Complex during the phallic stage. It is from the resolution of this conflict that morality, mature sexuality and eventually the adult personality emerge after the hiatus of the latency stage.

A major hazard for English speakers lies in the translation of Freud's works by James Strachey. At a time when psychoanalysis was banned by the Nazis as a Jewish science, Strachey was particularly anxious for Freud's writings to be accepted in mainstream Western society, and he made his translation with this aim in mind. Whereas Freud had written in simple everyday German with a total absence of jargon, Strachey introduced an obscure Latinised terminology (Bettelheim 1982). Thus, the simple term *Ich*, or 'I', was translated as 'ego'; the *Es* or 'it' became the 'id'; and the *Uber-Ich*, or 'over-I', the 'super-ego'. These and other translated terms have neither the feel nor the directness of Freud's writing, and it can be helpful to re-translate them into the more accurate and evocative 'I', 'it' and 'over-I'.

The Structure of the Mind

Freud first put forward his three-part mental structure in *The Ego and the Id* (Freud 1923, S.E. 19). In the late *Outline of Psychoanalysis* (Freud 1938a, S.E. 23) he imagines this structure as a link between the physical organ of the brain and the subjective experience of consciousness.

Freud defines the id as the primitive and unchangeable ground of the mind. It is unconscious and therefore always deduced rather than experienced directly. He describes the id as a seething cauldron of instincts, or drives (*Triebe*). The aim of the id is the fundamental aim of the person: gratification without thought, compromise or qualification. Freud took the term from the eccentric psychiatrist Georg Groddeck:

> I hold the view that man is animated by the Unknown, that there is within him an 'Es', an 'It', some wondrous force which directs both what he himself does, and what happens to him ... Man is lived by the It. (Groddeck 1949: 11)

The id and its drives are all that is most powerful within us. They are inherited psychobiological characteristics like nesting or feeding behaviour in other animals, inhabiting the borderline between the mental and the physical, the abstract and the concrete.

The ego is evoked rather than defined through the simplicity of the term 'I'. It is the organised part of the mind that makes decisions, consciously and unconsciously. Its function is to preserve both the organism of which it is an aspect and also its own existence as a differentiated part of the id. The origin of the ego is unclear in Freudian thought: in the same paper he describes it as existing in its own right from the beginning, on the one hand, and as developing out of the id after birth, on the other (Freud 1938a, S.E. 23). What is clear is that Freud saw it as a comparatively fragile structure. Under sufficient stress it can lose ground, become incapable of thought and decision and be to some extent weakened by the super-ego and submerged by or re-absorbed into the id.

Since the ego's primary function is self-preservation, it has to take external factors into account. Its ultimate aim is for the id to gain maximum satisfaction consistent with survival and well-being. The ego recognises that one cannot have one's cake and eat it, and mediates the demands of the id, the constraints of external reality and the pressures of the super-ego. It works by compromise and by the postponement or denial of gratification, placing thought between impulse and action. An id impulse would send us running straight across the road after a lost football; the ego makes sure we wait for the cars to pass first.

The super-ego develops last, and is most clearly the product of society. Like the id it is largely unconscious, although we consciously experience the guilt which derives from it. The super-ego is the internalisation of the forbidding voice of the parents, stereotypically the father. This embodiment is part of the resolution of the Oedipus Complex, where the paternal voice is transformed into a capacity for inner control. Freud mentions its more positive counterpart, the ego-ideal, far less frequently. He sees the ego-ideal as the internalisation of the gentler parental voice, stereotypically the mother. The super-ego provides negative control in the form of self-discipline backed up by guilt. The ego-ideal provides ideals to which we can aspire.

The ego's task is to reconcile the demands coming from the id, the super-ego and external reality. If this is impossible, anxiety results: realistic anxiety, if the unavoidable danger comes from the external world; moral anxiety, or guilt, if the super-ego's demands are overridden; and neurotic anxiety, or a neurotic symptom, if the id's needs are insufficiently recognised.

The aim of psychoanalysis is to strengthen the ego, and modify the super-ego if it is excessively harsh or particularly weak. The external world can only be changed in minor ways by any individual, and the id is unchangeable: its forces can simply be managed or held at bay. All psychoanalysis can do is facilitate the ego's capacities to bear conflict and contain anxiety, to think before acting. It is with this in mind that Freud expressed its goal: 'Where id was, there ego shall be' (Freud 1933a, S.E. 22).

The Instincts

While these formations are the mind's structure, the instincts or drives provide its energy. Freud's views of the drives changed over time, but he always classed them into two opposing groups. He first defined these as the ego-instincts such as hunger and aggression, with the purpose of preserving the life of the individual, and the sexual instincts, which existed to ensure the continuation of the species (Freud 1914, S.E. 14).

He later moved to his final definition of the instinct groups as Eros, the life instincts, with their energy termed libido; and the death instincts, usually spoken of as a single death instinct and sometimes termed Thanatos (Freud 1920, S.E. 18). Located in the id, the instincts are the power of all mental life. They are deeply biological metaphors, based on the physical parameters of life which for Freud were the foundations of the mind. The instincts are not separate from each other: Freud envisaged them to be in a state of perpetual fusion from the start of life, taken by Freud as birth.

The thrust of the death instinct is towards the disintegration of current states, leading through regression to earlier states of being. Its ultimate aim is to achieve the state that prevailed before life itself: inanimacy, represented by death. On its own, the death instinct would thus result in the individual peacefully relinquishing life; and Freud believed that this internal destroyer of life is always with us as part of our make-up. We can only survive our drive towards death by externalising the death instinct to produce an urge to disintegrate and destroy other beings or states of being. At the end of life, the instincts finally fall into defusion, with the death instinct bringing about what we may call a natural death as the fulfilment of an inner need.

Eros must be behind the externalisation of the death instinct, as it is this alone, in Freudian theory, which enables the individual to stay alive at all. Eros is in many ways the equal and opposing force to the death instinct, though Freud also illogically suggests that the death instinct must predominate because inanimateness always triumphs over animateness. Whereas the death instinct tends towards disintegration, Eros is the drive to bring things together to create new unities. Eros appears most decisively in sexuality, seen by Freud as the force which brings two beings together for the purpose of procreation.

However, as Freud regards the instincts as fused, in practice sexuality also contains some death instinct. Freud describes the sexual act from his own male, heterosexual point of view as an act of aggression (that is, penetration) in the service of the deepest intimacy. All impulses, sexual and non-sexual, would have similar mixtures. We can see the act of eating an apple, for example, as motivated by both the desire for the apple and ultimately union with it, and also by the urge to destroy the apple as a separate entity. The fused Freudian drive includes the creative and destructive urges to which any impulse can be reductively analysed.

It is not surprising that even in his own time the death instinct was a controversial idea, often viewed as anti-biological and idiosyncratically pessimistic. Many people feel that unity must ultimately underlie duality, with a life instinct alone at the root of being. Aggression can sometimes be considered a positive rather than a negative force, or secondary rather than primary, as a response to frustration. We may also appreciate that the idea of a death instinct (or for that matter any 'instinct') could be used to block further understanding of apparently negative behaviour: it could be put down simply to 'instinct'.

If we remember Freud's life experience, however, his conviction that destructiveness is a primary force is unsurprising. He grew up in a disintegrating society where old certainties were being destroyed at a faster rate than ever before. The 'Great War' or 'World War' of 1914–18 must have been as devastating as a nuclear war would be today, stark evidence of human beings' capacity to destroy themselves and the planet. In Freud's old age, the anti-Semitism which had grown ever more virulent through his life resulted in the attempted destruction of his people and the banning of his life's work. When he died in 1939, he had been suffering from an increasingly painful cancer for sixteen years; and the Second World War had begun a few weeks earlier. In these circumstances, Freud's balancing of the death instinct with Eros looks almost optimistic.

The death instinct is often seen today as an historical anachronism, but in disregarding it we may be throwing out too much. One way of understanding Freud's view of instinctual conflict is to paraphrase it as the difficulty we all struggle with between moving forward to new experiences, new understanding and new ways of being, and retreating to the safer, simpler, more familiar patterns of the past – the pull of inertia.

Through making space for the possibility of a concept such as the death instinct, even if we do not wholly subscribe to it, we acknowledge the depth of the destructiveness within us and between us. It is only realistic to suppose that although the battle it gives rise to must never cease, it will never be won: at most we may achieve temporary truces. A death instinct offers a perspective on personal death, species extinction, even our possible destruction of the planet and the inevitable end of the universe as natural rather than horrific events. With such a concept, death does not sneak up and kill us; the movement towards death is within us, giving us the capacity to come to terms with dying both personally and more broadly. It may help us find the possibility of seeing death alongside life as an acceptable state of affairs, and enable us to go beyond a sentimental view of humanity in which its most sinister traits are explained away.

The Topographical Division of the Mind

The Freudian mind is thus a kind of machine driven by fused opposing forces within an overall structure. The third division Freud introduced is that between consciousness and unconsciousness.

The unconscious was a current philosophical concept which Freud integrated with his other major concepts (see Whyte 1962). He expected his promotion of the unconscious to be among his most unpopular ideas because of its inference that we are not in control even of our own minds. An 'unconscious' means that we hold responsibility for feelings we are not even aware of and make decisions in which we have taken no conscious part.

It is still difficult to accept the implications of an unconscious part of the mind, even though it is now such a familiar notion. How much sense do we really feel it makes to speak of unconscious choice or even unconscious thought? The attribute of 'being in touch with one's unconscious', sometimes paraded as a psychological virtue, is an impossibility: anything we become aware of, however dimly, has by definition ceased to be unconscious. These difficulties underline the metaphorical status of Freud's theories.

Freud divides the mind horizontally, or topographically, into the unconscious, of which we have no awareness; the preconscious, of which we can more or less easily become aware; and the conscious, which is simply the fleeting awareness of the moment. Like icebergs, the unconscious regions are immeasurably more extensive than our possible knowledge of ourselves. Even psychoanalysis only makes a small enlargement to the preconscious field.

The unconscious is divided into the unconscious proper and the repressed unconscious. The unconscious proper is that which has never been conscious, and includes innate knowledge – 'primal phantasies' of 'phylogenetic origin' (Freud 1916–17, S.E. 15) – very reminiscent of Jung's collective unconscious and also of currently held ideas of deep psychological structure. The repressed unconscious holds what has once been conscious but which we have pushed into unconsciousness: disowned impulses and their associated memories of which we are not usually aware, but which reach towards expression through dreams, neurotic symptoms and free association. The urge of what is repressed to regain consciousness demonstrates that repression is an active process. Psychoanalysis seeks to induce the patient to allow the most urgent repressed material into consciousness so that less costly compromises or resolutions to internal conflicts can be made. Sometimes sublimation is possible, where repressed impulses may be diverted to socially acceptable or even useful ends. Freud thought of friendship as a sublimation of sexuality, and art as a sublimation of impulses of all kinds.

The unconscious works through primary process, with the pleasure principle dominant. Primary process means that the constraints of external reality are absent, resulting in irrationality, with no negatives, no logic, no time or space, no thought or delay. The pleasure principle means that immediate gratification is the only aim. In the preconscious, secondary process includes the reality principle: the awareness of external reality and its constraints and demands. Under its aegis, the ego develops the capacity for thought. In the space it creates between impulse and action, the ego previews both internal and external consequences, making possible logic, rationality and self-discipline. Survival and well-being take precedence over instant pleasure when the ego is in charge, and the reality principle hopefully predominates over the pleasure principle. However, this predominance is always precarious, as reading any newspaper demonstrates. Outbreaks of anti-social sexuality and aggression are the media's most popular themes.

Dreams and Symptoms

The evidence of the unconscious and primary process was clearest, Freud suggested, in the everyday phenomenon of dreams and in neurotic symptoms which are structured in a similar way. Freud postulated that the dream and the neurotic symptom both express and repudiate repressed impulses.

The original impulse, pushed down into the unconscious, presses upwards into consciousness. At the same time, the super-ego censors its direct expression. The ego mediates between the upward pressure from the id (the instinctual impulse) and the downward pressure from the super-ego; in a compromise formation, the ego distorts the impulse into something more acceptable to the super-ego and therefore less anxiety-provoking to the ego.

Freud coined the terms 'manifest content' for the story of the dream, and 'latent content' for its underlying meaning. Latent content is transformed into manifest content through the dreamwork, using the processes of condensation, displacement and symbolisation. A single component of a dream may thus embrace many allusions. Wishes and actions may be displaced from one person to another, disguising the forbidden impulse, and primary process can include symbolisation at an individual, personal level while also drawing on an ancient and universal language which Freud attributed to our genetic heritage.

The neurotic symptom is analogous to the dream. The symptom contains in a single structure the repressed wish trying to emerge into consciousness and the ego's distortions of that wish.

Both dreams and symptoms therefore express a wish which conflicts with the individual's moral code. Lady Macbeth's handwashing, for example, holds her conscious desire to cleanse her soul of evil: the fact that the 'blood' will not wash off reveals the persistence of her murderous wishes.

The dream of six-year-old Chantelle demonstrates the beginnings of dreamwork. She was on a ship in the middle of the sea, and her younger brother fell overboard. Just before he hit the water, the fairies with their magic pipes started piping him upwards again towards the deck of the ship. But they didn't stop piping, and little brother was piped ever upwards, 'almost all the way to heaven'. At the last moment, they let him down again.

The conflict between the little girl's wish to get rid of her brother and her disownment of that wish is poignantly clear. Dreamwork led to elements such as the ship and the sea, the fairies, their pipes and 'heaven'; and the fact that her brother fell rather than was pushed. In Freudian theory, dreamwork is minimal before the super-ego comes into being with the resolution of the Oedipus Complex at about this age, and becomes increasingly complex as the moral code is internalised. This dream illustrates how wish-fulfilment can be suffused with anxiety: Chantelle woke up crying that she had had a nightmare.

The assumption that dreams and symptoms hold deep personal meanings has passed into society's understanding of the person and the complex layers of human consciousness. Many psychotherapeutic approaches give these phenomena a special importance as spontaneous utterances of our hidden natures.

Sexual Development

Freud developed an account of the development of the mind and its instincts in a conceptual frame developed further by Karl Abraham (Abraham 1927). Interestingly, the erotic instincts are the focus of this developmental scheme, perhaps because Freud saw the death instincts as unchangeable and unchanging. Freud's concept of infantile sexuality, though not original, was and remains controversial, mocked in the cliché that psychoanalysis is only interested in sex. Infantile sexuality has important differences from adult sexuality, and may be more accurately defined as the bodily pleasure which precedes and leads towards adult sexuality.

Freud saw the young infant as predominantly self-centred, or auto-erotic, ruled by primary process and the urge to instant gratification. The ego is rudimentary or unformed, so there is little capacity for thought. Following an initial 'primary narcissism', where there is no sense of distinction or externality, the baby seeks gratification from her own body, or from the mother's body which is barely differentiated from the baby's own. The baby is 'polymorphously perverse', meaning not that her capacity for pleasure is distorted, but that she is able to gain pleasure from many parts of her body. Following this auto-erotic beginning is the oral stage, when the baby's most intense excitement is centred on her mouth and the activity of feeding.

During the baby's second and third years, Freud suggests that the mouth gives way to the anus as the focus of satisfaction, leading from the oral to the anal stage. In this phase, the process and control of defecation is the central physical experience for the child, heightened by external demands in the form of toilet training which typically occurs around this age in Western society. This develops into the phallic stage, which Freud sees as common to both boys and girls, although it is of course a male-centred concept. The focus of excitement is the genitals, with the wish to penetrate and possess with the penis. The phallic stage is the backdrop for the drama of the Oedipus Complex, out of which the full person, the social being, is born.

The Oedipus Complex is broadly accepted but intensely debated in its details. Freud sees it as reaching its peak between the ages of about three and seven. Its resolution marks the beginning of the latency period, when sexuality recedes into the background until puberty and the emergence of adult sexuality. Freud suggests that as bisexual beings, everyone goes through double versions of the Oedipus Complex, with desire and hatred focused conflictingly on both parental figures. However, the male version is by far the most coherent account. The female version is not convincing, and Freud does not consider separate homosexual and lesbian versions: he tended to see these orientations in terms of incomplete developmental processes.

In the classical Oedipus Complex, the mother is the boy's first object of love: the purveyor of satisfaction in the oral stage and frustration in the anal stage. In the phallic stage she becomes the longed-for prize whom the boy wants to possess with his penis, as a sexual object devoted to his own gratification. The father now comes into focus as a hindrance and a rival because it is he, in the boy's mind, who possesses the mother in the way that the little boy would like to. The father apparently owns not only the mother, but the means of gratification, which is the aim and purpose of life. The boy attributes his own passionate feelings to his father, and this increases his fear of his father's rivalrous retaliation. As the boy would like to get rid of the father, so he assumes by projection that the father wants to eliminate him. The threat of destruction is focused on the penis, or more symbolically the phallus, as the tool of sexual possession and locus of power. Freud called this fear the 'castration complex'. It may be aggravated by overt threats or subtle discouragement of the boy's masturbation, coupled with his anxiety that the female genitals could be castrated male genitals.

The fear of real castration induces the boy to castrate himself symbolically. He gives up the hope of possessing his mother sexually and may turn against her, despising her as a 'mere' woman. He identifies with his father rather than opposing him, on the principle 'if you can't beat them, join them', or identification with the aggressor. He introjects – takes inside him – the paternal prohibition of sexuality and aggression to keep himself safe, making use of his own forceful feelings to help maintain inner control. The father thus becomes part of the son, who gains satisfaction vicariously through identifying with him. At the same time, the boy has to turn outside the immediate family for his actual gratification, hopefully preserving enough acceptance of his own sexual potency to achieve extra-familial sexual relationships in adulthood. The super-ego, or conscience, thus derives from a battle with society which is resolved through the accepting of society's mores.

Alongside this classical Oedipus Complex, Freud envisaged the boy as simultaneously taking the father as his focus of desire, with the mother as the hated rival. This is not elaborated by either Freud or his followers, but is assumed to add to the turmoil of the Oedipal stage.

The female Oedipus Complex has always appeared secondary. The girl, like the boy, must take the mother as her first love object. How then does she move to the father? Freud's inevitable basis in heterosexual male experience does not help him here. He believes that at some point the girl, like the boy, sees that the genitals of the opposite sex are different from her own. She interprets the male genitals as whole, and herself therefore as castrated. She blames her mother for her mutilation, while also seeing that her mother is herself mutilated. The mother is thus the damaged persecutor, and to keep her as an erotic focus would be to court both danger and humiliation. The only way for the girl to achieve completion in the form of the penis she lacks is through fantasised sexual possession of or by the father. This develops into the fantasy of giving birth to the father's male child, possessor and symbol of the missing penis.

The main issue for the girl in the Oedipal stage is penis envy rather than the fear of castration. Having already lost the prize, the girl has little to fear from the future. She therefore has less incentive to internalise the prohibiting voice of the parent, and Freud considered the female super-ego to be correspondingly weaker and less developed than the male super-ego. He correlates the sexual inhibitions expected of the woman in his social context with her belief that she has been robbed of the major means of sexual satisfaction and power. He sees little need for her to turn away from her father as the focus of desire. It matters little if she views her husband as a substitute father and her son as the purveyor of significance in her life.

In the opposite Oedipal development, the girl continues to take the mother as her object of desire, and the father as the rival and intruder. Even the heterosexual version, however, lacks the force and drama of the primary male Oedipus Complex: with the original lack of the penis, the story is truncated from the start. The feminist tradition has laid out the inadequacies and male-centredness of Oedipal theory, though not all feminists throw out Freud or the

Oedipus Complex in its entirety. While the female Oedipus Complex strikes most people today as unconvincingly as the death instinct, we should again beware of throwing out the baby with the bathwater.

Oedipal ambitions may be brazenly voiced by today's more outspoken toddlers, and many parents can attest to the power of their feelings. I am thinking of a four-year-old who scratched her mother's brand new boots all over with a fork, howling that her daddy had said he would not marry her, not then and not ever. Variations on this common theme occur in Western families of all kinds, suggesting a typical developmental stage in Western childhood and the dominance of the nuclear family structure within all Western families. Children who are parented by adults in a same-sex relationship often show a typically Oedipal pattern of possessiveness towards one parent and jealousy of the other; single parents may be the focus of extremely conflicting feelings for their children, or the alternative parental role may be projected on to an external figure, if not the other parent; children of separated parents may dream of reuniting their parents rather than, or as well as, dividing them. No doubt the familiarity of the Oedipus Complex as a concept helps adults to be more accepting of the intensity of their children's feelings, although some family circumstances may make the conflict more painful for them as well as for their children.

Freud's Oedipal theory can also be viewed metaphorically. Juliet Mitchell (Mitchell 1974) suggests that his grim analysis of the female character, with its childishness and moral weakness, may be read as the analysis of an oppressed class. If the penis is the symbol of social power, envy of that power will be expected in the underclass: 'penis envy' is power envy. If a social group is barred from the access to power, members of that group will be less devoted to upholding society and its customs, as Freud suggested was the case in his differential view of the male and female super-egos. The characteristics which second-class status engenders will be cited as proof of inferiority, while those who do hold social power will always fear losing it in a metaphorical castration complex. The social application of Freud's ideas throws light on the conflicts endemic to a class-ridden society. His Oedipal views may tell us more about his social context than biological fate.

Freud's Oedipal theory took the place of his previous Seduction Theory, where adult neurosis was seen as the outcome of sexual abuse in childhood. Freud has been widely blamed for the cover-up of child sexual abuse over decades. For too long, children who were sexually abused were either not believed or were blamed for the actions of adults. Their accounts were seen as wish-fulfilling Oedipal fantasies or enactments.

It is commonly understood that Freud simply stopped believing the stories of abuse told to him by his mainly women patients, and reframed their allegations as Oedipal fantasy. The truth appears more complex, as it usually is. It seems that his patients had never given straightforward, overt accounts of sexual abuse in childhood: what they said was always subjected to Freud's interpretations (Crews 1993). Initially, he tended to understand their thoughts, feelings and associations as unconscious communications of actual sexual activity in childhood; later, he took their words to indicate unconscious phantasies of sexual possession of a parent.

As far as child sexual abuse was concerned, his position is again less clear-cut than either his opposers or his supporters tend to present. He did downplay his views on it publicly, partly no doubt to mitigate the negative effects on his reputation and that of psychoanalysis. The case study of 'Dora' (Freud 1905a, S.E. 7), in particular, indicates that although he believed her story, he harmfully misinterpreted her reaction to the sexual advances of a family friend. But in letters he expressed the view that the sexual abuse of children was more common than normally supposed and was always harmful. It was later adherents of psychoanalytic theory who denied its occurrence, using the Oedipus Complex as an explanation of children's allegations. It is unreasonable to blame the originator of the concept for what was done with it later.

The Oedipus Complex dates from the period after Freud's father's death in 1896, when Freud pursued his self-analysis with particular intensity. Although there were compelling theoretical grounds, we may speculate on the extent to which his abandonment of the Seduction Theory and the exploration of his own Oedipal conflicts could also have arisen from reactions to this bereavement. He may well have felt guilty at implicitly attributing blame to his father when he observed that his siblings, and even he himself, showed some hysterical tendencies (Sulloway 1980: 206).

Psychoanalysis as Therapy

Freud's application of his theories went hand-in-hand with their development. He started with the then popular use of hypnosis, but relinquished it in the belief that its results did not last. In a rare and touching expression of his softer, feminine side, Freud developed the technique of free association. The patient, lying on a couch with minimum distraction, the analyst out of view, simply gives words to her awareness. The analyst listens with non-prescriptive, non-judging 'free-floating attention' for the blocks, themes, modes and trends in the patient's words, manner and silences. This is a challenging and exposing procedure and is well worth trying out, alone or with a partner, for even ten minutes. It has remained a cornerstone of psychoanalytic technique to this day, and has been modified rather than abandoned in other forms of psychotherapy.

Sooner or later the words dry up, as the patient becomes unwilling or unable to voice her thoughts and feelings. Freud termed this 'resistance': conscious or unconscious censoring under pressure from the super-ego. It is an indication that repressed or less acceptable impulses are trying to emerge, and it is they which are most likely to be contributing to the patient's problems. If it is to be effective, psychotherapy of any kind must therefore at times be exposing, humiliating and nerve-racking, requiring courage and perseverance.

Freud discovered that the patient's free association typically turns away from the difficulties for which she has come for help, to feelings about the analyst. As though we cannot live without relationship, the analyst becomes the focus of hopes, fears, desire and anger. These feelings may be extremely strong, ranging from dependency and sexual obsession to terror and hatred. Freud saw this intensity as arising not from the present but from the emergence of past experience under primary process. Because there is no appreciation of time in primary process, past and present are not felt to be different. The patient is thus reliving unresolved conflicts originating from childhood relationships with the parents, so accounting for the strength and irrationality of her feelings.

Freud termed this phenomenon 'transference': the unconscious transferring of past relationship into the present, especially as it appears in the psychoanalytic or psychotherapeutic setting. Transference is both positive, with the patient feeling love and dependency on the analyst as the giving, nurturing, perhaps sexually exciting parent; and also negative, with the analyst being experienced as the withholding, forbidding and cruel parent. Counter-transference is the analyst's transference on to the patient, widened later to include all the analyst's experiences in relation to the patient.

Initially, transference appeared as a setback, hindering the unravelling of hidden memories and blocking the patient's desire to overcome her difficulties and complete the analysis. While Freud's colleague Breuer fled from the intense erotic transference of the famous 'Anna O.', one of their early patients, Freud explored this phenomenon (Breuer and Freud 1895, S.E. 2). Through his steadfastness, transference was transformed into psychoanalysis' most effective tool and organising principle: if early conflicts could be resolved live, as it were, the results would always be more lasting than if they were merely described.

Later Kleinian approaches held psychoanalysis to be essentially analysis of the transference: the effects of unresolved experience on current perceptions of reality and relationship, as communicated verbally and non-verbally between patient and analyst.

* * *

This brief résumé of Freud's most influential ideas may give some feel of the range and originality of his work, in a field delineated and explored by himself in his inventive, dogmatic personal style. We may consider the effect on his thinking and writing of his life experience with its strange and extreme conjunctions of power and oppression, centrality and exclusion. He and his followers did much to promote the myth of Freud as a superhuman scientist, outside the constraints of time, place and gender (Jones 1957; Sulloway 1979). While we do not have to go along with this, neither do we have to rise to the Oedipal bait he unwittingly dangles. All self-proclaimed kings court their own downfall through their followers' envy and fear. Perhaps we can maintain our awareness of Freud's inevitable limitations as a man of a particular society. While we may not agree with all the concepts he offered us as he laid them out, nevertheless we may resonate personally with the deeper strata of his mind from which they emerged and express these resonances in our own ways.

Ideas such as childhood emotional development, the mind as a structured entity, repression and resistance, the unconscious, are part of the way Western society now thinks. The Oedipus Complex, particularly in its female form, the biological basis to the mind, and especially the death instinct, may seem out-dated concepts, but even these give us insight into Freud's view of the human condition which may in turn throw light on our own.

Towards the end of his life, Freud moved increasingly towards a more philosophical, less concrete conception of the person. He gave more focus to the ego as the centre of experience, rather than the id as the biological given out of which psychology emerges. Building on the interpersonal structure of the Oedipus Complex with the super-ego as an internalised object, he went on to pave the way for the development of Object Relations. In two of his last papers we see Freud subdividing the ego rather as the molecule and then the atom were subdivided (Freud 1938a, 1938b, S.E. 23). The concepts of a structured ego and internalised object relationships bridge his earlier drive-based theory to the relational psychology which was most fully expressed and elaborated by the Object Relations school.

2

MELANIE KLEIN:
SUBJECT RELATIONS

LIFE

Melanie Klein is a tragic figure in psychoanalysis. Her life of loss and turmoil is reflected in the grim picture she paints of her special area: the early months of infancy and the psychotic anxieties that relate to them.

Born Melanie Reizes in Austria in 1882 – a generation after Freud – she was the youngest of four children in a Polish-Hungarian Jewish family. They lived in Vienna, making out through Klein's mother's efforts as a shopkeeper. Her father's medical career was curtailed by anti-Semitism and he had to work mainly as a dentist. Klein's mother let her know that her conception had been unintended; and she was deeply jealous that her father preferred her sister Emilie, while her mother adored her brother Emanuel. Another sister, Sidonie, died at the age of eight, the first of many bereavements that Klein was to suffer.

The family is revealed in Phyllis Grosskurth's comprehensive biography (Grosskurth 1986) as entangled and neurotic. It revolved around the powerful figure of Libussa, Klein's mother, an expert in manipulation who provided the emotional and practical focus: it was she who managed the money and kept the family going. Klein aligned herself with the prestigious grouping of Libussa and Emanuel, making a powerful trio against the weaker duo of Emilie and Moritz, their father. Klein idealised her mother as loving and self-sacrificing, and she grew up to adore Emanuel as her mother did. He was the father-substitute who noticed her intelligence and encouraged her learning, unlike her father whom she felt ignored by. After being diagnosed with tuberculosis in his early twenties Emanuel became a self-destructive drifter, exerting heavy emotional pressure on his mother to provide the means for him to travel in the style of the dying artist. When that was not sufficient, he pressured Klein to get more money out of the family for him. He died in 1902, and this was one of Klein's most painful losses.

Klein's father had died two years previously, leaving the family struggling financially. She wondered later whether the financial constraints resulting from her father's death were the reason she abandoned her plan to study medicine. She could also have been flattered and comforted in the wake of Emanuel's death by the attention she was given from the coterie of young men who admired her dark and striking beauty. She married Arthur Klein, a chemical engineer, in 1903.

The marriage was never a success and Arthur's travels meant they saw little of each other in the early years of their relationship; but Klein grew particularly fond of his sister Jolande and other relatives. They had three children between 1904 and 1914, and Klein found her new life fraught and joyless. 'I threw myself as much as I could into motherhood and interest in my child', she wrote of the period after her daughter Melitta's birth; 'I knew all the time that I was not happy, but saw no way out' (Grosskurth 1986: 42). She sank into deep depressions and Libussa sent her on numerous holidays and 'cures' during the earliest years of her children's lives. Probably post-natal depression exacerbated her general low state and Libussa, of course, was there to hold the fort, often urging her to stay away longer than she wished.

We get a picture of a lost and frightened woman, unable to manage without her mother, without a direction in her life. The imaginative and intellectual forces she unleashed later must have been tied up in her paralysing depression. In 1914, Libussa died, and it was in this period of crisis that Klein discovered psychoanalysis. She was inspired by her first reading of Freud, and entered psychoanalysis with Sandor Ferenczi in Budapest where they had recently settled. He was a warm and compassionate man who believed that people became neurotic not through instinctual conflict but through a lack of love, and Klein became greatly attached to him. He supported her resolve to become an analyst, and this must have been a crucial factor in overcoming her depression. Encouraged by Ferenczi, she began to work in an undeveloped field: psychoanalysis with children.

To do this, she needed patients who, not surprisingly, were hard to find. She solved the problem by analysing her own children and presenting them in disguised form as case studies. Though this strikes us today as shocking, it was then not unusual. Freud and Abraham, for example, both analysed their own daughters. It is also likely that having received effective analytic help herself, she wanted her troubled children to benefit from it.

Klein thus embarked on her own way of working with children, reaching further back than the Oedipal stage of development which Freud viewed as central to the formation of neurosis. She penetrated the primitive anxieties she felt her young patients were presenting with an outspoken directness that alarmed and embarrassed her colleagues. They feared that her explicit spelling-out of psychotic and infantile terrors could drive children mad.

In the meantime, Klein's marriage was deteriorating. Her husband moved to Sweden and she and the children moved to Berlin in 1921. She and Arthur were finally divorced in 1926, after protracted custody disputes. Klein entered analysis with Karl Abraham in 1924, and like Ferenczi, he became her mentor as well as her analyst. Her strong attachment to him, as to Ferenczi, perhaps reflected her professional isolation and her feeling of neglect by her father. Poignantly, the analysis had to end when Abraham became terminally ill only fourteen months later.

Klein had an extraordinarily difficult time in Berlin, and it is a mark of the effectiveness of her analyses that she never relapsed into the aimless depression of former years. Rather than turn her forceful energies against herself, she now presented as a flamboyant figure, tactless and intuitive. The German psychoanalysts did not take to her: she was a woman, comparatively uneducated and certainly not medically trained, divorced at a time when all divorce was a scandal, and from a Polish background that was low in the Jewish class hierarchy. It is interesting that her analysts, having far closer contact with her, did not have this reaction. Perhaps she felt safe enough with them to drop some of her intimidating eccentricity and reveal the depth of her suffering, her thoughtfulness and her creativity.

It must have come as a relief when Ernest Jones, the stalwart of the small British psychoanalytic scene, pressed her to move to London. He felt that her work offered a genuine new direction and should be encouraged. She moved to London in 1927 with her youngest son Erich, while her two older children remained in Berlin to finish their education.

Klein's life in Britain brought forth an extraordinary flowering of disturbing, intuitively-driven interpretations of the most primitive layers of life, which she organised into a radical set of new theoretical concepts. The British psychoanalytic world was torn in two, into those for and those against her ideas and style of working (King and Steiner 1991). The fervour she inspired in equal and opposite directions was fuelled by the insecurity of the pre-war years. Increasing numbers of Jewish analysts moved from central Europe to Britain. As the war proceeded there were no illusions about the fate of the Jews if a German invasion of Britain were successful, and a shortage of money and very soon of patients meant that the pool of available work was spread ever more thinly.

The theoretical divide increased sharply after the arrival of the Freuds in 1938 – again engineered by Jones, to Klein's dismay. Anna Freud and her followers became personally involved in the battle against Klein, made more intense because Anna Freud was developing her own very different approach to child analysis. Finally, three separate groupings formed as the only way of keeping the British Psycho-Analytical Society in one piece: the Kleinian group; the Viennese (classical Freudian) group; and the Independents, who hoped to bridge the gap. To this day the divide remains.

Klein's personal losses continued. The only man she was romantically involved with after separating from her husband did not take their relationship as seriously as she did. He was married and had numerous affairs, of which his relationship with Klein was but one. He jilted her in 1926, and her letters to him show how agonising she found this rejection.

Klein's relationship with her daughter, probably highly vulnerable after its dubious start, soured after Melitta became established as an analyst. She, her husband Walter Schmideberg and her analyst Edward Glover led the opposition to Klein's work, making every attempt to get her thrown out of the British Psycho-Analytical Society. Klein herself never answered their attacks, but at times they were so vitriolic that others were obliged to step in. Evidently the enmeshment and deprivation which had begun with Klein and Libussa continued with Klein and Melitta, turning inside-out to force the world to witness the hatred and envy which were its underside. This was a breach that never began to heal. Melitta did not attend her mother's funeral, nor did she answer letters of condolence, even from her brother.

Klein lost her elder son Hans. He died in a climbing accident in Czechoslovakia in 1934, and Melitta made sure to suggest that he could have committed suicide. Only her youngest son Erich remained to her, and it was his children to whom she was close in her later years. The deaths of her ex-husband Arthur in 1939, and her envied sister Emilie in 1940, were further uneasy losses.

Klein was thus in a continuing state of mourning through much of her life. She used her pain to investigate in detail the early states of loss, guilt, loneliness, envy and persecution that make up her theories. Her description of her disorientation and agony following Hans' death, in which she thinly disguises herself as 'Mrs A', makes poignant reading (Klein 1940). Although she achieved recognition and success, she was anxious that her work would not long survive her. She was revered by some, abhorred by others, and intimate with no one. In her last weeks in hospital, the crying of a baby in the next room worried and distressed her. Perhaps this response sums her up as a person. She died in 1960.

Maladroit and hostile with adults, she inspired awe or fear or hatred. In turn, she treated her colleagues less as people in their own right than as potential allies or enemies. She seems to have felt closest to children, other than her own, who were suffering. Many of her child patients remember her with affection; most of her colleagues remember her with admiration or with dislike.

THEORY

Overview

This chapter aims to explain basic Kleinian theory as it was created by Klein and her colleagues. Kleinian theory is a rich and complex field which has been intensively elaborated since its inception, focusing particularly on the functioning of groups and institutions and on the detailed analysis of psychotic and borderline states and their intrapsychic and interpersonal processes. Elizabeth Bott Spillius (1988a, 1988b) has gathered together a selection of work by some of the most influential British contributors to later Kleinian theory, giving an effective overview of how this tradition has developed.

Klein always saw herself as a follower of Freud: 'I'm a Freudian', she declared, 'but not an Anna Freudian!' (Grosskurth 1986: 455–6) She did not understand why he dismissed her work as a deviation rather than a development of psychoanalysis. This must have echoed her feeling of neglect by her father, and no doubt the theoretical conflicts between Melanie Klein and Anna Freud were fuelled by the personal rivalry between these two gifted women, both of whose fathers had openly preferred their sister.

Klein did not appreciate the magnitude of the change she wrought at the roots of psychoanalytic theory. As a non-scientist, she felt no need to work within Freud's biological framework. Instead, she used his ideas to listen to the *experience* of what her patients told her. She was imaginative, intuitive and bold, making wild leaps that could be backed up only by inner resonance. The premises of her theory are philosophical rather than scientific, and subjective rather than objective. She complained, in fact, that the classical theorists were stuffy and dry; her theory, by contrast, was vivid and alive.

The subjective base to her work means that the ways in which she uses terms such as 'instinct' and 'ego' differ from the Freudian usage. She envisages the person as a subjective agent within a subjective world of relationship, conflict and change. The outer world is experienced through the medium of this subjective world; the outer world also reaches into the inner world, influencing its nature and structure. Klein's work is a theory of 'subject relations' which marks the beginning of the Object Relations school.

In Kleinian theory, the ego, the sense of separate identity, is oriented towards external reality from birth which, like Freud, she takes as the beginning of mental life. She thus contradicted the official Freudian view that the baby is born into an initial state of non-differentiation (primary narcissism), out of which a sense of self and acknowledgement of reality gradually emerge. The ego, rather than the id, is the centre of Klein's theory, together with the libidinal and death instincts.

Klein's instinctual impulses, however, are not physiological drives, but hopes, fears and wishes experienced in bodily terms. Every inner movement is felt as an urge to connect with the object (the other) in desire or in destructiveness. The infant feels his impulses as the exchange of body substances (milk, faeces, urine) or the use of them as a weapon. Love is taking in good milk or feeding the mother with the baby's own stored-up goodness. Urine and faeces are valuable gifts, and in giving them in reality or in fantasy the child feeds – loves – the mother. Anger is a poisonous attack on the self or other by the same body substances now bad and destructive.

Klein believed the infant was born with pre-programmed 'knowledge' of the existence of the mother and basic body parts or functions, termed breast, penis, vagina; and that this preprogrammed knowledge enabled him to experience life in physical terms. Klein called this primitive and largely unconscious experience 'phantasy': Susan Isaacs (1943) gives a lucid account. Phantasy is the mental aspect of instinctual impulse, sensations interpreted pre-symbolically as actions. Strange though this may sound, there is some support for such ideas from developmental psychology, which has established that new-born babies 'recognise' the human face, 'know' how to feed from the breast, and are in fact pre-equipped with considerable knowledge and capacity (see Stern 1985). Klein, of course, was not worried about objective truth. She was getting at the subjective experience.

Like Freud, Klein saw life as the managing of the conflict between the urge to love and the urge to destroy. She assumed that the strength of the instincts was determined constitutionally, but she makes little other reference to biology. The life instinct receives scant explanation from her, beyond the assumption of Freud's view of a basic tendency to unite and create. She describes the death instinct in experiential terms as a desperate attempt at the beginning of life to undo the fact of birth and reach back to the pre-natal state with its supposed absence of conflict and frustration. (Klein began to wonder about intra-uterine life towards the end of her life, but she did not write about it.) Her conception of mental life is therefore a post-birth picture, comprised of a mixture of pre- and post-birth life instinct and an opposite reaction against it from the death instinct. The life and death instincts remain in conflict and in partial fusion until the person dies.

Although Klein may have seen this as a simple re-interpretation of the Freudian instincts, Freud must have seen it for what it was: a virtual removal of the physical roots of psychoanalysis, which in turn connected it with universal natural laws. Without these roots there was no hope of psychoanalysis being seen as a science alongside other scientific disciplines. No wonder he could not endorse her ideas.

Development of the Self

Klein saw all experience as arising from an interplay between internal and external reality. She writes of the projection into the other of innate and acquired feelings and images, and the introjection, or taking in, of external reality into the inner world of the self. There is a constant interplay, a recycling almost, of perception and feeling between the outer and inner worlds, so that both are experienced partially in the light of the other (Klein 1959).

The urge to relate, to join with the other in this projective and introjective exchange, arises partly from the presence of the death instinct. Because Klein's death instinct is the urge to abolish post-natal life, the baby feels a dread of destruction from within. There is an absolute necessity to channel this annihilating urge away from the self and into what is perceived as external; but as a result the world is turned bad through what the baby has projected into it. He therefore has a compensatory need to soften a potentially totally hostile world by projecting goodness and love into it from the life instinct. This accounts for the basic and unavoidable internal conflict in Kleinian theory, and for the subjective nature of perception. Each person's external world is in part a reflection of his inner world, while at the same time it reaches into his inner experience and changes it.

Psychological health, in this framework, lies in the capacity to see beyond what we project, and in the ability to appreciate that there is a difference between the badness which we wish to put into the world and what is really there. Psychological ill-health arises to the extent that we see, and thus induce, the confirmation of our negative expectations which arise from bad internal object relations.

Klein regarded the body as the vehicle of mental life and the raw material of primitive experience. Phantasy is a bodily-framed language in which body parts and products stand for gifts or weapons. It is not a symbolic language: these exchanges feel as though they are actually being carried out, in what Hanna Segal termed a symbolic equation, the equating of sensation with its interpretation (Segal 1957). There is no difference between thought and deed: an angry impulse is felt *as* a poisonous or explosive attack on the other through urine or faeces, teeth or limbs; feeling loved *is* the imbibing of sweet milk, or urine or semen as milk-equivalents. It is only when the capacity for true symbolisation develops that ideas can be communicated as ideas rather than experienced as actions; phantasy retains a basic concreteness.

Klein's developmental scheme differs from the Freudian stages of libidinal development. She focuses on the baby's first year, Freud's oral stage. She came to see this phase of life as a movement between the relative predominance of two mental standpoints: the paranoid-schizoid position and the depressive position (Klein 1952). She relates all later psychopathology to the baby's early attempts to deal with the anxieties endemic to these two positions.

The positions are therefore like stages of development, and indeed at times Klein refers to them as stages. However, a stage is grown through and subsumed into a later stage, whereas a position is a perspective that can be returned to, with a specific set of attitudes through which events are interpreted. Klein also uses 'paranoid-schizoid position' and 'depressive position' as ways of capturing configurations of anxieties and defences which come into focus at certain points of early development. The emphasis on anxiety rather than well-being is typical of the overall emphasis in Klein's work on the painfulness of life rather than its joys. 'Paranoid-schizoid' and 'depressive' hardly sound attractive alternatives. Winnicott made an unsuccessful bid to have the depressive position renamed 'the stage of concern' (Grosskurth 1986: 400).

Klein therefore viewed early development not in terms of the ways in which sexuality is experienced, but in terms of how anxiety is experienced and managed.

The Paranoid-Schizoid Position

In Kleinian theory, the paranoid-schizoid position predominates in the baby's first three months, with the baby also experiencing some more realistic depressive functioning (Klein 1946). The paranoid-schizoid position or perspective is the way in which the baby attempts to manage the disruption, deprivations and anxieties which Klein assumed were crucial features of birth and early post-natal life.

The urge to make sense of chaos leads the baby to order his experience by splitting or dividing it into what he feels is good and what he feels is bad experience. These two categories are then widely separated from each other, and kept far apart. The wicked witch and the fairy godmother of fairy-tales are the good and bad aspects of mother as she is thus perceived and divided. It is more important at this stage to achieve some order than make an accurate picture of reality, to the extent that the paranoid-schizoid position predominates over the depressive. In the paranoid-schizoid position there is no neutral zone, only good and bad. There is no experience of absence, regret or loss, because absence is simply felt as something bad rather than as something good not there, and relief as good rather than bad.

Splitting enables the baby to get started with trusting and loving. Given the high intensity of living under the sway of absolute impulses with little life experience to modify their extremes, it would be impossible to relax into trust and love with the dread of imminent annihilation lurking. So by separating everything bad from everything good, the baby has the chance of experiencing total goodness and can take in (introject) this goodness (good object) as a base for his sense of self.

The price of experiencing goodness uncontaminated by badness is that at other times the baby feels himself to be in the grip of pure evil. Our central fear in the paranoid-schizoid position is that we will be destroyed by a malevolent external force. Klein termed this 'persecutory anxiety', and it is the hallmark of the paranoid-schizoid position. This dreadful experience arises partly from externally-derived bad experience, but also, and Klein felt most powerfully, from the rebounding-back of the death instinct which we have projected into the other. Together these factors join forces to give a horrific picture of early infancy, a time that Klein's colleagues preferred to see as involving little anxiety or stress. Klein suggested that some babies die or fail to thrive because of a constitutional bias towards the death instinct: it may be impossible for them to trust or take in from a world which is shot through with badness, projected and perhaps also real.

This is the stuff of nightmare; and inevitably the baby will clutch at any straw in trying to cope with his dread, particularly if poor environmental conditions exacerbate the problems. He may resort to further splitting in an attempt to break down what has to be coped with into manageable segments, or in a destructive death instinct attack on the suffering part of himself. In an extreme, this results in the fragmentation and incoherence that we see in psychosis, where the person barely survives as a psychological entity.

The term 'part-object' describes a part or an aspect of the self or the other which may be all that the baby can perceive and relate to. The 'good breast' and 'bad breast' are the prototypical part-objects, the initial focal points of the baby's mental life. They refer not just to the actual breast, but to the mother in her feeding role, with no other characteristic included. The older baby or child may regress to part-object relating because he feels the world is so dangerous (probably through projection) that he can only deal with other people in bits. In later life, part-object relating results in other people feeling exploited by the person who simply uses them – for information, sex or money – rather than seeing them as people in their own right.

Projection and introjection arise from the same capacities as splitting. In projection, impulses which the baby cannot hold inside are split off and propelled into the other. Although the baby is doing this in phantasy, his perception is that it is really happening. Projecting hate and badness apparently rids him of his own badness, but goodness is also projected: partly to supply something good to rely on and relate to, but also to keep goodness safe from the badness that he feels is within. Introjection is another way of strengthening the division of experience into good and bad; it involves taking in goodness as a support, and taking in badness to make the outside world safer. Projection and introjection are rough-and-ready ways of coping with anxiety and making a link with another; but used excessively or destructively they sabotage the sense of a secure, coherent self and a reasonably reliable other.

Projective identification is a more complex and extreme form of projection. It consists in non-verbal communication in which one person picks up feelings or experiences from another. If the baby's anxiety is particularly intense, he may project into the other person not just impulses, but whole aspects of the self. This defence may allay anxiety by appearing to get rid of a part of the self that feels painful or unmanageable, and it may offer the illusion of having some control over the other person. Under pressure to fall in with his needs, the other person starts acting as though he or she has really taken in the unwanted part, experiencing the feelings and impulses involved. A mild and benign version of projective identification enables one to put oneself across to others and empathise with them. In the paranoid-schizoid version, however, the person projecting his unwanted parts may end up feeling empty and depleted, confused as to where he ends and the other begins. The person projected into may have the urge to push the intruding forces straight back to the sender, without recognising their projected origins.

Projective identification has an unparalleled value in psycho-therapeutic work, since the client or patient may transmit directly to the therapist the actual experience that he cannot manage. It thus forms a major part of the counter-transference, which later Kleinians extended to include all reactions and responses of the therapist in relation to the patient (Bion 1962a; Rosenfeld 1964). Projective identification has been taken up as a particularly useful concept by many schools of psychotherapy.

Denial, another primitive way of coping with anxiety, is the superficial plastering over of one state of affairs by another. The persecutory experience of frustration may be covered over with the imagined experience of satisfaction; because at this stage there is no difference between what is imagined and what is real, this is called an hallucination. When we see small babies apparently interacting with space, or sucking without being fed, they may be warding off anxiety through denial. In later life we use the same device when we act as if we do not need to attend to something which makes us anxious: going to the dentist, for example.

Klein speaks of greed as an expression of the death instinct, aggravated by anxiety and frustration. It is the ruthless exploitation of the source of goodness (in phantasy the breast) regardless of its real capacity or of one's own immediate need. It is fuelled by the anxiety that the counterpart of the good feeding breast – the bad depriving breast – will spring forth at any moment. The phantasy of greed is that we can take in not just the good milk from the good breast, but the whole good breast itself so that we can be fed continuously from an inner wellspring over which we have total control. Of course, this absolute security is never reached, and the greedy person continues to take and take, fruitlessly waiting for an omnipotent sense of invulnerability.

Envy is one of the most controversial of Klein's concepts, developed late in her life (Klein 1957) and taken up intensively by her followers. She describes envy as a powerfully destructive impulse, directed from the earliest months against the good breast as the source of life. It is the urge to spoil what is good because it is outside the self and because it supports the self. The very goodness of the breast is a constant reminder of the separation and relative deprivation resulting from birth. Before birth, Klein believed we knew neither need nor fear: it is only our need that makes the breast good. It is this symbol of post-natal life that we want to destroy, as the death instinct pushes to destroy the fact of birth. What makes envy so destructive is that it is an urge to destroy not badness, but goodness. Envy makes it impossible to benefit from goodness, leading us to discard or destroy possibilities of help and nurturance. The primary splitting into what is good and bad is threatened by envy, because we treat goodness as something bad. Klein relates later states of psychotic confusion to the insidious effects of envy. Envious external relationships lead to envious internal relationships, wreaking havoc on a sense of clear identity and basic self-worth, as good and bad objects are confused, attacked and fragmented.

The paranoid-schizoid position, with its persecutory anxiety, is not something that we grow out of, although its force may be lessened from our first stark dealings with living. Because survival is the main issue, the paranoid-schizoid mode is ruthless and self-centred. In the grip of persecutory anxiety, we have little regard for what is true and no sense of personal responsibility: everything bad is someone else's fault. We see signs of paranoid-schizoid functioning in all areas of life, reflecting the later conception of the Kleinian 'position' as a state of mind, rather than a developmental way-station. Splitting and projection, for example, are basic to political systems such as Britain's, where each 'side' is under pressure to automatically find fault with anything the other 'side' suggests.

Klein believed that Oedipal conflicts and processes developed from the very beginning of object relating (Klein 1928), rather than arising during early childhood as Freud imagined. In Kleinian theory, the baby's relation to the father follows and reflects the baby's primary relationship with the good/bad breast. The father is the first intruder into the baby's relationship with mother. The penis, the main paternal part-object, represents the differentiating and penetrating qualities of masculinity as the breast represents the feeding mother. The baby may experience the penis as nurturing and healing, or at other times as a scything weapon attacking his own body parts and his mother's.

Klein invokes early Oedipal phantasies in the wild and fantastic terms in which she conceived infantile experience. She envisages that bodily sensations meet with innate ideas of body parts and processes. Relationship is imagined – felt – as breast and mouth, penis and vagina, milk, urine, faeces and unborn children, in all possible combinations (Klein 1959). An early realisation of the parents' independent relationship is experienced by the baby as a gigantic combined figure, penis joined with breast, stomach, mouth or vagina in endless mutual gratification, creating ever new riches in the form of faeces-babies. Under the influence of anxiety induced by the death instinct, the baby projects his envy and rage into this monstrous figure, which then appears as a powerfully evil force, conjoined in mutual destruction and threatening to annihilate the baby and his world.

As the child begins to differentiate between the parents, he is able to distinguish the various part-objects in their phantasied relations and have different feelings towards them, partly driven by his own gender-specific sensations and corresponding desires. Klein makes a far more convincing differentiation between the girl's and the boy's Oedipal processes than Freud had managed. In Klein's thinking, the girl's phantasies are dominated by her envious attacks on her mother's insides, containing milk, father's penis, faeces, unborn siblings; this projection rebounds in an acute reflected fear about her own insides, leading to a continuing insecurity about the intactness and fruitfulness of her internal physical and experiential world. The boy's particular fear is of the father's castrating retaliation on him, following a phantasied attack on the father inside the mother. This makes him fear as well as desire what may be inside the mother. Like Freud, Klein assumed that both Oedipal processes unfolded alongside each other whatever the child's gender, resulting in children experiencing all possible desires, fears and roles in relation to their parents.

The Depressive Position

The depressive position comes into ascendancy in the second half of the first year, having begun to emerge more strongly at around three months (Klein 1935). Again, it is a matter of relative dominance:

paranoid-schizoid elements remain and we may revert to them particularly when under pressure. It is when things go well enough that the baby is able to come to terms with the worst of the paranoid-schizoid anxieties and begin to take his survival more for granted. He has less need for the splitting, denial and projective defences which kept persecutory anxiety at bay. A new view of life opens up with different things to worry about: the depressive position, with its array of depressive anxieties.

With less need to distort his perceptions, the baby in the depressive position experiences inner and outer reality more accurately. He recognises that the part-objects resulting from his splitting, the good and bad mother, father, self, are complex, whole people about whom he has mixed feelings. The early stages of this realisation bring particular anxieties: as internal and external objects become more integrated, the baby experiences absence as the loss of the good rather than simply a depriving attack by something bad. Instead of anger, his reaction is grief. It is around three months when babies begin to cry with tears; perhaps this is an expression of their greater capacity for sadness.

As splitting diminishes, different experiences fit better together. The bad is less bad, but by the same token, the good is less good. The myths of the lost Garden of Eden, the land flowing with milk and honey, evoke powerfully the mourning that we have all had to go through, leaving a sense of bliss and innocence which is real but lost for ever. We have grown too wise to see that experience as the whole picture; yet once we did.

As the world's goodness becomes tainted, so also does the baby's goodness. He realises with a shock that the malefactors he has done his best to destroy are the people he most loves and needs. This realisation makes him terrified of his anger, and this is the central fear of the depressive position. Though dreadful, it is somewhat less disastrous than the paranoid-schizoid fear of total annihilation, although the baby still feels his survival is in jeopardy through the threatened loss of his main objects. The fear of the loss of the internalised good object (person) also carries a direct threat to his identity: without it, he would feel he was wholly bad and worthless.

The baby's fear of his anger forms a major part of the super-ego and of the feelings of guilt and remorse which are further emotional challenges of the depressive position. Because he is afraid of directing his anger outwards, he turns it inwards instead, berating himself rather than the other person for being selfish and bad. This is the core of depression, and leads to the term 'depressive position'. As the depressed person knows, it is all too possible to become paralysed by depression: pulled towards action, relationship and the outside world by anger and need, pulled against expressing feelings through fear of the consequences, sunk in obscure resentment, guilt and dissatisfaction. Melanie Klein points to the sad expressions and occasional withdrawal which we sometimes see in a baby nearing the end of his first year (Klein 1959): he is now capable of inner conflict, low self-esteem, sadness and guilt.

The pain of guilt gives rise to the new capacity for reparation. The baby comes to realise that even though anger can damage, love can mend. It is belief in reparation that prevents us getting quagmired in depression, a continuing danger for those who have not yet discovered or do not trust their ability to make amends. These people feel that their anger is too overwhelming or destructive for repair to be possible; they may have lost sight of, or never really gained, belief in their own goodness as the basis for reparation; or their guilt may itself feel too persecutory and attacking. This is especially likely if the earlier paranoid-schizoid anxieties are only partly resolved and a persecutory flavour to life continues, leading to the repressing of guilt as an intolerable feeling and a reversion to paranoid-schizoid defences.

We see young children repeatedly working through experiences of persecution, loss, guilt and reparation: tantrums and conflict alternate with an absolute need for love and an urgent necessity to give. Many are the cold cups of 'tea' which parents have been roused with at 5 a.m., and the grubby bits of biscuit offered for their enjoyment. Parents know, without necessarily knowing why, that to reject these gifts would be a crushing blow to their child's sense of having something good to give. These early forms of reparation develop into helpfulness and individual interests and talents, all ways of contributing to society. The capacity for reparation is thus a vital emotional achievement which Klein viewed as the basis of constructive living and creative power.

Klein suggests – demonstrating the cultural specificity of Object Relations – that depressive anxieties come to a crisis and may be symbolised in the experience of weaning. In Western societies, this commonly takes place at the end of the child's first year when the child may have reached the readiness to live through an experience of loss, anger and grief, and to emerge from it with increased maturity and greater appreciation of self and other. If the baby is weaned before this readiness is reached, the loss of breast or bottle feeding would simply be a depriving attack, reinforcing insecurity and the feeling that the world was hostile. Conversely, a baby who has not enough opportunity to come to terms with loss and separation in some arena may find it relatively more difficult to develop a secure knowledge of the limits of his destructiveness and the power of his reparative love. Comparatively early weaning may be part of the tremendous emphasis placed on separateness and independence in Western society, which is also reflected in the importance allotted to the depressive position.

With the rise of the depressive position, the child's Oedipal dilemmas are initially exacerbated (Klein 1945). Rather than loving and hating the split parental part-objects while envying the powerful combined figure, he realises that the mother and father whom he loves, hates, fears and needs, are whole people in a relationship from which he is excluded. His conflicting feelings are compounded by guilt and a fear of his own destructiveness, and these are a spur to the re-finding of loving feelings in his wish to protect his parents, both internal and external. In a rare optimistic moment, Klein suggests that the child comes to accept the parental relationship not simply through fear, as Freud believed, but also through love: he wants the parents he loves to be happy, to love each other and to love him. In managing to overcome his jealousy, the child is in turn reassured that he has goodness inside him; his internalised parents feel safe and good rather than dangerous and bad, and his fears of their ghastly retaliation reduce. A gratifying form of the combined parental figure may have been what was symbolised in four-year-old Stefan's exciting dream of 'five hundred ice-creams on wheels'. Thus the child's Oedipal conflicts resolve into a greater security and confidence in himself, his parents and the world.

The paranoid-schizoid and depressive positions with their attendant issues and anxieties are in continually shifting balance through our everyday lives. At different times we feel more or less secure in ourselves and in the world, seeing things with more or less clarity, facing up to issues or hiding from them with more or less courage.

Later Kleinians have described a fixed pattern that is often dominant in those people termed 'borderline', in which paranoid-schizoid defences are used in a consistently destructive way. Reality is not denied, as in the psychotic paranoid or schizophrenic state, nor is it recognised, as in the depressive position. Instead, perceptions are perverted or distorted, so that rather than moving towards the greater integration of the depressive position with its painful experiences or loss and guilt, the person escapes backwards into the more familiar and less demanding paranoid fears and schizoid defences. Steiner

(1993) terms this state a 'pathological organisation' of the personality; Rosenfeld (1971) likens it to a Mafia-like 'narcissistic gang' controlling the mind in an inner conspiracy dominated by the death instinct. These patients and clients may be dispiriting to work with therapeutically, as their fear of further integration is immense and there may be a perverse excitement in distorting the truth which is very hard for them to resist. Intense envy makes helpful responses from the therapist particularly hard to bear; they may be heard as gloating, patronising, cold or irrelevant. The therapist may then be pulled in the counter-transference into fury and helplessness which it is tempting to give in to rather than observe and monitor. The survival of the therapeutic relationship may be all that can be achieved for a long time.

From a Kleinian point of view, psychotherapy and counselling aim to help establish the depressive way of being more securely – for it is never fully secure. Under loss and disappointment, as well as under real persecution, we more or less easily revert to the belief that the world is against us. Compassion and empathy decrease, blame increases; the experience of other people becomes less important as our own experience fills all our mental space. The way to a more secure and balanced humanity involves acknowledging and accepting our ordinariness and shortcomings, yet without turning upon ourselves in hatred and contempt. Humility is the hallmark of the depressive position.

Kleinian Psychoanalytic Work with Children

Klein's psychoanalytic play technique is one of her most important innovations, and has influenced all later therapeutic work with children (Klein 1955). Her rich experience with young children led directly to the Kleinian view of infancy.

Klein treated children as soon as they were old enough for some verbal communication to be possible – from the age of two and a half onwards. Essentially, free play takes the place that free association holds in the analysis of adults. Spontaneous play is the child's natural way of externalising his preoccupations and working through his anxieties, and offers a window on to his psychological processes.

Klein supplied each child patient with a collection of small, simple, non-mechanical toys which lent themselves to imaginative rather than technical play: figures representing adults and children; cars, boats and trains; animals, fences and bricks; and also water, sand

and clay, and paper, scissors and glue. The analyst puts into words – using the child's language and expressions as far as possible – the concerns the child demonstrates through what he does or does not do with the materials, together with what he says and expresses non-verbally. Each child's toys are kept in his own locked drawer in the consulting room. The drawer and its contents represent the inner world the child shares with the analyst, charting its change and development. Toys may be damaged, scratched or broken, and later attempts made to mend them. Drawings can be scribbled over, torn, sellotaped up or done afresh. Figures can be relegated to the back of the drawer, perhaps to be retrieved later. The drawer itself can be tidied or left in a jumble. All is under the child's control, with no one apart from the analyst having access to it. The medium of play has proved itself a simple and obvious means of communication at conscious and unconscious levels, though Klein expected the child to communicate verbally as well. Her aim was for the child to develop the ability to express and resolve his anxieties, feelings and thoughts in words as well as play, to his full individual potential.

Typically, when a child first enters the analyst's consulting room, he will hesitantly select one or two toys, place them in a configuration or begin to use them in a way which gives a clue to his state of mind. Very often and especially at the start, the child's anxiety will be evoked by the unfamiliar situation he finds himself in. He may retreat behind a door, draw with a tense and anxious concentration, or place a toy in potential danger. The Kleinian analyst tries to pick up on the child's most intense anxiety, which in a Kleinian framework may be understood as arising from fears about his sexual, needy or angry feelings towards the important people in his world, reflected in the transference. By putting his anxieties into words, Klein believed the child could feel understood and supported so that his fears would be less overwhelming.

Insensitively handled, this approach may be intrusive rather than containing, and many of Klein's contemporaries were frankly alarmed at the thought of articulating children's unconscious fears so directly. However, an important feature of Kleinian work, then and now, is the close and thoughtful attention given to the details of the psychic experience of both patient and therapist. The Kleinian practice of infant observation in psychotherapy training contributes to the capacity for accurate and empathic observation, and has been increasingly taken up in other forms of training. Kleinian theory continues to derive as directly as possible from clinical experience rather than abstract speculation (Schoenhals 1994).

Anna Freud was developing her own psychoanalytic work with children at that time, and much of the controversy surrounding Klein's work was between those who espoused Anna Freud's approach and those who supported Klein's. Both have developed into effective work with children through different institutions and have over time become less divergent. Comparing Anna Freud's approach (A. Freud 1927) with Klein's brings out the essence of Klein's approach.

Anna Freud concurred with her father's view of the centrality of the Oedipus Complex, with its crisis and resolution between the ages of about three and seven. In her view, therefore, there was little point in full psychoanalytic work with children before the age of six or seven, because until they had lived through their major formative experience they were in a sense incomplete people. Without a stable ego or super-ego, their future personality could be endangered by over-attention to the id drives which they could not yet be expected to control. As we know, Klein thought that Oedipal conflicts and primitive ego and super-ego structures developed from the beginning of object relating, at birth. There was therefore every reason for her to recommend working with troubled children as early as possible, before their difficulties proliferated and became established.

Anna Freud pointed out that children were most unlikely to initiate their own psychotherapeutic treatment: it was far more likely that the parents, rather than the child, would be suffering from their child's disturbed behaviour and would therefore seek treatment for him. The analyst's first task was to make a relationship with the child in order to create a motivation for the analysis; this might be done through playing with him or making things with or for him. The analyst should present herself as a friendly and reassuring figure, rather like a favourite aunt; and in order to avoid impossible confusion, the rules of behaviour for the consulting room should be similar to the expectations of the outside world. The aim was to foster the child's liking and respect.

Klein, on the other hand, felt that only the disturbed child's inexperience and helplessness prevented him from seeking help. It was counter-productive to try to make the child like the analyst, which would only mask his problems. She thought that when children experienced how analysis could help them with their anxieties, they would develop their own motivation for the therapeutic work with its inevitable tribulations.

Their views on transference were also opposed. Anna Freud believed that as the child lived with and depended on his parents he would not transfer these relationships on to that with the analyst, making transference interpretations misplaced. Klein, however, understood the child to be as involved in transference as the adult. The relationship transferred was not so much the child's external relationship with the parent as his inner relationships with the internalised parents and part-parents. These inner objects may have formed before the depressive position predominated, as all-powerful fragments of good or evil within. It was the extreme and unrealistic fears and wishes associated with these inner objects which the child relived in the transference relationship. It was therefore crucial, in Klein's view, to interpret the child's transference.

Because Anna Freud believed that the Oedipus Complex was not resolved before six or seven, she also assumed that the child's super-ego only came into being then and remained undeveloped for some time, especially in those children who were disturbed enough to need analysis. The analytic task was therefore in part to help reinforce the child's weak super-ego. She suggested that the analyst may need to hold more authority than the parents for the period of analysis in order to influence the child's development; whereas delving into the unconscious could overwhelm the child's fragile personality.

Klein, on the other hand, believed that children needed exactly the same approach as adults. For her, children were not incomplete people, but young human beings experiencing life with particular intensity and with an openness to unconscious processes which adults rarely retain. She believed that from their earliest years children could feel harshly persecuted by a super-ego infused with persecutory anxieties. Like many adults, children often needed to develop more compassion for themselves through modifying the ruthlessness of their inner judgements. The analyst's task was not to help socialise children. This role belonged to their parents and the world outside therapy, and Klein believed that even two-year-olds could differentiate between what was appropriate in the consulting room and what was allowed elsewhere. She believed that the analyst's task was to help the child face his deepest anxieties; by naming them and working them out through play and words, he could further resolve them. Although she prevented children from injuring themselves or her, attacks on toys and attacks with words were essential to the realisation of these goals. Reassurance, she felt, had as little place in the analysis of children as in the analysis of adults. She thought it would give the child the impression that the analyst could not bear his feelings or fears, forcing him to bury them once more rather than confront them.

Both approaches have developed since then. The Anna Freudian approach has taken up parts of the Kleinian approach, such as working with younger children and recognising that children develop transference relationships, while the Kleinian approach may now take more account of the child's external environment and look beyond the world of transference.

Klein's approach demonstrates her respect for the child as a person with the capacity to endure and develop through his own experience, given recognition and support. Her opposers, from her own time to the present day, feared her approach was an ill-advised opening of Pandora's box; but the children she worked with, now middle-aged adults, remember her with fondness – partly because she did not in practice keep so severely to the rules she outlined. She would offer comfort as well as analysis to a child in deep distress, extend hope to a child who felt life was not worth living, start playing with a child who was too inhibited or too unrelated to express himself. Her beliefs and her humanity shine through most clearly in her work with children. With the sad exception of her own children, she seemed to understand and feel at ease with them.

Commentary

Kleinian theory makes a leap from biology to psychology (Greenberg and Mitchell 1983). Instead of seeing the workings of the mind as fundamentally an aspect of the body, meaning, relationship and subjective experience become the touchstones for understanding human beings. Psychoanalytic theory gained emotional vividness and depth, though at the expense of a more systematised theory. Kleinian theory perpetuates the mind–body division of Freudian theory by replacing a physical predicate with a mental bias. The Object Relations school was a direct development of this crucial shift of focus.

While Freud reached back to the child in the adult, Klein reached the infant in the child and therefore also in the adult. Her play technique forged a means of communication which has shaped all later psychotherapeutic work with children, and her grasp and articulation of primitive processes have structured and deepened the understanding of psychotic and borderline states. She provided a framework for conceptualising and thus tolerating early and disturbing levels of experience, extending the range of disturbance that psychotherapy can address.

Klein's theoretical focus on the mother–child relationship and on the girl's development as a process in its own right redressed the male-centredness of Freudian theory. Her psychoanalysis does not otherwise address difference, rooted as it was in the social assumptions which were reflected in current theory. The biological premises of psychoanalysis and the influence of Darwin's evolutionary theories meant that homosexual and lesbian development were inevitably seen as deviant; and because of the supposed universality of psychoanalysis, little attention was paid to class, national or ethnic groupings (but see Klein 1959: Postscript). Klein commented, however, that she would be very interested to analyse a person from a different culture, indicating that she thought there would be at least some important differences. She also remarked that she had found working with highly religious people difficult: the Freudian view of religion as illusion, which she shared, would have brought about a philosophical clash (Grosskurth 1986: 443).

Klein's neglect of environmental factors has been widely criticised. In her theory it is the baby's nature that gives rise to his suffering, and the hate which derives from the death instinct is a psychoanalytic version of original sin. This pathological view of the human condition reflects Klein's anxious adherence to Freudian theory. In order to be fully biological, conflict is regarded as intrinsic to the person rather than a function of the individual's relationship to the environment. Perhaps she might have modified these premises of psychoanalytic theory had she felt freer to depart from the accepted Freudian views: her case studies demonstrate the significance she actually allotted to the child's experiences in his family. Individual psychology, she suggests, is made up of 'internal processes arising from constitutional and environmental factors' (Klein 1945). She saw psychological experience, therefore, as a third area, influenced by but not reducible to either the innate capacities or environmental forces which contribute to it. Original sin seems to be joined by free will.

Early critics of Kleinian theory objected to her concrete and crude expressions of selfhood, with internalised penises, breasts and vaginas and preoccupation with faeces, urine and unborn babies, which sound more like actual objects than mental phenomena (King and Steiner 1991: 405). Klein replied that she developed her psychoanalytic language directly from her work with children, whom she talked to in their own words and their own ways: these were not symbolic and delicate, but earthy and blunt. Klein presents her theory as what a baby or a child would say if he were able to, rather than as an academic deduction or abstraction of what she found. Her theory is more descriptive and evocative than explanatory. In recent years, however, Kleinian work with children has become less of a focus, with more attention being given to primitive processes and states of mind in adults. The language of Kleinian theory now involves fewer references to concrete part-objects such as penis and breast, and more to psychological functions such as seeing and hearing, thinking and experiencing. Part-objects are seen more in terms of a mode of relating than as the building blocks of phantasy.

Klein took the ego for granted, with its libidinal and death drives manifested as autonomous capacities for loving and hating. To some degree we must accept this starting place: any theorist must choose her premises and areas of focus. However, the assumptions Klein made undermine her stated adherence to drive theory. If the 'instincts' only become active at birth, what was their status before? If, as she suggested, there was no cause for the foetus to experience separateness and thus object relationship, what were the drives doing then? Her theories imply a state of pre-natal suspended animation which does not ring true with personal experience or later research. She seems to be caught between her wish to be faithful to the drive premises of Freudian theory and the fact that her framework holds together better with a basis in object relation, which would allow love and hate to be seen as phenomena in their own right rather than as manifestations of quasi-biological instincts. Explicit references to the death instinct are now seldom made, although constitutionally-based intrapsychic conflict and primitive destructive processes remain central to the Kleinian view of the person.

It has often been said that Klein attributes impossibly sophisticated and complex processes to the young and inexperienced infant. Daniel Stern (1985) suggests that early phantasies and the defences of splitting and projection imply an awareness of duality and spatial organisation, together with a capacity for symbolisation, which do not develop before the second year. He post-dates Kleinian psychological processes to the period when the child is beginning to use language rather than the months after birth. This would imply that Klein mistook the young child's current internal reality as expressed through his play and his words for a regressed or earlier reality: paranoid-schizoid processes appeared because the child was now able to think and feel in this way, revealing nothing about how he experienced life as an infant.

Very similar points were made by Klein's contemporaries, who also viewed the Kleinian phantasy world as impossible to attribute to the infant (King and Steiner 1991: 348–52; 434–8). Where, they asked, would the baby learn about penises and vaginas, let alone unborn children? Where would he have experienced the drowning and the poisoning, the floods, fires and explosions that were supposed to arise from his own faeces and urine? Surely these were sophisticated verbal phantasies, probably the analyst's own, which were being foisted on those unfortunate patients who found themselves in Kleinian clutches.

Phantasy is unconscious and pre-symbolic; but our only means of articulating it is language, which is conscious rather than unconscious and presupposes a more sophisticated mind. Verbal expression brings an unavoidable baggage of structures, processes and capacities from a differently organised mentality. The most words can do is give an obscure sense of what the phantasy could be if it were conscious and able to be articulated. The body parts and violent processes of Kleinian language are evocations rather than content. They refer obliquely to the experience rather than bearing a direct equivalence, and changing Kleinian language reflects the conceptual and linguistic changes in Western society.

Klein also suggests that while the baby has some vague awareness of what we would later call separateness, cognitive structures such as spatial and temporal awareness resonate with rather than precede phantasy, echoing something already felt. It is for this reason that Klein postulates an innate knowledge of an object and some of its functions (part-objects) as the *sine qua non* of phantasy. Later research has gone on to establish that the new-born baby is indeed equipped with capacities and presumably unconscious 'knowledge' which enables him to survive through perceiving, feeding from, interacting with and making sense of another person (Stern 1985).

Fairbairn (1952) disagreed with Klein's concept of the primary good internal object. He could see no reason for the baby to internalise another person, or aspects of them, unless the relationship between them had become blocked. In his view the internal object is a sign of pathology, albeit universal; whereas in Klein's theory the child builds his whole sense of self around the good internalised object. She saw this as a benign rather than a destructive attempt to reverse the separation brought about by birth, beautifully expressed in one of her late papers: 'The good breast is taken in and becomes part of the ego, and the infant who was first inside the mother now has the mother inside himself' (Klein 1975: 179).

Klein's colleague Ella Sharpe argued that the illusory nature of this post-birth union provides a shaky foundation for the identity (King and Steiner 1991: 337–40). While it may be temporarily expedient, she felt that people should grow out of their childish clinging to the parents within. True maturity involves autonomy and separation, and the acceptance that each individual is fundamentally alone.

It is arguable that to base our most intimate sense of self on something imported is alienating, but Sharpe's objection is hard to uphold overall. Her viewpoint assumes that it is possible to relate to another person without at some level identifying with them (Bion 1962b). Klein felt that in perceiving and wanting something outside our control, we already have an internal sense of what that something could be, or at least how it could make us feel. Thus the mouth in wanting the nipple experiences a gap, an idea, which is nipple-shaped. The feel, smell and appearance of the real nipple and milk that the baby physically takes in, colour and elaborate the 'idea' the baby already has in his aching lips, palate and throat. The next time the baby's need to feed, suck or take in gives rise to the 'idea' of the feeding breast, it will be a fuller, more embodied breast that he wants and seeks. This process of idea and realisation is what Klein refers to as the constant interplay between projection and introjection, between the baby finding what he expects to find, and expecting to find in part what he has already found. Relationship arises through experiencing what is inside and what is outside as in some way the same: in other words, identification. Klein's concept of the self built around the good object expresses her commitment to the primacy of relationship. The core of the self is the confluence with another, underscoring our inescapably social nature.

Perhaps the most difficult aspect of Klein's work lies in the emotional demand she makes on her readers. The unrelenting horror and suffering that she presents as unavoidable and perhaps predominant in any human life strike us as chilling and, we may hope, misguided. Can the zenith of achievement really be the capacity to bear depression and ambivalence?

Of course the capacity for depression means that we can be more secure, related and happy, but Klein's terminology indicates that this was not what drew her interest. The loneliness arising from her tragic losses and from her difficult, conflicted, self-centred personality must have been a potent influence on her theories. Yet in shining a torch on these most shadowy corners, she left us a stark clarity that would have been compromised by a more balanced approach. Klein's eccentric courage led her to face suffering and destructiveness more directly than did her colleagues, without deviating from the values of self-responsibility and ethical concern for others which are the hallmark of the resolved depressive position. Having a personal understanding of Klein inside us can help us, in turn, face the extremes of our own and others' hate, fragmentation and despair. Her theory can help us bear the most dreadful parts of human beings.

3

RONALD FAIRBAIRN:
THE DYNAMIC STRUCTURE OF THE SELF

Fairbairn is arguably the most neglected figure in Object Relations. His retiring personality, his residence in Edinburgh and the dizzying challenge he made to orthodox psychoanalytic theory all contributed to his marginalisation. It is only in recent years that his work has been published in its entirety, with the recognition that he was the first person to set out a full Object Relations theory of the personality.

LIFE

Ronald Fairbairn was born in Edinburgh, Scotland, in 1889, the only child of well-to-do parents (Sutherland 1989). His father was a strict Calvinist, his mother an English woman with strong ambitions for the family. Fairbairn became the focus of his mother's attention and hopes, growing up to be idealistic and serious-minded. The rather pompous entry in his diary on his twenty-first birthday expresses his wish for a 'muscular Christianity' rather than the glum passivity of church culture. After initial plans to become a lawyer he decided to enter the church.

Fairbairn shared his mother's wish that he should go to Oxford University, but his father opposed the plan on the grounds of expense and Oxford's dubious moral climate. He remained in Edinburgh to study philosophy, going on to study theology and Hellenic studies in London, Manchester and abroad until the outbreak of the First World War. During his period in the army he encountered 'shell-shocked' soldiers, and soon came to the view that psychological knowledge offered more than religion in addressing emotional and social problems. Another factor in his change of direction may have been his growing fear of preaching, an early example of the phobic symptoms he developed in later life. In his exploration of psychological theories he discovered Freud and decided to pursue psychoanalysis.

Ernest Jones advised Fairbairn to qualify as a doctor before training as a psychoanalyst, so in 1919 he embarked on an intensive four-year medical qualification course. Given the many years he had already spent as a student, this was probably a less daunting prospect to Fairbairn than to many: James Strachey, for example, only lasted six weeks into a similar course. Fairbairn did not have access to a training analyst, supervision or formal training, but he was in analysis for two years with Ernest Connell, an Edinburgh psychiatrist who had been psychoanalysed by Jones. By 1925 Fairbairn was seeing his own patients for analysis.

Despite several attempts to move to London, Fairbairn remained in Edinburgh for the rest of his life. For some years he combined psychoanalysis with the medical care of terminally ill patients, teaching and psychiatric work at Edinburgh University and the clinic attached to its psychology department. His work with traumatised soldiers, with physically and sexually abused children, with disturbed and psychotic patients and with sexual offenders (Fairbairn 1952) demonstrates a conviction that psychoanalysis should make a social contribution beyond the benefits to the tiny number of people with access to psychoanalytic treatment.

At a mature thirty-seven, Fairbairn married Mary More Gordon. She was intelligent and cultured, and enjoyed the upper-class social and cultural life in which she had been brought up. As was expected of a woman of her social class, she gave up all thought of a career after her marriage, despite having trained in medicine. She and Fairbairn had five children between 1927 and 1933, two of whom were twins who died at birth in 1928. This trauma must have contributed to the difficulties in their relationship which continued until Mary's sudden death in 1952. It seems likely that their youngest son Nicholas, who became an eccentric and cynical Conservative politician, suffered particularly badly during his formative years when his parents' relationship was deteriorating.

Mary's antagonism to Fairbairn's work, and her eventual alcoholism, are often seen as the cause of their marital problems. However, the empty life imposed on the middle-class woman of her time, with no focus outside the home and nannies and servants within it, must have been hard for an intelligent woman to bear. When we also learn that Fairbairn regularly worked a ten-hour day with only a short lunch-break, spending the evenings until after midnight writing, it seems inevitable that she should be frustrated and unhappy. Fairbairn took his children to school and for outings at weekends, but he was unable to build with Mary the kind of empathic shared relationship he wrote of so eloquently in relation to his patients. His most vivid life may have been lived within himself and his work, which could have served to some extent as an evasion of his difficulties with Mary.

The idea of separation was impossible given Fairbairn's religious convictions and his concern for his children. He and Mary reached an uneasy compromise, with Fairbairn participating in visits, holidays and cultural events which he would probably rather have avoided. Mary, however, remained angry and unhappy, while Fairbairn may well have taken up an irritating attitude of distance. They seem to have been kept from disaster by a companion-secretary who lived in the household for many years and who managed to get on with both of them.

Fairbairn's teaching and psychiatric work were also beset with difficulty. Although a few of his colleagues were open to psychoanalysis, most viewed it as a controversial innovation which was not wanted in their institutions. They had almost no direct contact with psychoanalysis other than through Fairbairn, and given his shy personality he may not have been an effective ambassador. We get a picture of Fairbairn as isolated and with little support, the butt of hostility and ridicule, which no doubt increased his tendency to turn inwards rather than outwards. It is not surprising that in 1934, when his personal and work circumstances were at a very low ebb, he developed the same neurotic symptom from which his father had suffered: an inhibition which increased to an inability to urinate when others were nearby. His anxiety in this situation could rise to suicidal proportions, and while it fluctuated, this phobia never left him.

Fairbairn's symptom has been analysed exhaustively for its symbolic meaning (Sutherland 1989). What emerges most forcefully is his acute tension and literal fear of letting go in what he experienced as a dangerous situation: the presence of other people. Perhaps the constraints put upon his social and professional life through his inability to travel or stay away from home could be read as expressions of both his anger and his guilt towards his wife, depriving her of the activity she craved and depriving himself of professional opportunities and the recognition that comes from public involvement.

Fairbairn's most active and original clinical work was during the 1930s and 1940s, although he continued in later years to develop his theoretical ideas through his writing. Harry Guntrip, whom we shall meet in a later chapter, was in analysis with Fairbairn during the 1950s. He describes a formal and introverted figure, 'more orthodox in practice than in theory' (Guntrip 1975), a picture which is at odds with the bold challenger of Freudian theory but consistent with the thoughtful, anxious, conflicted man attacked from inside and outside home. Mary died during this period, and Fairbairn began to suffer increasing ill-health. He had several near-fatal bouts of influenza and developed Parkinson's disease.

In other ways, however, Fairbairn's life became easier. He gained some professional recognition in Britain, and also in America. His colleague and biographer Jock Sutherland, as well as Guntrip, remained in close touch with him until the end of his life. In 1959 he married his secretary, Marian Mackintosh, who had succeeded the original companion to himself and Mary; Marian remained an important support until his death on the last day of 1964. It is touching to learn that despite his poor health and his difficulties with travelling, he made the journey to London for Melanie Klein's funeral in 1960.

Fairbairn's life in Edinburgh, far from the discussions and controversies of the London psychoanalysts, was demonstrably not a bar to the development of his original and innovative ideas. Although he had to do without the feedback and stimulation that day-to-day contact with colleagues could have provided, he might have felt less free to carry out his deconstruction of Freudian theory had he been under constant pressure to conform to accepted views. Although some analysts responded to his papers, it was from within himself and from the writings of Freud and Klein that Fairbairn fashioned his critique of classical psychoanalysis.

Fairbairn comes over as an introspective and intellectually brilliant man with a richer inner than outer life. His early call for a 'muscular Christianity', for keeping a light touch alongside a serious commitment, was perhaps a call to himself. His friends and colleagues, though they were rather few, spoke of a man of warmth, humour and kindness, despite his tendency towards distance rather than intimacy. His social conscience and his commitment to the alleviation of suffering go side by side with a rigorous scrutiny of ideas and the development of original thought. It is not surprising that much of his theoretical interest is focused on the schizoid way of being, when primal disappointment in life turns us away from relationship with others on to a path of withdrawal and internal conflict. His work with children and with psychotic and traumatised patients offered him opportunities to explore and conceptualise the primitive emotional needs and defences with which he found himself uniquely able to empathise. Like Freud and Klein, Fairbairn offers us an insight into what it was like to be him.

THEORY

Overview

Fairbairn began his psychoanalytic studies with a thorough and critical reading of Freud. As a German-speaker the original version was available to him, and his training in philosophy enabled him to pick out the assumptions and structures underlying Freudian theory.

Fairbairn concluded that the scientific foundations on which Freud's work rested were out of date. As science had developed further, so the discipline of psychoanalysis required revision and updating. Freud's theories were based on nineteenth-century Newtonian physics, where energy and matter, force and substance, were seen as fundamentally different phenomena. Freudian theories of the personality and the instincts rest upon this separation, with instinctual energies channelled into the static id, ego and super-ego. By the 1930s, physics had moved on. Einstein was presenting matter and energy as aspects of the same phenomena: light, for example, could now be viewed either as energetic waves or concrete particles, depending on the circumstances. The traditional scientific dualism could no longer be upheld.

In a gradual, radical reworking of Freud's framework, Fairbairn argues that the distinction between matter and energy, structure and instinct, should be abandoned (Fairbairn 1952). He suggests that the ego (the 'I') is present at birth, which he took as the symbolic beginning of the person as Freud and Klein had done before; and that libido is simply its activity. The person *is* structured energy, or dynamic structure. This means that when we think of the self in structural terms, the word 'ego' should be used; when we think dynamically, 'libido' applies. This change had far-reaching implications which were obscured and confused by Fairbairn's use of the same words in the same translation as Freud had used, but carrying different meanings and resting on different premises.

Fairbairn saw the person as the libidinal 'I' with the overarching aim of relating to another 'I'. Libido, or the person in her libidinal capacity, is primarily not pleasure-seeking but object-seeking. Fairbairn is suggesting that our deepest motivation is for contact with others and that this need overrides our wish for physical gratification. Our most basic anxiety, therefore, is separation anxiety: the dread of the loss of the other, on whom our physical and psychological survival depends.

What of the death instinct and the aggression that derives from its externalisation, bulwarks of both Freudian and Kleinian theory? Fairbairn could not conceive of aggression as a primary phenomenon because it would be antithetical to the need for libidinal connection. He saw aggression as a reactive rather than a fundamental phenomenon, arising when libidinal contact is blocked or frustrated. There is thus no place for a death instinct or primary destructive urge and Fairbairn rejected this concept, in absolute opposition to the established Freudian and developing Kleinian schools.

The id, too, is redundant in Fairbairn's structure. Whereas Freud saw the id as the container of the instincts, the 'seething cauldron' of unconscious energy, Fairbairn's synthesis of structure and energy removes its *raison d'être*. If a container is not separable from what it contains, if there is no death instinct and if libido (Eros) is simply the active aspect of the ego, there is no place for the id. Fairbairn also redefined the super-ego, rejecting its Freudian genesis as the product of the Oedipus Complex. What Freud and Klein refer to as the super-ego he saw as a complex of structures arising from the early division of the self.

The Schizoid Position

Freud suggested that at birth the baby is an uncoordinated being whose disparate fragments gradually cohere and integrate. Fairbairn suggests by contrast that at birth, our hypothetical beginning, we are whole and undivided; but that through the traumas and stresses of post-natal life our primary unity is broken along predictable lines, and we become divided within ourselves and against ourselves. He terms this primary division the schizoid position, postulating the same basic patterning in all human beings. He is suggesting not that we are all schizoid personalities but that we are all split and conflicted, and that these inner splits and conflicts structure the self.

What is the nature of the primary trauma leading to this internal rupture? Fairbairn suggests it is that which impels the baby to withdraw from whole-hearted connection with the object, the person in the outside world. Withdrawal from relationship involves a basic conflict because the baby's fundamental motivation is to relate to others. The compulsion to go against this basic urge arises, Fairbairn suggests, from two possible, and inevitable, scenarios: if the baby is not convinced that her object (for example, mother) loves her for herself, and if the baby is not convinced that her object accepts her love as love. These simple and profound definitions of primary trauma bring out the subjective nature of failures in relationship that cannot but be universal. No one feels an unending certainty of being loved and valued simply for being who they are: we sometimes feel valued for our services, our looks or our talents, as the extension of someone else's hopes or as a means of demonstrating their importance. Actual and perceived indifference, neglect or exasperation cannot but occur rather frequently in our closest relationships from babyhood onwards.

From the baby's point of view these early abandonments are shockingly intolerable, but she is forced to find a way of managing them. She has to construct a way of being which encompasses her absolute need to relate as well as offering some protection from the emotional consequences of her unmet relational needs. Fairbairn suggests that the only way of doing this involves separating off the traumatic experience and relocating it inside. The trauma is incorporated in the baby's subjectivity by way of damage limitation, paid for in internal conflict. The baby is able to continue relating to the external person, while the split-off bad experience takes up her retreat from the dangers of relationship.

Fairbairn offers us a diagram to help explain how the schizoid position (the split position) first comes about (Fairbairn 1952: 105). We can build up the diagram in stages, following this process. The whole and intact ego (the self) is originally in full and unproblematic relationship with the other person (Figure 3.1):

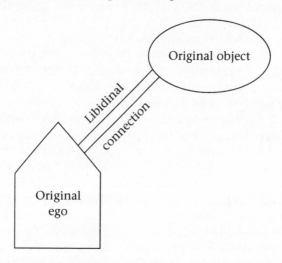

Figure 3.1: The earliest relation of ego and object

When the libidinal, or loving, connection is broken, blocked or compromised, the baby takes inside the relationship which has now become ambivalent. She divides this jumbled mixture into its tolerable and intolerable parts. The tolerable aspect, termed the 'ideal object', stays connected to the main part of the ego, which we now term the 'central ego'; there is thus a constant internal relationship between the central ego and the ideal object (Figure 3.2). The central ego is the self that we like to think of ourselves as: 'I feel myself again today'. The ideal object is the way we would like others to appear to us. These two elements together represent the mode of relationship in which we feel most comfortable: comparatively smooth, without an over-intensity of either anger or need. The central ego/ideal object set-up is the manageable inner relationship which we salvage from a bad experience.

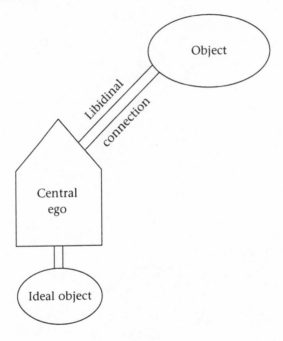

Figure 3.2: The central ego and ideal object

The intolerable aspect, also internalised, is further subdivided into two elements. The intolerably tantalising aspect of the other person, connected to the intensely needing self, is internalised as an inner bonding of the 'exciting object' and the 'libidinal ego' (Figure 3.3).

The libidinal ego is a fragment of the original ego that has been disavowed and driven apart from the official, accepted self, the central ego. The baby thus splits off her unbearable neediness in a withdrawal from external relationship. Her neediness implies the original object of her need: the person who excited her beyond what she could endure. The libidinal ego/exciting object configuration may emerge from repression as intense dependency cravings. We feel it at a more conscious level where it merges into the central ego/ideal object, as painful yearning in situations such as waiting endlessly by the phone for the lover who had promised to ring, but who we know from experience will not.

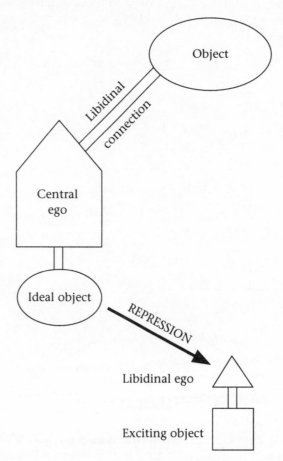

Figure 3.3: The libidinal ego and exciting object

Simultaneously, the intolerably depriving, rejecting aspect of the other person is internalised as the 'rejecting object', attached to the 'anti-libidinal ego' (Figure 3.4). The anti-libidinal ego is the split-off ego fragment that is bonded to the rejecting object. We can think of it as the 'anti-wanting I', the aspect of the self that is contemptuous of neediness. Rejection gives rise to unbearable anger, split off from the central self or ego and disowned by it. Fairbairn originally termed this element the 'internal saboteur', indicating that in despising rather than acknowledging our neediness, we ensure that we neither seek nor get what we want. The anti-libidinal ego/rejecting object configuration is the cynical, angry self which is too dangerously hostile for us to acknowledge. When it emerges from repression we

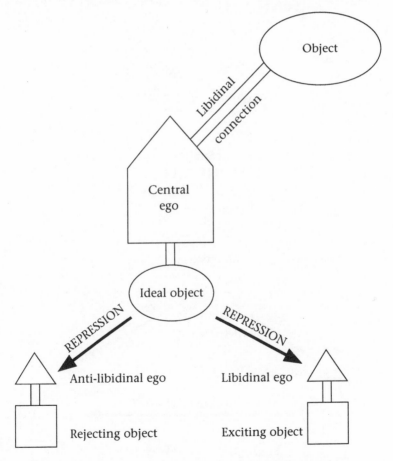

Figure 3.4: The anti-libidinal ego and rejecting object

may experience it as chaotic rage or hatred, sometimes with persecutory guilt. As it merges with the conscious central ego/ideal object, it appears as the despising of oneself and others as wimpish and pathetic; 'I never wanted her anyway', we declare brazenly, berating our pathetic neediness of the tantalising exciting object whom we attempt to render worthless.

The libidinal ego bonded to the exciting object and the anti-libidinal ego bonded to the rejecting object are repressed and split off: the central ego/ideal object duo drives them out of acknowl-edgement. The libidinal ego/exciting object (need) is further rejected

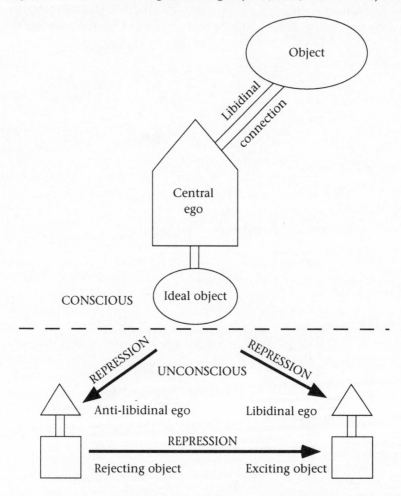

Figure 3.5: Fairbairn's complete ego/object structure

and disowned by the anti-libidinal ego/rejecting object (anger), a process Fairbairn describes as secondary or indirect repression (Figure 3.5). The central ego/ideal object is the main part of the self, acknowledged, accepted and conscious, fading into the other constellations which are essentially repressed and unconscious.

The diagram thus represents the original splitting of the ego which leads to a differentiated complex of internal relationships representing the continuing necessity of relationship in the face of blocked external relationship. By taking the burden of badness within, we can continue to see the needed external person as good enough, and can therefore continue trusting them and relating to them. We maintain an outward sense of security at the price of inward insecurity and conflict. Fairbairn calls this relocation of badness the 'moral defence', and connected it with the Freudian super-ego (Fairbairn 1943). He suggests that in order to cope with this inner persecution, we back up the repression of the disavowed ego/object constellations by internalising good experiences; this consolidates the ideal object and offsets the intolerableness of the rejecting and exciting objects and their respective ego fragments.

Fairbairn ends up with a tripartite structure which bears a superficial resemblance to Freud's tripartite personality structure. The central ego/ideal object and the Freudian ego, the anti-libidinal ego/rejecting object and the super-ego, the libidinal ego/exciting object and the id correspond to the aspects of the mind which Freud and Fairbairn understood in different ways. The central ego, however, is a far more dynamic and substantial centre of operations than Freud's ego, which is a secondary structure besieged by external and internal pressures. The id is the centre of Freudian theory as the source and container of all mental energy, a tumultuous, chaotic instinctual jumble; the libidinal ego/exciting object, by contrast, is simply repressed dependency in continual relationship with a tantalising other within the self. Freud's super-ego develops at a later stage than the anti-libidinal ego/rejecting object; and Fairbairn considered what Freud saw as the super-ego to include this duo together with the aspirations and expectations supplied by the ideal object in relation to the central ego.

Fairbairn's structure also bears comparison with the three ego-states articulated by Eric Berne (Berne 1961). Berne left psychoanalytic training to establish Transactional Analysis, and like others in American psychoanalytic circles he was familiar with Fairbairn's work. The anti-libidinal ego/rejecting object correlates readily with the moralising Parent, the libidinal ego/exciting object with the needy and spontaneous Child, and the central ego/ideal object with the reality-based Adult. The 'top dog/underdog' polarity looks very like the opposition between the anti-libidinal ego/rejecting object and the doubly-oppressed libidinal ego/exciting object. Berne's ego-states are tools rather than theoretical constructs, and are not differentiated into conscious and unconscious as are Fairbairn's ego constellations; it would be interesting to explore the relations between these practical and theoretical ideas (to which Kathi Murphy (personal communication) drew my attention).

The Schizoid State

The schizoid position is the primary structuring of the self which Fairbairn took as the basis for personality development of all kinds. The schizoid personality develops when the original splitting and repression are maintained and increased to an extreme, yet without the psychotic fragmentation of schizophrenia (Fairbairn 1940). The hallmark of the extreme schizoid position, the schizoid state, is a sense of emptiness, deadness and futility. While this state is experienced transiently by many people, the schizoid person experiences it as a normal way of being. In Fairbairn's terms, so much personal involvement – need and anger – has been split off and repressed that the central ego/ideal object is left empty. Many people in a schizoid state express this as feeling unreal and cut off, as though separated from the world and their own feelings by a glass screen. The sense of futility arises from the poverty of their relationships, which in Object Relations theory are the centre of human life. Love and relationship are dangerous for the schizoid person because it was her need for others which brought about her hopelessness; this in turn led to a vicious internal war of attrition. If love itself is destructive, life has neither meaning nor purpose.

Because relationship with others has proved unendurable, the schizoid person substitutes inner relationships which are themselves conflicted, problematic and repressed. The focus on the inner rather than the outer world is manifested in the characteristic schizoid introversion and narcissistic valuing of the self over others. The schizoid person scorns physical need and passion as gross, shunning dangerous emotions and preferring to occupy only the more rational and intellectual layers of the psyche. Reverting to the simpler view of the other as a function, the schizoid person tends to treat others as adjuncts to the self – part-objects – rather than as people in their own right. The apparent schizoid indifference or contempt for others led Freud to the view that such patients could not be treated psycho-analytically as they seemed unable to form a useful transference on the analyst. Fairbairn's vivid and empathic articulation of the dreadful inner state of the schizoid person opened the door to a fuller understanding of the schizoid state and how to work with those suffering within it.

Fairbairn contrasts the schizoid position, where love appears to be the agent of destruction, with the depressive position, which arises at a later stage of infancy. The dilemma of the depressive position, so fully articulated by Klein, is how to manage anger and hate. In the depressive state we feel that while our love is good, our hate is bad. We cannot avoid being angry and so we fear that we will drive away or destroy the person we love. The feeling that this leaves us with is not futility but despair. We still believe in the value and goodness of relationships but feel we are not capable of sustaining them.

Fairbairn suggests that the schizoid and depressive positions and anxieties face us with our ultimate fears: the destruction of the self and the other through our love or through our hate. Being caught in either is an intolerable experience which we defend against in any way we can. While both are unbearable, the schizoid state is the more fundamental and terrible because of the conviction that love itself is bad; thus a schizoid state exacerbates the depressive position before it has even begun. In the schizoid state the libidinal ego/exciting object, our needy self, is the threat; in the depressive it is the anti-libidinal ego/rejecting object, our angry self, that is feared and therefore kept under repression. Fairbairn suggests that all psychotic and neurotic states relate to these two basic human positions; people usually tend more towards one than the other, depending on whether their greatest problems arose in the primitive experience of need, leading to the schizoid position, or the later experience of hating the person they needed, leading to the depressive position.

Fairbairn considered that twentieth-century Western childcare engendered an alienated, schizoid mode of being through the isolation suffered daily by babies. The schizoid sense of meaninglessness has been explored in depth and detail by the existentialists (see Sartre 1938), who view it as the core of the human condition: for them, our only choice is to struggle with it or deny it.

Emotional Development

Fairbairn rethought the Freudian stages of libidinal development, elaborated by Abraham as the oral, anal, phallic and genital stages of sexuality. In this model, the child's focus of excitement moves to different body parts or erotogenic zones, setting the tone and structure for interaction with external objects (people) who are important only insofar as they are agents of the child's instinctual gratification or frustration. The different neuroses – depression, hysteria, obsessional neurosis – are seen as arising from fixations or arrests at specific points in libidinal development, as a result of either too much gratification or too much frustration of the child's instinctual urges. Thus people fixated at the anal stage are continually preoccupied with cleanliness and dirt, order and mess, holding on and letting go. They may present as obsessive-compulsive in their unconscious and incessant efforts to undo their messiness through rituals of checking or cleansing, as rigidly inhibited in emotional expressiveness, frequently being physically constipated as well, or as messily defiant in their refusal to 'follow the rules'.

Fairbairn describes libidinal development in emotional rather than sexual terms, reflecting the primacy of relationship over drive (Fairbairn 1941). He suggests that we move from 'infantile dependence' to 'mature dependence' via a transitional stage. He does not see maturity as independence because we never grow out of our need for others, although the way we experience others and our need for them changes over time. He places the neuroses in the transitional stage, suggesting that they are based on paranoid, phobic, obsessional or hysterical techniques. These techniques are not the result of fixation, but different methods which we use in the struggle to move from infantile to mature dependence. Neurosis represents both the achievement of going beyond infantile dependence and the failure to reach mature dependence.

Infantile Dependence

Fairbairn describes infantile dependence as a libidinal connection – a wanting connection – based on identification with the object and expressed through an attitude of taking. He terms the structure of this connection 'primary identification' (Fairbairn 1941). In this state, the baby experiences the other more as an aspect of herself than as another person. She feels her attachment as a need to feed from and be nurtured by the other, essentially to take from the other. Mature dependence, by contrast, is a libidinal connection based on the recognition of the other person's separateness; mature attachment means wishing to give as well as take.

In infantile dependence, the baby perceives little difference between self and other. She drinks in the parent's attitudes, tones, movements and emotions and these suffuse her being. She sees no conflict between her own needs and her parent's. Like her own body parts, the other is there simply to give to her in the way she wants to take: her pleasure is the other's pleasure, the purpose of whose life is in perfect harmony with the baby's needs. Taking from the other is a truly loving act, bringing two beings together in a unity of shared fulfilment. We can see how inevitable it is that parents or carers honoured in this way will not always experience such taking as an expression of love. Sometimes their own needs will predominate, and the infant's will seem a nuisance, a demand, or even an attack. The original splitting of the ego, while theoretically pathological, is thus unavoidable and universal in the real world.

Transitional Stage and Transitional Techniques

With the schizoid position set up, the baby tries to relate to the other as before while containing the traumatic experience within. She feels the badness is safer and more controllable inside than outside because she can continue to see the parent as good and thus feel secure. In the separation process which follows the most primitive stage of infantile dependence, the baby begins to realise that the other is not the same as her. As her sense of control is threatened she feels increasingly vulnerable and powerless. At the same time the repressed ego constellations, like all repressed elements, press upwards into consciousness. These two factors come together in a tendency for the baby to treat external objects as if they were her own internal objects; she projects her rejecting or exciting inner objects on to the people around her and relates to them in those terms.

The transitional stage is thus a process of emotional separation between self and other. Projecting elements of the inner world on to the external world eases the internal battle while offering the illusion that we may be able to get rid of our difficulties. The transitional techniques are the ways in which we manipulate our internal object relationships in our efforts to ward off the full force of the schizoid state, with its relentless persecution covered by inner deadness, or depressive anxieties with their unresolved internal conflicts.

Fairbairn sees the phobic technique as a dilemma between recognising the separate nature of the object and regressing to primary identification. Both the exciting object, promising fulfilment and safety, and the rejecting object, threatening destruction, are projected on to the world outside which then seems to hold both danger and salvation. The phobic person flees in terror from the person or the situation on to which she has projected her rejecting object, and clings regressively to the person or situation representing her exciting object. She is drawn into identification with this object until the fear of losing her identity and individuality turns the exciting object into the rejecting object. Claustrophobia, for example, can be seen as the longing to be merged indistinguishably with the object, together with the dread of being engulfed in the process.

The obsessional technique, like the phobic, represents a conflict between separateness and identification. This time, however, the rejecting and exciting objects are experienced as internal rather than external and are not clearly separate from each other. The obsessional predicament is being torn between holding on to their attractive exciting aspect, and evacuating into the external world their dangerous rejecting aspect. There is a direct relation here to Freud's and Abraham's anal stage, where the central conflict is whether to hold on to or push out the faeces which are experienced both as poisonous weapons and as precious gifts. The rituals of the obsessive-compulsive person express her inability to resolve this question. Constant washing, for example, does not result in the relief sought, although it may briefly give the illusion of doing so. You cannot wash feelings off – particularly if you do not want to let them go.

The hysterical and paranoid techniques are based on the conflict between accepting the object in its exciting aspect and rejecting it in its frustrating aspect. In the hysterical mode, the person identifies her own central ego with the rejecting object, while projecting the exciting object on to the other. She thus rejects herself as a resource and clings desperately to the other who appears as a tantalisingly elusive saviour.

This fragile state of affairs easily tips over into the paranoid state, where the person identifies herself with the exciting object and projects the rejecting object outside. The world then seems full of hostility and danger, while she herself is completely good. The paranoid state may be a comparatively stable way of being or it may arise when the hysterical technique breaks down. Those who represent the hysteric's exciting object are always in danger of falling off their pedestals when they fail to provide sufficient relief. The hysterical person, now paranoid, experiences them as malevolent and evil while she is their innocent victim.

Fairbairn draws a parallel between the schizoid state of inner division and the hysterical state of dissociation. He was one of the earliest psychoanalysts to recognise the connection between these two ways of being and the frequency with which they alternate. It is a common pattern to yearn for the other, experienced as the exciting object, only to withdraw in dread if she responds. The conflict between the desire for relationship and the fear of intimacy becomes exaggerated through projection into a conflict between being rescued and being trapped. This has been variously described as the 'in-and-out programme' (Guntrip 1968), the 'hystero-schizoid split' (Lake 1966) and 'claustro-agoraphobia' (Rey 1994), all of which are subsumed in the borderline and narcissistic states which have become a focus in modern Object Relations.

While the schizoid state involves internal preoccupation and external detachment, the hysterical state involves the distortion of relationships over and above the projection of internal objects. The hysterical person retreats from the dangerous world of the emotions to the safer world of sensations. She only feels safe while actually holding on to the needed other, regardless of whether there is an emotional connection. This parallels the regression to part-object relationships: as well as treating others as less than whole people, the hysteric treats her problems as physical rather than emotional and therefore seeks external relief. The mysterious physical symptoms commonly manifested in hysteria represent a 'substitution of a bodily state for a personal problem' (Fairbairn 1994a: 29).

The hysterical person's bodily focus can look like the Freudian pleasure principle in full swing – the seeking of relief or gratification regardless of personal relationship. Fairbairn regards this as a deterioration of object-relating arising from the abandonment of full emotional contact: pleasure-seeking is simply a poor substitute for person-seeking.

Fairbairn did not examine the process of moving from the transitional stage of relating to that of mature dependence. However, as the transitional techniques are the major neurotic modes, the process of psychotherapy must parallel this move. Fairbairn's psychotherapeutic aim is to help the patient to give up her closed system of internal ego/object structures and come to rely instead on undistorted relationships with real people. He sees the therapeutic relationship as facilitating the patient's change to the extent that it is genuinely good rather than solely transference-based. Fairbairn suggests that maturation means becoming more able to manage experience without resorting to the splitting and repression of the schizoid position or the projection of the transitional stage, and that psychotherapy can help people grow further towards mature dependence (Fairbairn 1994a: 73–92).

Fairbairn gives surprisingly little attention to the development or treatment of psychosis, but leaves a pithy definition:

> Whereas the psychoneurotic tends to treat situations in outer reality as if they were situations in internal reality (i.e., in terms of transference), the psychotic tends to treat situations in inner reality as if they were situations in outer reality. (Fairbairn 1994a: 85)

The extent to which we are dominated by our inner conflicts therefore determines our psychological well-being. In psychosis, the outer world all but disappears as the inner world takes over; in the ideal state of full mature dependence, we manage our own feelings and recognise other people for who they are. That leaves most of us, most of the time, somewhere in between: treating other people to some degree in terms of our own expectations and needs, our view of them depending partly on our mood. All of us who have moved beyond gross infantile dependence will tend to favour one or more of the transitional techniques and distort our perceptions accordingly.

The Oedipus Complex

Fairbairn paid brief but crucial attention to the Oedipus Complex (Fairbairn 1952: 119–25). Rather than placing it in the centre of emotional development as in the Freudian scheme, he viewed it as a culturally variable aspect of relating in the transitional stage. He links the Western child's desire for one parent and fear and hatred of the other with the inner exciting and rejecting objects.

He postulates that the child experiences both parents as frustrating and fulfilling, exciting and rejecting, sometimes more intensely than she can manage. The child's inner rejecting object and exciting object will therefore each contain aspects of her experiences with both parents, layered and fused over the primary division of her early relationship with the mother or mothering person. To simplify this complexity, the child comes to identify one parent predominantly with the exciting object and the other predominantly with the rejecting object, projecting these objects on to the parents in transitional-stage relating.

Fairbairn sees the Oedipus Complex, like all relationship, as centred on emotional contact rather than instinctual gratification. He suggests that when the Oedipal polarisations are played out in a sexualised manner it is as a consequence of parental seductiveness, together with the child's defensive attempts to replace emotional contact with physical excitement. He sees the intense, painful, crisis-ridden Oedipus Complex of Freudian theory as the outcome of earlier deprivation and inner splitting. Where relationships have been more fulfilling, the Oedipal stage is less difficult and less important.

Fairbairn briefly comments that individual experiences of Oedipal relating are connected with later sexual orientation. The child's experience, as well as her biology, will influence which parent she sees as more exciting and which as more rejecting and how exclusively this happens. His comment indicates his view that the Freudian double Oedipus Complex, where the child sees both parents as objects of desire and also as potential rivals, arises simply from the child projecting both her exciting and rejecting objects on to each parent. Heterosexual orientation would arise from experiencing the opposite-sex parent predominantly as the exciting object and the same-sex parent predominantly as the rejecting object, with the situation reversed for lesbian and homosexual orientations, while bisexuality simply presupposes a more equal balance between the two.

Fairbairn did not elaborate on his ideas, nor did he relinquish the homophobia endemic to his social class and group. However, his fleeting attention to this subject offers a genuinely pathology-free construct of sexual orientation. It is very unfortunate that his ideas have not been developed further.

Therapy

Prior to Fairbairn's influence, psychoanalysts believed that technique was what made psychoanalysis effective. The analytic setting provided a neutral screen on to which the patient's unconscious conflicts and preoccupations were projected and which the psychoanalyst elucidated. The analyst would interpret, or spell out, the transference in particular: the feelings and perceptions the patient transferred on to the analyst from her childhood relationships with parents or other significant people. The relationship between patient and analyst was not in itself important, and was kept neutral so that the patient's projections would show up clearly. The analyst's interpretations were the active ingredient, the factor which most assisted the patient in becoming aware of her hidden assumptions and impulses, enabling her to work them through and come to a more satisfactory resolution.

Fairbairn's view of the primacy of relationship over impulse changed the psychoanalytic rationale. He believed that the single most important factor in helping the patient to change was the real relationship – not the transference relationship – with the analyst. If the patient was to become able to let go of her attachments to her internal bad objects, there had to be a genuine relationship with the analyst to take their place. The relationship with the analyst was more important than the correctness of the interpretations offered, which were mainly useful in communicating the analyst's understanding and concern.

With this in mind, Fairbairn modified the conventional analytic setting, although, characteristically, in a less complete way than he imagined. He felt strongly that to have the patient lying down with the analyst sitting behind her, out of view, replicated the patient's early traumas of abandonment and deprivation. He therefore offered the option for patients to sit in a chair, half-facing himself; he put himself, however, behind a large desk (Fairbairn 1994a: 80–1). Fairbairn obviously saw this as a more friendly arrangement, without considering the effect of such an imposing barrier (Guntrip 1975). His empathy seems to have been greater than his ability to communicate it; but his own difficulties with intimacy must have contributed to his acute sense of what his schizoid patients were suffering.

Fairbairn (1943) believed that the greatest resistance to change lay in the patient's loyalty to her internal objects. Our persistence in holding on to our inner world of unsatisfying relationships leads us to view the external world in the same terms. The risk of disregarding our normal way of being, with its familiar judgements and predictions, feels extraordinarily dangerous because of our absolute need as children to preserve our external relationships through the only means available to us. If we open up our closed systems we are likely to encounter an acute fear of falling into a spinning vacuum of emptiness, disorientation or humiliation in a resurgence of early trauma. It is for this reason that the real relationship with the analyst is so important. Without a secure trust in the analyst or therapist, we will not risk abandoning our internal objects to turn more fully to the other person.

In terms of Fairbairn's diagram, the purpose of psychoanalysis or psychotherapy is to help the patient, through genuine concern, understanding and challenge, to re-own her split-off capacities for anger and need and integrate them into her central ego/ideal object. She will then be able to relate to others with more richness, while her internal world will be less divided and conflictual. She will experience both herself and other people more fully and more truly.

Commentary

Fairbairn's theories represent a revolution in psychoanalysis, yet many of his papers remained unpublished until 1994 (Fairbairn 1994a, 1994b). Geographically and psychologically distant from the mainstream psychoanalytic world, he was not a natural communicator like Winnicott nor a pioneering fighter like Klein. He was not interested in creating a large body of written work and must have reworked each paper painstakingly until he was satisfied with it. He did not travel the country promoting his ideas and he had no interest in founding a Fairbairnian school of psychoanalysis. These factors, together with the startling challenge his ideas posed to Freudian theory, combined to postpone serious engagement with his work.

Some analysts did nevertheless write reviews or critiques of his work, some of which he answered. The best known of these is a book review by Winnicott and Khan (1953) in which they criticise aspects of Fairbairn's ideas, concluding that his attempt to challenge the Freudian basis of psychoanalytic thinking was misguided and mistaken. In particular, they point out that Fairbairn's view of the person as essentially and primarily object-seeking appears to conflict with his view of infantile dependence and primary identification. If our need for others is originally based on identification rather than separateness, if there is no sense of differentiation between subject and object at this primitive stage, in what sense can there be a relationship between the infant and the other, and in what sense can the infant be said to 'want' or 'need' a relationship? Surely, they suggest, what the infant seeks is pleasure, which is what contact with the mother happens to provide. Therefore, Freud's conception of the libido as pleasure-seeking has to take precedence over the libido as object-seeking. Balint (1957b) came to a similar conclusion.

This apparent contradiction is partially resolved in a recently published paper in which Fairbairn makes it clear that he saw primary identification as an emotional rather than a cognitive process, and typically partial rather than total in post-natal life (Fairbairn 1955). The baby may be aware at a perceptual and cognitive level that the other is a separate being. Emotionally, however, it is as though the other shares the same world as herself. For the baby, the other has no interests, no feelings, no perceptions and no thoughts which conflict with her own wishes and needs. Love means taking in from a being within the baby's own orbit and whose sole interest is in meeting the baby's needs. The baby is similarly wide open to the smallest nuance of feeling and atmosphere that comes to her from the other, drinking them in without criticism or questioning, accepting them as fully as she accepts her own feelings and perceptions. With this understanding, we can see infantile dependence not as a mystical state of union but rather as an immature mode of relating towards which we are always slipping back, even as adults. We often fail to acknowledge sufficiently that those who are important to us also have a life, a subjectivity, a world of their own, and that they are not there simply to serve our needs.

However, Fairbairn does indeed assert that before birth the baby experienced a full and total identification with the mother, emotionally and cognitively. He even writes (Fairbairn 1946) of the efforts of the child to return to the pre-natal state of bliss and security through the illusion of identification with the other. Unless Fairbairn is suggesting that the child does not become human until after birth, the confusion remains as to how the baby could experience her need for an other when she has no conception of otherness.

In answer to his critics, Fairbairn explains that he views identification as an act rather than a state, an illusion created by the child's absolute need for the other: 'the dynamic of identification is a need' (Fairbairn 1955). This suggests that he thought of primary identification as an early defence against the unwelcome reality of separateness and vulnerability. Through identifying with the other, the child creates an illusion of infinite closeness and therefore security. From this perspective, pleasure is only pleasant because it confirms the relationship which is our true primary need.

Elsewhere, however, Fairbairn indicated that he also thought of primary identification as a state of affairs which preceded any awareness of separateness: 'I employ the term "primary identification"', he wrote, 'to signify the cathexis of an object which has *not yet* [my emphasis] been differentiated from the cathecting subject' (Fairbairn 1941). In other words, the baby only becomes aware of the possibility of differentiation at a certain stage, probably through the trauma of birth. She defends against this knowledge through her identification with the other, which now appears to be secondary identification; or, to put it in another way, through a slowness to fully acknowledge the other's otherness and thus move beyond primary identification.

Because Fairbairn, like Klein and Freud, took birth as the starting point, his brief look at pre-birth experience is a casting-back rather than a comprehensive scrutiny. Since this was not the main area of his study, he did not explore the contradictions between his various statements. As Klein depended on the fact of birth to set the instinctive drives into operation, so Fairbairn depended on the birth trauma to set primary identification going as an active mode of relating.

We can therefore take the meaning of the pre-birth state, hypothesised as blissful, in two ways, confirming either the Freudian pleasure-seeking or the Fairbairnian object-seeking view of our basic nature. In the Freudian view, the absence of otherness means that the baby can only be aware of wanting pleasure; objects, or others, become attached to pleasure secondarily. This viewpoint is built on conscious psychological experience.

In the Object Relations view, the baby's bliss is simply the absolute fulfilment of her relational needs. She is not aware of otherness because she has experienced no break in her fulfilment, no trauma of deprivation. Her felt desire for the other arises as a result of the other's absence which creates the category of separateness. It is not that she was not object-needing before she experienced separation, it was just that she had no way of becoming aware of her need. This viewpoint encompasses both conscious and unconscious processes.

This difference is taken up in James Grotstein's contribution to a recent gathering together of a variety of reflections on Fairbairn's ideas (Grotstein and Rinsley 1994). Grotstein suggests that Freudian and Kleinian theory should be taken not as objective fact but as a retrospective account of how the child or the baby would explain her experience. 'There is something creative in me and something destructive', she might say. 'I am moved by forces beyond my control.' These unconscious forces are seen as biological because they are outside conscious awareness.

Fairbairn's ideas depend less on what is conscious. This gives him the freedom to see the self from the outside and encompass both conscious and unconscious levels in the psychological domain. It is paradoxical that a less experience-centred view gives a more psychological theory, reflecting the vastness of the unconscious and the ultimate impossibility of reaching the roots of the self directly. Freud and Klein saw this inaccessibility as the fading of psychology into biology; Fairbairn, as the desperation with which we close off parts of ourselves which can then only be reconstructed from an external point.

Other problems arise from the intense focus Fairbairn gave to such a defined and limited area. He did not pursue the origins of the ego beyond stating that it is 'present at birth' (Fairbairn 1994a: 155). Nor did he explore the needs of the developing child for anything other than nurturance and acceptance. There is no suggestion that the child may benefit from differentiated parental roles or that the father can be anything other than a second mother. He gave little attention to mature dependence compared with infantile dependence, and his transitional stage also gets rather short shrift. His table of neurotic techniques, while interesting, is less elaborated and less connected with clinical experience than his full and empathic analysis of the schizoid state.

Fairbairn's view of internalisation as a pathological process, and a structured psyche as somehow unnatural, has been criticised by psychoanalysts from Klein onwards. Fairbairn in his turn objected that Klein's internal objects were mere figments of the ego's phantasies rather than distinct parts of the ego, able to think, perceive and interpret.

Richard Rubens (in Grotstein and Rinsley 1994) clarifies the distinction implied in Fairbairn's theory between internalisation which leads to the impoverishment, and internalisation which leads to the enrichment of the self. Rubens uses the term 'structuring inter-nalisation' for the internalisation which arises from bad experience and leads to the splitting-off and repression of parts of the self. 'Non-structuring internalisation', on the other hand, is an internalisation into the central ego/ideal object, enriching it and its connections with the world. Few would maintain that self-fragmentation is a constructive process; and few would deny that we can be enriched by any experience that we can bear. Fairbairn did not address this beneficial kind of internalisation in any detail, giving the impression that he saw no difference between mental development of any kind and a riven subjectivity.

Fairbairn's theory of the schizoid position is built on the assumption that an untraumatising environment is theoretically feasible and would not lead to split-off structures within the self. However, the only environment that Fairbairn conceived as untraumatising was one which is absolutely continuous with the self. Yet if that were the case, it would not constitute an environment: the distinction between organism and environment implies a disjuncture. It seems a weakness in Fairbairn's theory that the basis for emotional development is stigmatised as pathological, with theoretical 'normality' based on a logical impossibility.

Fairbairn's monumental revision of Freudian theory had a hidden but far-reaching effect on psychoanalysis and thence on psychotherapy. While his theories were ignored or dismissed, their implications for practice spread. Psychoanalysts of all persuasions began to accept that their patients needed a genuine relationship with the analyst rather than simply a good technical job of accurate interpretation. Although he was not acknowledged, this rippling out of a more humane approach indicated his colleagues' silent agreement with at least some of his ideas.

Practitioners of different approaches are now turning to Fairbairn's long-neglected theories. While incomplete and puzzling at times, they nevertheless offer the first coherent analysis of human experience built on a relational rather than a physiological basis. The content of Fairbairn's work explains and confirms our primary need for relationship with others; his reserved style conveys the pain of being without it.

4

DONALD WINNICOTT:
THE EMERGING SELF

Winnicott is an elusive figure in Object Relations, at once extrovert and enigmatic. He pursued his own idiosyncratic course amidst the political and theoretical storms of the war years. He was perhaps unique in staying close to Melanie Klein for many years, even analysing her son, whilst maintaining his autonomy. Winnicott was a leading member of the middle or independent group, analysts who refused to take either side in the Freud–Klein controversies and who valued flexibility and open-mindedness over dogmatism. His enquiring, experimental approach brought together his two specialisms, paediatrics and psychoanalysis, in highly original ways. He produced talks and papers, brief and lengthy, on a multitude of subjects. Gripping and evocative, his musings roam the world of applied psychoanalysis as well as his rich clinical experience.

It is a paradox that the accessibility which is such an attractive feature of his writing is limited to his professional style. His personal life has tended to be presented in an idealised fashion by himself, his widow Clare Winnicott and other advocates of his work (Davis and Wallbridge 1981; C. Winnicott 1983; D. Winnicott 1989). It is therefore difficult to make an appraisal of his personal life and its relationship with his work.

LIFE

Donald Winnicott was born in 1896, the youngest child and only boy in a middle-class business family in Plymouth, England. Clare Winnicott (1983) describes his parents as religious but not rigid, and his upbringing as free, open and loving. Winnicott seems to have been the focus of attention of his mother, sisters, aunt, nanny and governess, who with his more distant father formed a large and relaxed household; there were also older cousins who lived close by.

The Winnicott family comes over as a warm and rather female-dominated community in which Winnicott developed as a valued and cherished individual. There is little suggestion of conflict or unhappiness, except briefly when as a nine-year-old he decided he was 'too nice'. Going to boarding school at thirteen was an adventure: his father had decided to send him, according to Winnicott, when he was disturbed at hearing his son say 'drat'. Although this can hardly have been the deciding reason, Winnicott seems to have found this act of paternal authority reassuring, agreeing in later life that he had indeed been associating with the wrong kind of boy. His letters communicate his enjoyment of the larger school community as well as the closeness he maintained with his family.

Winnicott first thought of becoming a doctor when he had broken his collar bone, because he did not want to be dependent on doctors throughout his life. He was fearful about the disappointment this would cause his father who naturally expected his only son to enter the family business, and needed the support and intervention of a friend before he felt able to commit himself to this decision. He studied medicine at Cambridge University and served briefly in a medical capacity during the First World War while he was still a student. The friends and contemporaries who were killed remained a sadness which haunted him throughout his life (Winnicott 1989: 11).

Winnicott's first marriage is seldom mentioned. He married Alice Taylor in 1922 when he was twenty-seven, having had some difficulty, according to Clare Winnicott, in becoming independent of his family. Alice has been variously described as a potter, as an opera singer and as psychologically disturbed (Goldman 1993: 68–9). The marriage was difficult from the outset, and Winnicott is said to have stayed with her until he felt she could manage without him. He may also have been waiting until after his father's death, in what would be a close parallel to his anxiety about disappointing his father's hopes that he would enter the family business. Winnicott and Alice did not have children and they eventually separated in 1949; he maintained contact with her even after he remarried two years later. The psychoanalyst Margaret Little, who was then his patient, reports (Little 1990) that when his marriage ended, Winnicott sank into a depressed state and suffered the first of the coronaries which afflicted him over the last twenty years of his life.

His second wife, Clare Britton, was a psychiatric social worker with whom he had worked during the Second World War. They had been involved in the setting up and running of hostels for children who had been evacuated but who were too disturbed to be cared for in foster homes. Clare also became a psychoanalyst and remained a staunch supporter and advocate of his work throughout his life and after his death.

Like Fairbairn's first wife, Alice Winnicott is commonly seen as the cause of the difficulties in their marriage, with her husband being portrayed as sacrificing his youth to her care. However, this must be a partial view, as his distress when they separated makes clear. In a paper entitled 'Hate in the Countertransference', Winnicott describes a disturbed and difficult nine-year-old boy who lived with them for three months during the war and whom Winnicott hoped to treat: 'My wife very generously took him in and kept him for three months, three months of hell', he wrote. 'He was the most lovable and most maddening of children, often stark staring mad ... It was really a whole-time job for the two of us together, and when I was out the worst episodes took place' (Winnicott 1975: 199–200).

This suggests that Alice was not completely incompetent and dependent; and in emphasising both her generosity and her willingness to look after this child, Winnicott indicates that he felt he had asked a lot of her.

This boy was not the only patient to be taken into their home. A colleague, Marion Milner, published an account of her work with a regressed and needy schizoid patient, 'Susan' (Milner 1969). Winnicott had in fact asked her to work with Susan and paid for her treatment, and she lived with the Winnicotts for six years. Milner indicates (1969: 3) that it was Alice who pressed for Susan to leave hospital and come to live with them. The greatest burden would again have fallen on her as Winnicott would have been working or writing all day. The length of time Susan stayed was remarkable, only ending when the Winnicotts' marriage broke up. Dodi Goldman (1993) speculates on how the presence of another woman could have contributed to their separation after twenty-seven years of marriage.

Winnicott clearly saw himself as a carer, and in other cases too he seems to have become highly involved and perhaps entangled with some of his regressed patients (see Little 1990). Alice also, in her willingness to bring needy people into the household, took up a caring role. In part this demonstrates an unusual kindness and generosity in them both and a way of expressing their concern for others in the absence of children of their own. Perhaps they also had the need for a vulnerable other into whom they could project their own feelings of dependency, creating a buffer between them in the process. Their childlessness is often put down to Alice's problems, but Goldman wonders additionally whether Winnicott would have found real fatherhood demanding and constricting: it might have cramped his style. As it was, he took a role which was in some ways analogous to his experience of his own father as an idealised distant figure.

Winnicott turned to psychoanalysis partly through the influence of Thomas Horder, an innovative physician who encouraged him above all to listen to his patients. He also seems to have encountered some personal difficulties, alluded to vaguely as feeling inhibited and being unable to remember his dreams (Hughes 1989: 19; Jacobs 1995: 10). Probably more significantly, it was shortly after he married Alice that he entered analysis. On the advice of Ernest Jones, he saw James Strachey, the translator of Freud's work who had himself been analysed by Freud; Strachey then recommended Klein as a supervisor for his work with children, which as a paediatrician he was in a good position to develop. He must have started working with Klein soon after her arrival in Britain (Winnicott 1962a). He had a second analysis with Joan Rivière, a leading Kleinian.

Winnicott thus had early and full experience of both Freudian and Kleinian psychoanalysis. Both analyses seem to have been problematic for him at times and his ten years with Strachey and five years with Rivière left him unsatisfied. Strachey, he wrote rather ambivalently to Jones, 'adhered to a classical technique in a cold-blooded way for which I have always been grateful' (quoted in Goldman 1993: 74). He felt that Strachey underestimated the importance of relationship in development and overestimated the power of interpretation in the analytic process. Strachey, for his part, had his own difficulties with Winnicott, finding him misguided in his deviation from Freudian orthodoxy and late in paying his bills.

Winnicott found his analysis with Joan Rivière both enlightening and disappointing. He was inspired by Klein's ideas, but was unsuccessful in his attempts to induce either Klein or Rivière to offer some endorsement of his own very different work. The psychoanalyst John Padel has suggested that many of Winnicott's papers were written with the aim of getting Klein to modify her theories (Grosskurth 1986: 399). If this was the case, it was clearly a non-starter as a plan. The ideas he was building – based on the importance of the environment as against instinctual conflict – were in blunt opposition to Klein's. For her to have accepted his views would have weakened both the thrust of her theoretical views and her political position in the British Psycho-Analytical Society. Winnicott may have become involved in an opposition which was not going to be resolved, but in defining his own ideas against those of Klein he probably attained a greater clarity than he would otherwise have done.

Winnicott maintained the two strands of his working life, paediatric medicine and psychoanalysis, throughout his career, to the enrichment of both disciplines. He held a clinic at Paddington Green Children's Hospital in London for over forty years and also worked at The Queen Elizabeth Hospital for Children in the East End of London. His wife and colleagues estimated that he had seen over sixty thousand cases in his working life, giving him a far broader experience of ordinary people than other psychoanalysts gained. He improvised ways of using psychoanalytic concepts and attitudes to help families and children for whom psychoanalytic treatment was not an option. Many of his papers describe brief interactions with a baby or child, or intermittent and intuitive family support to help disentangle a block in a child's development (Winnicott 1955, 1960a). He also experimented with irregular, 'on demand' treatment of children, again as an alternative to normal ongoing treatment. One such treatment was written up as *The Piggle* (Winnicott 1977).

Winnicott worked extensively during the Second World War in the management of child evacuees. He was involved in setting up and consulting to hostels for children whose placements in foster families had broken down as a result of their disturbed behaviour. The primary importance he attributed to the environment in children's development is demonstrated in his focus on the management as well as the treatment of delinquent children (Winnicott 1984).

Winnicott also distinguished between management and treatment in his psychoanalytic work with borderline patients, whom he considered were often unable to benefit from the therapeutic distance suitable for the less disturbed. His view of regression as a therapeutic opportunity rather than a defence led him to experiment with different ways of facilitating psychic growth in highly dependent patients who had regressed to early stages of development. His responses to such patients included open-ended sessions of sometimes several hours in length, physical holding, sessions on demand and support outside sessions. These experiments have been welcomed as bringing a new humanity to psychoanalysis, but Winnicott has also been criticised for holding an arrogant attitude of omnipotence and failing to learn from previous similar experiments which had mostly turned out badly.

Again, the truth is likely to be complex rather than simple. Many of Winnicott's patients must have benefited from his genuine care and concern, and his efforts to meet even the extreme needs of his patients in an imaginative and flexible way are impressive. Other patients, however, must have suffered from his keenness to provide all the care himself. This led him to propose irregular treatment with him rather than referring patients to colleagues who could have offered them more consistency.

Winnicott is commonly described as playful, spontaneous, sparkling and deeply empathic; perhaps a bit of a *puer,* a Peter Pan, even a 'crypto-prima donna' (Grosskurth 1986: 399). Some people saw him as a loner, for all his apparent sociability. His work is strangely silent, in content and tone, on the devastating effects of the two world wars through which he lived. Perhaps his pessimism was to some extent split off from his optimism; this would make his hopeful side particularly attractive, while his more cynical side would recede from view.

There is more to Winnicott than the spontaneous and generous man who emerges most clearly in his writing. He was canny in the way he limited the situations and patients he worked with, consciously preserving his sensitivity. The ease with which he let go of patients with whom the reader has become quite involved can jar. This is not surprising in view of the huge numbers of patients he saw, yet it indicates a shrewd self-interest which is not immediately apparent from the empathic warmth of his writing.

It sometimes seems as though there is a thread of self-consciousness running alongside his wonderful imagination. The double negatives, the poetic language, even the paradoxical prayer in his autobiographical writing: 'Oh God! Let me be alive when I die' (Winnicott 1989: 4), can seem contrived. Perhaps his warmth and imagination were in part techniques to cover his isolation: ways of bringing people not exactly under his control, but into his realm. His sometimes patronising tone when talking to mothers in particular – even the term 'the ordinary devoted mother' – gives the same impression of subterranean arrogance. This more complex side of Winnicott is also betrayed by the personal difficulties he fleetingly alludes to, which suggest buried pre-symbolic wounds. He mentions a disturbing symptom of following every sound he heard with his larynx as though subvocalising (Winnicott 1963a), and a persistent sense of something rotten in the centre of his head (Winnicott 1968). A poem reveals the thought that perhaps his life, even his very joyfulness, was a way of restoring a depleted, depressed mother: 'to enliven her was my living' (quoted in Goldman 1993: 45).

A picture emerges of a creative and idiosyncratic man, devoted to his work, who developed a unique capacity to slip into immediate communication with anyone from a baby to a delinquent to a borderline adult. The narcissistic strand in Winnicott's make-up was probably connected with the difficulties that enabled him to tune into primitive states of being. It may have linked up with his unexpected view of the core of the self as private, out of reach, 'incommunicado' (Winnicott 1963b). This hidden, perhaps troubled side of Winnicott contrasts with the playful old man described by Clare – riding down London's Haverstock Hill with his feet on the handle-bars of his bicycle, or climbing to the top of a tree (C. Winnicott 1983).

Winnicott died peacefully in 1971. He left followers and dissenters who held him in affection and respect, and some who saw him as misguided and a lazy thinker. The Squiggle Foundation in London, devoted to the dissemination of his ideas, was named after the doodling game he played with children (Winnicott 1964–68). The name captures the simplicity and imagination of his kind of psychoanalysis. It also offers the temptation to accept at face value the childlike Winnicott so often presented to us, leaving aside the complexities which make him a person rather than a myth.

THEORY

Overview

Guntrip described Winnicott as first and foremost a clinician, a people-person, and, unlike Fairbairn, 'more revolutionary in practice than in theory' (Guntrip 1975). Winnicott's contribution to Object Relations lies more in the field of practical application than in theory. He emphasised above all the necessity of making concepts one's own before they can be used creatively.

Winnicott's writing style is impressionistic rather than analytical. He aims to re-create in the reader the state of mind he is writing of rather than to present a clear argument. This makes him emotionally attractive to read, but maddeningly elusive to grasp.

Winnicott focuses on paradox, transition and ambiguity. He charts the emergence and vicissitudes of the self in early development, in disturbance, in delinquency and in psychosis. His arena is the borderline between inner and outer, self and other, the subjective and the objective. 'There is no such thing as a baby', he asserts strikingly and provocatively (Winnicott 1952a), because where there is a baby there is always a caring adult. He is pointing out the absolute sociability of human beings; the individual emerges, always incompletely, from a matrix of communality which is also held within the self. He thus places himself firmly within the Object Relations school, but does not throw out drive theory and instinctual gratification. Instead, he sees physical life as a challenge to our capacity to contain and make meaning of our excitement. While it can easily overwhelm the sense of self, physicality is also the core of realness which he characterised rather than defined as the 'true self'.

Winnicott disagreed, diplomatically, with Freud and Klein on the primacy of instinctual conflict; he suggested (Winnicott 1959–64) that the concept of the death instinct was superfluous rather than wrong. He sought to balance Klein's emphasis on unconscious phantasy arising from internal conflict with a far greater inclusion of the environment and its effects. In his optimistic fashion, he made a plea for Klein's depressive position to be renamed 'the stage of concern'. Unusually for a psychoanalyst, he saw human beings as on the whole healthy. The human race is a going concern because of the good-enough care given to children through the generations. Many of his case histories include such comments as: 'he comes within the wide definition of the term normal' (Winnicott 1971: 8).

Winnicott's infant becomes a personal self through the protective care of the 'good-enough mother'. Through her initial close identification with her baby, which he termed 'primary maternal preoccupation', she fosters an illusion of oneness with her baby which makes him feel secure and even omnipotent. As this intense and intuitive early relationship develops it broadens out into a less focused, more everyday mode of being together. Gradually the baby moves through bearable experiences of frustration and disillusionment to the realisation that his own powers, while real, are limited. The mother enables this to happen through her natural recovery from her near-obsession with her new-born baby. As she begins to take up her own separate life again, the baby learns to develop his own resources. Winnicott suggests that with an 'average expectable environment' of loving care, the baby gathers a sense of continuity and coherence which coalesces into personal identity, with an emotional core of togetherness which he terms 'ego-relatedness'. This sense of inner relatedness is the foundation on which autonomy and independence rest.

This profoundly social view of early development is difficult to reconcile with Winnicott's view of the centre of the self as unsocial (Winnicott 1963b). There is no account of where this totally private self comes from or what sustains it. Perhaps, like Freud's death instinct, the idea derives from emotional conviction rather than intellectual thought. His descriptions conjure up the still centre of a dynamic sphere, a point rather than a zone.

Winnicott takes this developmental process of moving from illusion to disillusion as a recurrent focus of attention. Although he did not develop a coherent theoretical structure, he evolved ideas and perspectives which have stood the test of time, entering into mainstream psychotherapeutic thinking and sometimes into social awareness too.

Privation and Psychosis

Winnicott described psychosis as an 'environmental deficiency disease' (Winnicott 1949a, 1952b). He did not discount genetic factors, but he saw the primary cause as deficiencies in care during the earliest stages of self-formation, 'absolute dependency' (Winnicott 1963c). At this stage, the baby is not yet aware of the differentiation of self and environment and therefore does not perceive an environment, or an other, as such. The wound that the baby suffers is thus not an external lack to which he could react but a trauma, a brokenness, which runs throughout his subjectivity. He termed this deficiency 'privation': the absence of factors which were needed for the child to develop and mature in a straightforward way. Winnicott thus defines psychosis as arising from a disastrous early failure of relationship, albeit a failure that may be particularly hard to avoid with some children who may be especially vulnerable.

What is the nature of the relationship between the infant and mother before the infant is aware of anyone separate to relate to? Winnicott suggests that while the infant has drives, he should not be seen as a bundle of bodily needs seeking gratification, but rather as a person who is perpetually 'on the brink of unthinkable anxiety' (Winnicott 1962b). The 'good-enough mother' holds the baby together through her attunement to his needs and inner states; the baby perceives her not as a distinct object, but as a surrounding presence. Winnicott refers to the mother thus experienced by the young infant as the 'environment mother' (Winnicott 1963d).

The baby is at first aware only of his relative well-being or, conversely, the threat or actuality of falling into an unbearable state which Winnicott calls 'annihilation'. Winnicott describes this experience in graphic terms, as the 'primitive agonies' of going to pieces, falling forever, having no relation to the body, having no orientation in the world and complete isolation with no means of communication. These are horrors which surface in later life as psychotic or borderline-state anxieties in which one's very being seems threatened.

Winnicott identified three ways in which the mother protects the baby from these experiences: 'holding', 'handling' and 'object-presenting'. Problems in these areas correlate with specific anxieties and the stunting of differing emotional capacities.

Holding is both physical and emotional. The good-enough mother contains and manages the baby's feelings and impulses by empathising with him and protecting him from too many jarring experiences. Her protective holding is expressed through the way she carries, moves, feeds, speaks to and responds to her baby, and in her understanding of his needs and experience. She forestalls the shock of sudden movement, physical pain or distress, loud noises and bright lights, until the baby is able to manage these without shutting down his being. This means that the baby is able to remain in a state of 'unintegration', a relaxed and undefended openness in which his different experiences can join together in an unbroken stream. The mother's holding enables the baby's 'true self', the spontaneous experience of being, to develop coherence and continuity. During periods of unintegration the baby lays down his sense of existing over time and space as one being, existentially real and personally authentic.

When the mother cannot give the baby the kind of holding and protection he needs, he is jolted into shock and reaction. Rather than simply 'going on being', he has to try to hold himself together against the threat to his being, a threat which may be external, like a sudden noise, or internal, such as hunger or a need for contact. Not to react would result in the appalling experience of unintegration without being held, an experience of annihilation that is fought against at all costs. But while fighting against it, there can be no simple continuous state of being, and the baby cannot develop a sense of effortlessly existing as a real, alive, continuous, unified being. If these states of reactivity are frequent and prolonged, the baby, and then child, will feel to some extent unreal, inauthentic, afraid of 'going to pieces'. He may cover his 'true self' with a 'false self', hiding his fraught inner state behind an outward appearance of coping and compliance (Winnicott 1960b). If even this fails, the fragmentation of psychosis may be revealed, with the psychotic person experiencing himself in bits and speaking as different people, unable to maintain a sense of wholeness, coherence and continuity of self.

The second aspect of this early, pre-differentiated relationship arises from the mother's handling. At its best, her sensitive touch and responsive care of the baby's body will enable him to experience physical and emotional satisfaction in an integrated way. This will help the baby to bring together the worlds of sensation and emotion, building a stable unity of mind and body. The person who received enough sensitive handling in early life will experience his mental, emotional and physical capacities as connected and personal in 'true self' living.

By contrast, the baby may feel that his bodily functions are managed impersonally, or he may be left alone, emotionally or physically, for longer than he can bear. He may attempt to cope by identifying with his mind rather than his body, despising his physical needs and distancing himself from physical experience. He may feel that his 'true self' is ethereal rather than corporeal. He is trying to cope with the agony of 'having no relation to the body', an experience which may surface in later life as feeling unreal, depersonalised, floating in a void without being anchored to the bodily self. This feeling of disembodiment and unreality can include 'having no orientation': no sense of specific connection to the world which includes the body. At its worst, this can be a literal sense of not knowing which is up or down, inside or outside, forwards or backwards. All feels vague and disconnected, as though floating or spinning in an endless vacuum without a reference point or anything distinct.

Object-presenting is the third aspect of mothering Winnicott defines. It is the way in which the mother brings the outside world to the baby. When this goes well, the baby is ready to receive and explore and the mother is happy to allow him some independence. Winnicott often describes object-presenting in terms of feeding. The sensitive mother allows the baby to actively find and feed from the breast or bottle, rather than thrusting the nipple in his mouth before he knows it is there or keeping him waiting for longer than he can manage. Similarly, if the baby is allowed to reach for and find a toy, smile or burble to a mother who then responds, bring about change and satisfaction through his own efforts, he feels as though he is actually creating the world. He seems to be living in a world of 'subjective objects', at once part of him and yet novel, which are under his magical control. Through presenting objects and experiences in a way which is sensitive to her baby's state, the mother helps him build a primitive conviction of omnipotence and 'dual unity' which is an essential prelude to disillusion. The baby develops a sense of oneness and trust in the world, which grows into an appreciation of both his connection with others and his separateness. He gains a confidence in his ability to reach out, connect and make changes in the world, and he expects to be met with understanding and responsiveness.

Various problems may arise in the arena of object-presenting. An anxious mother may forestall her baby's reaching out by feeding him before he is hungry, lifting him before he is awake, playing with him before he has a chance to want contact. Conversely, a depressed, harassed or self-absorbed mother may not respond sufficiently to her baby's demands or may not be attuned to him. In all such cases, the baby may find difficulty in developing a realistic self-confidence. The baby whose autonomy was smothered may expect the world to fall in with his needs without effort on his part. He may fear being engulfed and taken over by others and have an undeveloped sense of his personal boundaries. The child whose parents could not respond to him sufficiently may not expect the world to understand and empathise with him. He will feel safer relating to the world from a 'false self' position, adapting to the needs of the other rather than expressing his true needs. At its worst, failure in the area of object-presenting results in the conviction that people are not only separate, but isolated. This is the primitive agony of not being able to communicate because there seems to be no way of connecting with anyone, even oneself. More commonly, there is a sense of distrust, futility and loneliness. If there seems to be little point in trying to relate to others, the person may elevate self-sufficiency from a necessity to an ideal.

Privation of attuned holding, handling or object-presenting will not feel like an external failure to the baby who has not yet become aware of separateness. Rather, he will be overwhelmed by stimuli from internal or external sources which he cannot manage, at an intensity that breaks up his peaceful state of simply being. Winnicott termed these traumatic experiences 'impingements', fractures in the wholeness of being which the baby has no option but to accommodate. At an extreme, he will not be able to develop further on an unanxious basis, and will have to construct a defensive mode of survival over the top of unbearable anxiety. False-self living, emotional withdrawal and actively-induced disintegration are all protective devices for the traumatised true self, which may remain hidden, broken or unestablished, but is never extinguished. Winnicott's passionate belief in the true self led him to make horrified protests about the psychiatric treatment of leucotomy (Winnicott

1949b), which he saw as the barbaric destruction of what is most preciously human.

Winnicott was acutely sensitive to the hazards of this early stage of life and the kind of suffering that arose from it. This made him highly empathic to his psychotic and borderline child and adult patients, whom he thought of in terms of the baby at the stage of absolute dependence. He remarked that the patient who is afraid of breaking down does not fear an unknown situation, but a return to a previous, unbearable state of dereliction (Winnicott 1963e), an insight which can be a real help when people are afraid of falling apart. Winnicott emphasised that under the threat of psychotic anxieties (the primitive agonies), we do not need the analysis of our problems, but rather the kind of sensitive, involved and unsentimental care that the 'good-enough' mother gives naturally to her young baby (Winnicott 1967a).

If both therapist and patient can tolerate this regression to early dependence, the patient can perhaps be helped to repair some of the gaps and fragmentation in his being through experiencing more empathic care. A distant professionalism feels false and evasive: only a real person will do. As Winnicott put it:

> The borderline psychotic gradually breaks through the barrier that I have called the analyst's technique and professional attitude, and forces a direct relationship of a primitive kind, even to the extent of merging. (Winnicott 1960c)

Transitional Phenomena

Winnicott's theory of transitional phenomena (Winnicott 1971) is perhaps his most widely known idea. His ability to notice what was there to be seen brought into focus the rags, blankets and teddy bears to which young children are often almost addicted in their early years – an everyday aspect of young children's experience to which he was the first to give attention. Winnicott's thinking about these intense attachments developed in the context of childcare practices in post-war Britain, where the care of very young children was seen as the task of the mother alone. Babies experienced periods of excited and intimate contact, often around feeding, alternating with extended periods of solitude; they were normally weaned at around nine months. Children therefore had to cope with being alone on a regular basis, against a backdrop of intense involvement with one main carer. Transitional phenomena are culture-specific, although Winnicott presents them as universal (Jacobs 1995: 105–7).

Transitional phenomena belong to the border between the child's early fusion with mother and his dawning realisation of separateness, in the area of transition between absolute and relative dependency. In this transitional zone, the baby finds he can use a particular object, sound, ritual or other happening as a way of managing his fears of being separate or alone. The transitional object is the blanket, rag or toy that the baby needs to be holding or sucking before he can go to sleep and which he may carry around for most of the day as well. The transitional phenomenon is a non-material object of attachment such as a song or story which plays the same role for the baby.

The transitional object or phenomenon is the emblem of the child's internal unity with a giving, accepting, nurturing mother. It is this security that the child grasps on to while struggling to let the mother go, both physically and in his acknowledgement that she is separate from him. It is for this reason that a child may need his transitional object more than he needs the actual mother to go to sleep with, or to help him manage his anxiety. It is the outward sign of the early blissful fusion between mother and child.

The separateness of the transitional object signifies the limits of the child's omnipotence: the rag or blanket is real rather than imaginary. The object's externality stands for the mother's externality, whilst its embodiment of the 'soul' of their felt unity softens this realisation. Through his transitional object, the child creates a resting place between the comforting illusion of oneness and the separateness that he can no longer deny. In his relationship with this special object he is allowed to have things both ways, and is usually intuitively supported in this by any adults or children he encounters. Teddy bears are often brought spoons and plates in restaurants and given seats on buses, yet never have to pay for food or fare. In numerous enthusiastic accommodations, adults who may not even be parents share this special transitional area.

Winnicott outlines the transitional object's essential features. It must belong to the child, and the child must be able to treat it as he likes; but at the same time, it must not be so malleable that the child feels he has magical control over it. The child's relationship with the object may range from identification to love and hate, and the object must survive the rough treatment of primitive relating. It must seem to have a substance and a life of its own to contribute to the relationship, whether through sound, texture, movement or warmth. It must therefore be an external object or phenomenon – a blanket, toy, the sound of a musical box, shifting patterns on a rug – yet it cannot be copied or replaced. It carries its symbolic power only through the meaning with which the child infuses it.

The importance of the transitional object is that it both stands for and is not the mother. It is the beginning of symbol-making, of fantasy, play and thought. Winnicott places the start of transitional phenomena with purposeful vagueness, 'from four to six to eight to twelve months' (1971). Gradually, the child ceases to need a concrete embodiment of the transitional state as he becomes able to take both connectedness and autonomy for granted. The transitional object is not consciously given up, lost or mourned, but is slowly relegated to the margins, dropped behind a bed or left in a cupboard. The world now offers the child opportunities for broader transitional experience.

Winnicott suggests that we move beyond the single object to words, play, culture, art and religion as modes of experience which are not asocial but where we will not be challenged to account for our responses. In all these fields, the inner and outer worlds meet in a special area that is personal to each of us, and which offers particular meaning and enrichment to our lives. Yet even as adults we retain 'special' objects. The favourite mug, accustomed chair, the writer's pen, the musician's instrument carry rich feelings of kinship and intimacy which are logically spurious. They are relics of the fusion we originally felt with our earliest carer which we lovingly carry within us.

Winnicott describes the therapeutic setting as supremely transitional. The therapist offers himself and the therapeutic space explicitly for transitional experience. The client or patient responds most fruitfully by 'playing' with versions of reality, experiencing dependency, love, opposition, contempt and hate in a relationship which is tolerable through the patient's and therapist's knowledge that these reactions are not simply to be taken personally. Without play, Winnicott suggests, there can be no therapy; when the patient is enabled to play, growth and development naturally follow.

Deprivation and Delinquency

During the Second World War Winnicott acted as consultant psychiatrist to the British Government Evacuation Scheme in Oxfordshire, a post which involved the oversight of hostels set up for those children who were too disturbed to be cared for in foster homes. He noticed that most of these children came from backgrounds in which family life was disrupted or inadequate or had broken down. He thus had an early opportunity to explore the links between early deprivation and later delinquency, as well as the related difficulties arising from the separation of children from their families. He retained an interest in this area throughout his working life, treating some such children directly or through family support as well as considering how society manages its delinquent and criminal members (Winnicott 1984).

Winnicott sees aggression not as a wholly separate instinct as did Freud and Klein, but as a part of relating which only becomes distinct from love over time. He suggests it is originally an aspect of the ruthless, self-seeking excitement of primitive relationship, before the realisation that the object of love is a separate and vulnerable being. It is only through the gradual relinquishing of the illusion of fusion and omnipotence that the child becomes able to consider the impact on the other of his own fierce desire. As the baby gathers together his myriad different feelings, impulses and perceptions of his mother, he builds an integrated view of two distinct yet connected people who are both loving and hating, lovable and hateable. He becomes able to make up for his anger and destructiveness through creativity and reparation, taking increasing responsibility for his own part in relationship. Winnicott (1963d) termed this achievement the 'stage of concern'; it is analogous to Klein's depressive position when this has become reasonably stable through the working through of depressive anxieties.

The baby's concern for himself and for the other can only develop in the context of a continuous personal relationship in which he is sufficiently protected from the primitive agonies of earliest life. Without the security and trust this builds, he will not risk moving beyond an illusion of omnipotence that will itself be over-strained. He will not have had the consistent arena in which he and mother could survive and sort out the intense contrasting states which make up a full relationship.

The child who has not experienced stable and continuous care will thus have far greater difficulty in building a coherent sense of self and integrating the different aspects of relating and relationship. He will have had neither the necessity nor the opportunity to realise the effects of both his anger and his love on the same person, and will not therefore appreciate their difference nor bring them together to develop an attitude of concern. He will not feel a part of the family, group or society around him, and will not feel the obligation towards others that arises from this sense of belonging. This extreme circumstance is usually seen only in children who have been looked after by changing figures where close personal bonds have not had a chance to build up or have been continually broken. This was more common during the 1940s and 1950s than in the present day: the efforts of Winnicott and Bowlby mean that far fewer babies and young children are now brought up in impersonal and disrupted settings.

However, specific failure in relationship at the stage when the child is able to perceive his own separateness leads to a fault or gap in the development of the capacity for concern. Winnicott terms this failure 'deprivation', as opposed to 'privation'. It leads to an 'anti-social tendency', arising in the stage of relative rather than absolute dependence. Winnicott describes deprivation as the loss of good experience at a stage when the baby or child is able to perceive the loss as coming from the outside – usually from the parents. It is a loss which continues for longer than the child can manage, until his faith in his parents and in the world is broken. With this fracture, he is in danger of falling into a primitive agony of helplessness and inner collapse with no one to hold him together, and he tries to forestall this catastrophe by holding himself together and away from danger. He constructs a compliant self which is designed to fit in with a dangerous world, adapted to the external requirements rather than his own needs. Thus in the immediate wake of loss or disruption, a child may become unnaturally 'good'. Through inhabiting this 'false self', his 'true self' is protected; the price is a break in the continuity of living and relating from genuine need, love and anger.

The anti-social act or tendency emerges when the child becomes hopeful of a positive response from the world once more (Winnicott 1956, 1963f). His hope leads him to protest against his deprivation and try to put matters right. He may seek unconsciously to take back what has been 'stolen' from him in some form of stealing (often, of course, from the parents). He is reclaiming his right to take unreservedly from the other, as he did in the unconstrained good relationship he had before its traumatic break, and he is demanding that the other acknowledges his loss and makes amends in symbolic form as part of the re-establishment of a relationship of trust. Winnicott points out that many children have brief phases of demanding behaviour or actual stealing which is resolved through dependable loving care.

The anti-social tendency may also be expressed through destructiveness. The destructive act expresses not only anger but also a plea for strong parenting from an adult who can contain and control the child without hate or vengeance. In meeting with a firm response from a loving adult, the child once more becomes able to trust the world to hold him: he no longer has to hold himself in anxious tension. When the child is convinced of the adult's ability to take responsibility for him, he can live once more from his true self rather than the defensive false self.

Most anti-social behaviour is held and resolved within ordinary family life. Parents often know intuitively when they should allow extra leeway for their child, realising that he needs love, reassurance and the relaxation of expectations. They respond spontaneously to his need to reach back to the time before his trust in the world was threatened, to 'make up' to the child for the difficulty he experienced, although neither child nor parent may consciously know what that was. Parents also know when they must provide their child with extra-firm limits for a time and not let him get away with anything. This consistent firmness is their attuned response to the child's need for the strong parent who will not allow the child's destructiveness to get out of hand, thus allowing him to relax.

The anti-social tendency is a response to trauma which may be temporary and insignificant or severe and continuous, but which follows on from good-enough experience. It is not a psychotic structure, because the child has some sense of differentiation of self and other. It can become part of a personality ranging from the near-normal or the neurotic, to the fragmented and near-psychotic.

It is a relatively straightforward task to manage a child whose anti-social tendency has arisen from minor deprivation in a generally reliable setting, but it is a different matter when the child or adult has become anti-social as a way of life. The extreme anti-social set-up is deep-rooted and compulsive and becomes more fixed and complex the longer it continues. When the child is almost overwhelmed by the original deprivation, his destructiveness may be a desperate playing-out of an intolerable inner state in an attempt to externalise it and get others to contain him. The less he feels this happens, the more frantically he continues in an escalating attempt to achieve safety. The confirmed delinquent, like the very young infant, may feel himself permanently on the edge of unbearable anxiety with persecution and disintegration barely kept at bay. His stealing and vandalism offer him some outlet, while challenging society to impose the control that he cannot. At an extreme, acts such as stealing, drug dealing or violence, together with society's controlling response, give an illusion, a parody almost, of emotional satisfaction in a containing environment. This can become irresistible, especially when there is little opportunity for more wholesome satisfaction. The habitual criminal may have too much at stake to risk changing his ways. His delinquency gives him esteem from himself and his peers; it offers him a direction, even a career, in prison; and it gives him material goods through stealing, or an emotional buzz through excitement and power over others. With only despair, fragmentation and isolation underneath, giving these up is likely to be an unthinkable prospect.

With this in mind, Winnicott suggests that management should be differentiated from treatment in the area of delinquency and criminality. Treatment would be aimed at enabling the person to relinquish his anti-social defences, break down and experience being cared for in a way that would facilitate new growth on a basis of trust. This could only happen with strong motivation and excellent provision, and would involve the chaos of acute suffering. Management, on the other hand, is the structuring of the environment to take the place of the inner control the anti-social person lacks. In mild cases, this could be sufficient to help in the recovery of trust and connection, but the more dependent the delinquent is on external control, the more such control has to be a holding operation rather than a strategy to encourage change of anything deeper than behaviour. The less the person can make use of personal relationship, the more impersonal and strict management has to be. Within a regimented environment, the deprived person may feel sufficiently secure to experience a reasonable quality of life. With a relaxation of control, the unbearable agony will surge forth again, leading to renewed offending behaviour which ensures relief from internal pressure and the re-establishment of control from the outside.

For these reasons, Winnicott believed that some apparently rigid and Spartan régimes are effective and humane responses to some extremely anti-social delinquents. He points to the danger, now not uncommon within the care system, of the continued breakdown of deprived children's placements in potentially loving foster homes. The intimacy and flexibility offered to some frightened and angry children may seem threatening and not sufficiently containing, leading to a further breakdown of inner control. In this situation, an escalation of destructiveness may be less a sign of hope than an externalisation of inner disintegration and a desperate attempt to find more effective external control. Even if such a child does respond with hope to the possibilities of the new setting, his 'testing-out' is liable to be extreme. Whatever the mixture of hope and desperation, the ensuing manipulations, lying, stealing, destructiveness and violence may well be too much for the foster family to bear. All too often, such placements continue to break down until the security of a young offenders' institution is reached, followed by a graduation to prison.

Winnicott's views on deprivation and delinquency led him to disagree sharply with Bowlby. Bowlby's work on the far-reaching effects of maternal deprivation persuaded him to press for children to be kept with their own parents if at all possible, and for those who had to be taken into care to be placed in foster homes rather than institutions. This led to the closure of many children's homes in what Winnicott felt to be a decreasing appreciation of the needs of the most disturbed delinquent children.

Winnicott's view of delinquency has been highly influential. Parents and teachers are now more understanding of the unhappiness that often lies behind the brief phases of attention-seeking, disruptiveness and stealing through which many children pass. Judicial systems may still be mindful of the need to keep young delinquents from becoming confirmed criminals, often advocating social intervention rather than institutionalisation in a fixed anti-social community. However, the backlash against liberalism in recent years has turned against understanding towards incarceration and revenge. Winnicott spoke of punishment as largely irrelevant to the confirmed offender, but necessary to society. Systematised social retribution allows society to forgo the brutality of spontaneous vengeance in favour of a vicarious, controlled expression of hurt and anger. The urge for some form of retribution can provide the motivation to maintain and fund régimes which are sufficiently rigid for offenders to feel safe within. Winnicott might have suggested that this swing could have arisen in part from the overlooking of some delinquents' needs for strong control, as well as the inadequate recognition of society's needs.

Commentary

Winnicott is a maverick figure in psychoanalysis. His practice and his writing express a relational depth which encompasses the worlds of medicine and psychoanalysis, parenting and professionalism. As a psychoanalyst he brought an imaginative and creative optimism to the oppressive and pathologised Kleinian scenario. He did not revise the theoretical structures of Freud or the conceptual developments of Klein, but he used their work as a background for a new emphasis on the role of the environment in emotional development. Winnicott's psychoanalysis is art as well as science, requiring empathy as well as thought. He values emotional closeness, the capacity for relaxing personal boundaries and an imaginative and playful attunement to others. Marilyn Senf (1995) sees Winnicott's work as a growth of the feminine in psychoanalysis. The intimacy of his thinking, working and writing lends a refreshing intersubjectivity to the individualistic focus of Freud and Klein.

Winnicott's aim was very similar to that of Klein: 'I'm going to show that infants are ill very early, and if the theory doesn't fit, it's just got to adjust itself' (Winnicott 1989: 575). Like Klein, he had to place his ideas in relation to existing theory, a task which he carried out half-heartedly.

Winnicott differs from Freud in his practical and theoretical dependence on a relational rather than a mechanistic approach, and from Klein in his view that the environment is as crucial as instinct in emotional development. Yet he does not wholly abandon instinct theory, and he presents his ideas as built on Freudian foundations with only minor divergences from Kleinian theory. Goldman (1993: 137) brings out Guntrip's view that Winnicott maintained a dual relationship with Freud, disagreeing in private while upholding him in public. His sharp criticism of Fairbairn – 'He spoils his good work by wanting to knock down Freud' (quoted in Guntrip 1975) – demonstrates a powerful aversion to the overthrow of forebears, despite his declared independence of mind. His unwillingness to criticise both Freud and Klein may be partly rooted in his affectionate regard for them; together with Darwin, they were the foremost influences in his thinking. It also conforms with the conservatism of much of his world view and brings to mind his fear of opposing his father's wishes.

Greenberg and Mitchell suggest that Winnicott's unwillingness to oppose Freud and Klein results in muddled theoretical premises. They point to his subtle and gross misrepresentations of major aspects of Freudian and Kleinian concepts:

> He recounts the history of psychoanalytic ideas not so much as it developed, but as he would like it to have been, rewriting Freud to make him a clearer and smoother predecessor of Winnicott's own vision. (Greenberg and Mitchell 1983: 189)

They suggest that while his practice and the main thrust of his theory are relational, he maintains a spurious allegiance to drive theory: his ideas imply a dual track in development, presenting both biological urges and the search for meaning as primary.

The underlying premises of Winnicott's work are indeed ambiguous. He uses Freudian language and concepts, but alters some of their main properties without saying that he is doing so. The following passage, for example, gives no indication that he is using the term 'id' idiosyncratically to denote a particular type of bodily experience, rather than as the forever unconscious source of instinctual life:

> *Example:* a baby is feeding at the breast and obtains satisfaction. This fact by itself does not indicate whether he is having an ego-syntonic id experience or, on the contrary, is suffering the trauma of a seduction, a threat to personal ego continuity, a threat by an id experience which is not ego-syntonic, and with which the ego is not equipped to deal. (Winnicott 1960d)

Winnicott is suggesting that there are two strands in human development which only come together partially and gradually. On the one hand there is the personal strand of meaning and relationship, articulated with particular clarity and commitment in his account of true- and false-self development (Winnicott 1960b). On the other, there is the impersonal strand of bodily instinct which he relegates to secondary status but which he does not incorporate within the relational stream.

Winnicott views the ego as synonymous with the person, in that it is meaningless to speak of development without the assumption of an experiencing person. 'Is there an ego from the start?' he asks; and answers himself, 'The start is when the ego starts'; adding rather cryptically, 'It is as well to remember that the beginning is a summation of beginnings' (Winnicott 1965: 56). He gives an example of an infant born with much of the brain missing whose physiological functioning cannot be called ego-functioning because the infant has no capacity for experience. He thus gives relative primacy to ego development and subjectivity over instinctual development and biology, because it is the experiencing ego that renders the organism human.

This leads Winnicott to conceptualise 'id experience' as a factor which is external to the ego (the 'I'); and it is only when the ego has developed some resilience that instinctual demands can be a confirmation of personal identity rather than a threat to it. The 'instincts' resulting in 'id experience' are somatic urges which have a quality of seeking climactic relief, such as hunger, sexual excitement, the wish to move or the need to defecate. While the ego is still fragile, they may be felt to impinge on the baby's sense of cohesion and identity. It is therefore part of the mother's role to manage the infant's bodily states in an emotionally attuned way. Satisfactions such as being fed or touched can be experienced by the infant as 'seductions' in which his personhood feels overlooked, while his physical need and excitement are exploited:

> It is indeed possible to gratify an oral drive and by so doing to *violate* the infant's ego-function, or that which will later on be jealously guarded as the self, the core of the personality. (Winnicott 1962b)

Winnicott thus sees human development as arising from both object-seeking and gratification-seeking roots, a view he shared with Balint and which formed the basis of his rejection of Fairbairn's theoretical structure. He differentiates between ego experience which is concerned with meaning and relationship, and id experience which he seems to view as without meaning until it has become integrated with ego experience. However, his use of such terms as 'id experience' makes clear that instinctual life is only relevant insofar as it is experienced. This appears to undermine his dual view: if instinct can be incorporated within experience, his theory is founded on subjectivity rather than both drive and subjectivity. While experientially evocative, his formulations involve a theoretical confusion which he does not explore.

Winnicott's rejection of the death instinct is also problematic. He suggests that aggression is part of primitive loving and cannot be seen as destructive, being more akin to energetic assertion. He thought the death instinct was a psychoanalytic version of original sin, entailing a condemnation of the infant to which he was wholly opposed. However, he also suggests that aggressive impulses are initially separate from erotic impulses: he speaks of the 'erotic root' and the separate 'aggressive root' of instinctual life (Winnicott 1950–55). Taking up the Freudian idea of the fusion of the death instinct and Eros, he postulates an early stage of 'pre-fusion', when aggression and desire form distinct relational components. 'Fusion' is a psychological task which is closely related to the development of the capacity for concern. 'De-fusion' arises from the de-integration of love and hate in a partial or total breakdown of the capacity for concern.

If the desiring and aggressive components of object relating have separate roots and are brought together in a progressive integration, Winnicott's objection to the death instinct seems unfounded. A change of name, differentiating assertiveness from destructiveness, would seem more apt than an abandonment of the concept.

Winnicott's assumption of the initial merged state of the infant with the 'environmental mother' presupposes a position prior to Klein's paranoid-schizoid position. It was an assumption Freud also held in his view of primary narcissism, and which Klein and Fairbairn relegated to pre-natal life. The widespread assumption that early development involves individuation out of initial fusion is questioned by Stern (1985), who offers evidence for the merged state being a mode of relating that becomes possible after, rather than before, the differentiation of self and other. He suggests that infants are other-oriented from birth, with the sense of self and other emerging from nothing, rather than from a prior sense of unity. His comparison of research findings with psychoanalytic assumptions calls for a wholesale review of common psychotherapeutic views of early development. This material was not available to Winnicott, and he commented that it was easier to track early developmental processes through regressed patients than through direct observation of infants and parents. It is thus quite possible that his assumptions of merging and differentiation are over-simplified or wrongly ordered.

The unstated contradictions underlying Winnicott's ideas have been treated variously as pedantic, off the point or as evidence of a lack of systematic thinking. Winnicott is regarded by some as a visionary who writes poetically rather than analytically. The evocative power of his self-expression does indeed create in the reader an experience of the concept or the sense he is describing, whether this is the transitional area, the primitive agonies, a patient's state of mind, or even id experience. He is one of the most vividly communicative of psychoanalytic writers. Nevertheless, his declared allegiance to scientific method rather than creative expression alone means that the premises on which his creativity rests cannot be ignored.

Winnicott's detractors point to the lack of rigour in his theoretical structure, suggesting that this was paralleled by an overly indulgent attitude to patients. Guntrip made the suggestion that Winnicott, though 'clinically revolutionary ... [was] not really interested enough in pure theory to bother to think it out' (quoted in Goldman 1993: 137). Winnicott endorsed this impression at times by presenting himself, to the delight of his audience, as the charming, creative, naughty child who neglects to go through the literature or acknowledge his sources. His colleague Masud Khan recounts how he urged Winnicott to read a newly published book; his friend expostulated: 'It is no use, Masud, asking me to read anything! If it bores me I shall fall asleep in the middle of the first page, and if it interests me I will start re-writing it by the end of that page' (Winnicott 1975: xvi). Khan was responsible for much of the editing and preparation of Winnicott's writing, and prodded him to relate his ideas to those of others (Winnicott 1965: 11). Winnicott was particularly anxious about reading the work of Ferenczi, an early exponent of a relational approach to psychoanalysis, because of his fear that he would find his own ideas there; and in an informal talk he gave to his colleagues near the end of his life, he conceded with some humility that he had been remiss in his failure to correlate his ideas with theirs and acknowledge their contributions (Winnicott 1967b).

To condemn Winnicott as lazy and self-indulgent in his thinking seems no more adequate than it would be as an assessment of a patient. More enlightening are the numerous indications that Winnicott lacked confidence in himself as a thinker. The brevity of many of his papers suggests a nervousness about holding and developing a theme. Goldman, quoting various letters, draws out the sense of intellectual inferiority which hampered him in discussions with colleagues, and even 'inhibitions in regard to the reading of Freud' (Goldman 1993: 146). Winnicott joked about his headmaster's estimation of him: 'Not brilliant, but will do' (Winnicott 1989: 11), but it was a remark he always remembered. His dread of opposing or disappointing his benignly painted father may be a demonstration of his fear of competition; and it is interesting to learn that his father was himself sensitive about the learning difficulties that had hampered his education (Jacobs 1995: 3). Winnicott's capacity for lateral thinking, and also his symptom of following words in his throat, could well relate to specific learning difficulties, often subsumed under the term dyslexia; no doubt his father suffered from such specific difficulties and Winnicott may also have done so subliminally or through identification with his father. It would thus not be surprising if Winnicott played to what he felt were his creative strengths, rather than his intellectual weaknesses.

Winnicott's theoretical work may be re-evaluated by relating it directly to its context of Freudian and especially Kleinian dominance. While both he and Klein focused on the earliest stages of life with their primitive mental processes, Klein emphasised unconscious phantasy, aggression and the role of the instincts in emotional development. Winnicott, by contrast, speaks of his wish to balance Klein's emphasis with an intelligent attention to the effects of the environment.

This suggests the possibility of reading Winnicott as one component in a Winnicott–Klein conjunction. Seeing Kleinian theory as Winnicott's split-off pessimistic aspect, and even Winnicott's work as Klein's split-off optimistic aspect, may enhance both contributions. Winnicott's dismissal of the death instinct as unnecessary makes sense if his role was to provide a balancing additional focus; and the 'external' and seemingly contentless instinctual impingements he mentions can be recast as Klein's unconscious phantasies, the mental corollaries of instinct projected out because of the internal threat from the death instinct. His optimistic view of delinquency as a sign of hope, his cosy picture of nuclear family life and the well-being of Western society, could represent a necessary part of a larger picture balanced by Klein's grim internality and individualism. His conviction that the core of the self could never be reached from the outside is perhaps a rare glimpse of the essential isolation he shared with Klein. The increasing distance that grew up between Klein and Winnicott reveals the difficulty each had in accepting the theoretical mode of the other, despite personal liking and an early mutual feeling of affiliation. The position held by each may have been emotionally repugnant to the other.

The beguiling simplicity and immediacy of Winnicott's work bring a subtle challenge to his readers. He gives us every encouragement to take a one-sided view of his unusual contribution by idealising him and his theory, or conversely by dismissing it. By insisting on a more rigorous evaluation we might gain more than he realised he was giving: a structural expansion to theory which enhances his inspired creativity.

5

MICHAEL BALINT: THE HARMONIOUS INTERPENETRATING MIX-UP

Balint's contribution to psychoanalysis is seldom fully acknowledged. He is the only one of the early Object Relations pioneers who has not yet been the main subject of a biographical and theoretical study. His concern for the world outside the consulting room led him to develop accessible forms of psychotherapy through collaboration with other professions, particularly medicine. Within psychoanalysis, Balint developed his own perspective on early development and its implications for practice. Keeping a critical eye on the analyst's role, he pointed up with uncomfortable clarity the effects on patients of the psychoanalytic setting and its theoretical framework. His varied interests and controversial style set him apart from the mainstream psychoanalytic world. His colleagues mistrusted his moves beyond 'pure' psychoanalysis, and no doubt found his incisive criticisms disquieting.

LIFE

Michael Balint was born Michael Bergmann in 1896 (see Haynal 1988). His family was part of the German-speaking Jewish population of Budapest. The Hungarian capital, like Vienna a cosmopolitan cultural centre, was similarly shaken by the collapse of the Austro-Hungarian Empire. Besides Balint, a surprising number of psychoanalysts originated from Hungary: Sandor Ferenczi, Margaret Mahler, Geza Roheim and Thomas Szasz are among the most well known. All except Ferenczi emigrated to the United States, where, like Ferenczi and Balint, they developed original and independently-minded challenges to classical theory and practice.

Balint converted to Unitarianism, as did many of his Jewish middle-class compatriots, also changing his name in the Jewish protest against Germanification. While neither action was unusual in his social context, taken together they present a clear rebuff to his familial traditions in this paternalistic culture. Little is publicly known about

Balint's family life, but there are indications of an antagonistic relationship with his father, who was particularly distressed by the changing of his name, and a protective feeling towards his mother (Haynal 1988: 112).

Balint was the elder of two children, active, sociable and curious. He studied medicine, he half-joked later, to please his general practitioner father, in an early suggestion of an Oedipal conflict between appeasing and opposing him. He served briefly in the First World War, returning enthusiastically to his medical studies after an injury to his thumb. The two explanations for his injury – that it was deliberately self-inflicted or that it was a result of clumsy curiosity about a hand-grenade – reflect the ambivalence of his later colleagues, who seemed both to distrust him and to hold him in affection.

Balint's family and that of his first wife, Alice Szekely-Kovacs, were known to each other in Budapest, and he and Alice became close when they met at a seminar on Freud. Alice's mother was a psychoanalyst, and Balint seems to have fallen in love with Alice and psychoanalysis simultaneously. He writes with touching pleasure of their close, almost fused relationship (Balint 1952: preface). They trained in parallel analyses and their early papers resulted from constant discussion. Balint presents a picture of ideal love with their work and personal lives intertwined. His affection for Alice shines forth from a family photograph (Haynal 1988: 110); one wonders whether some of the conflict between them may have been exported to relationships with colleagues.

Because of the increasing anti-Semitism in Hungary, Balint and Alice moved to Berlin in 1919 to begin their psychoanalytic training while Balint simultaneously pursued a doctorate in biochemistry. They enjoyed the lively pre-Hitlerian Berlin, and Balint was one of the few analysts to express sympathy for Melanie Klein's plight. However, they found their analyst, Hanns Sachs, dogmatic and domineering, and returned to Budapest to train with Ferenczi.

A change of government resulted in a pro-Hitler régime in the 1930s and psychoanalysts became increasingly subject to restriction and persecution. The Balints moved to Britain in 1939 with their son John, escaping probable death at the hands of the Nazis. Unlike other European analysts who mostly settled in London, Jones arranged for the Balints to live in Manchester. This appears to have arisen from long-standing friction between Ferenczi and Jones in the wake of a bitter disagreement between Freud and Ferenczi. Balint was fervently loyal to Ferenczi, and the discord between Balint and Jones was exacerbated when Jones repeated the rumour that Ferenczi had been schizophrenic before he died. Balint publicly refuted this (Haynal 1988: 96) and criticised Jones' sneering portrayal of Ferenczi (Balint 1968: ch. 23).

Balint took up psychiatric work in hospitals and child guidance clinics and undertook research in infant development. Shockingly, Alice died of a ruptured aneurysm a few months after their arrival in Britain; although foreseen, it was a bitter blow. Then in 1945, Balint's parents committed suicide when they were on the point of being arrested by the Nazis, news which must have been particularly poignant so close to the end of the war. Balint's second marriage in 1944 lasted only a short time. He must have suffered lonely and painful years following these tragic losses, in a new country and with the sole care of his son.

Balint combined psychoanalytic work with efforts to bring the benefits of psychoanalysis to the larger society. He was at the Tavistock Clinic, London, from 1948–61, developing work with groups and couples and a form of brief therapy which could be used in the new National Health Service. It was at the Tavistock that he met his third wife, Enid Eichholz, a social worker who also became a psychoanalyst. She had founded the Family Discussion Bureau (later the Institute of Marital Studies), and she and Balint developed the case discussion seminars which were adapted with spectacular success for family doctors. A surprisingly large number of older general practitioners speak with enthusiasm of the 'Balint groups' they have either taken part in or heard of, and which had a definite though limited effect on British medical training.

Independent rather than partisan, Balint seems to have had mixed relations with his colleagues. Fairbairn's biographer Jock Sutherland described him as 'assertive by British standards' (Sutherland 1971). Klein, whom he knew from Budapest and Berlin, appreciated both his personal support and his outspokenness (Grosskurth 1986: 330); Winnicott, with whom superficially he had the most in common, seems a more distant figure. Competition may have been a factor: Balint complained that Winnicott acknowledged his debt to himself and Ferenczi only through poking fun at them (Goldman 1993: 6), and Balint may have been one of the analysts to whom Winnicott felt at a disadvantage in theoretical 'discussions'. Balint's closest friend and colleague, after Enid, was John Rickman, who had also been in analysis with Ferenczi and who had helped him come to Britain. Balint was respected in the British Psycho-Analytical Society, being elected Secretary of the Training Committee as well as President.

Balint was instrumental in forging links between British and European psychoanalysts after the Second World War, visiting the decimated Hungarian psychoanalytic circle and even supporting the rebuilding of psychoanalysis in Germany. He travelled widely in America and Europe, working and writing with Enid as closely as he had with Alice: a photograph from the 1960s (Haynal 1988: 114) shows him gazing at her adoringly. His relationships with Alice and Enid bring to mind the 'harmonious interpenetrating mix-up' from which he felt all object relations grew.

Balint developed diabetes and heart problems in his later years, and died in 1970. Enid Balint continued to work in the field of applied psychoanalysis and early development until her death in 1994.

Balint is remembered as a warm, volatile, expressive man, opposed to dogmatism and with an extraordinarily wide range of interests and enthusiasms. His idyllic relationships with Alice and Enid resonate the wistful love he expressed for his mother in a letter to his sister-in-law after his parents' deaths. The same letter demonstrates the ambivalence of his relationship with his father: 'It is true that I had neglected my father for a long time. We never got along too well', he wrote, adding conscientiously, 'But I inherited my intelligence, my logical mind, my capacity for work from him' (quoted in Haynal 1988: 112).

Ferenczi seems to have been Balint's good father, and perhaps his work with the medical profession brought his two fathers, both general practitioners, together in his mind. Much of his work involves attempts to reconcile oppositions, perhaps reflecting the inner and outer conflicts in his life. He seems to have made unusually creative sublimations of these in happy if one-sided relationships and worthwhile practical and theoretical contributions in his work. His relative marginalisation probably stems from his cross-professional work, his anti-partisan stance and his association with the neglected and unfortunate Ferenczi.

THEORY

Balint brought the Hungarian tradition to Britain and Object Relations. He was deeply influenced by Ferenczi, who was Klein's first analyst and a close friend and colleague of Freud until his independent thinking led to their estrangement. Ferenczi broke new ground in his work with those patients whom Freud deemed too narcissistic for psychoanalytic treatment. Ferenczi believed that they were traumatised through a lack of love rather than innate instinctual conflict, proposing an Object Relations hypothesis startlingly early. He spent his professional life following up the implications for practice of this reorientation. Ferenczi's attempts to supply the affection he thought these patients had lacked led to successes but also to difficulties. He ended up taking one patient on holiday with him, and became entangled in a double relationship with his mistress and her daughter who later became his patient. Similar scenarios disturbed and embarrassed his colleagues, especially Freud, and eventually his work was shunned until Balint brought Ferenczi's compassionate, enquiring approach to mainstream psychoanalysis.

Like Ferenczi, Balint's main focus was the effect of theory on practice rather than the creation of a new theoretical structure. As an Independent in the Freud–Klein controversies, he maintained a similar stance to Winnicott: that in their instinctual lives human beings are both pleasure-oriented and object-seeking.

Balint's ability to stand back from psychoanalytic habits and traditions, his focus on practice and his promotion of a wider view give his work relevance to practitioners inside and outside psychoanalysis. His frank discussions on touch, technique and closed-mindedness address concerns which are common to many of the caring professions.

The Harmonious Interpenetrating Mix-up

Balint's perspective on early development draws principally from his experience with patients. The accepted Freudian view was that object relationships develop after an initial period of self-absorption in which the baby seeks satisfaction rather than connection, termed 'primary narcissism'. The Kleinian view, on the other hand, proposed a rudimentary sense of separateness and an orientation towards object relationship from birth.

These divergent premises were argued out repeatedly (King and Steiner 1991), and little notice seems to have been taken of Balint's careful study of the implicit contradictions in Freud's various accounts of the primary human state. Freud suggests both that object relationship is primary and leads on to narcissism, and elsewhere that narcissism or auto-erotism are primary and lead to later object relationship (see Balint 1968: ch. 7). The unfinished 'Outline of Psychoanalysis' (Freud 1938a, S.E. 23) holds that primary narcissism precedes object relationship. This became the 'official version', and

Freud's earlier ponderings were forgotten. Balint used Freud's oscillations to support his own proposition of the earliest mental state being object relationship rather than primary narcissism, but object relationship of a special kind.

Balint took up Ferenczi's conception of 'passive object love' to describe a primitive attachment where the need is to receive rather than to give love (Balint 1935). He later coined the terms 'primary love', 'primary object relationship' and finally 'harmonious interpenetrating mix-up' in his attempts to articulate this first form of relatedness. He suggests that in this state the other is experienced neither as the self nor as a distinct object but as *matter*, a word which he points out has the same root as 'mother'. Our original relation to this 'matter' is a benign and low-key intermingling, a 'harmonious interpenetrating mix-up' so gentle that we only intermittently perceive it. He likens it to the fish's relation with water, or our own with air (Balint 1968: ch. 12). It makes as little sense to distinguish between self-matter and other-matter as it would to argue about whether the air in our lungs is part of us or part of the atmosphere. Most of the time we live in harmonious mutuality with our medium and are only sharply aware of it when it is lacking. In the same way, Balint suggests, the foetus is only aware of the environment as something distinct at moments of crisis, most dramatically the crisis of birth. Otherwise there is simply a background awareness.

Balint thus leads us eloquently to his vision of being-with: a quiet rightness that is easily overlooked in our everyday life and in the therapeutic setting. He sees the ground of our relatedness in the shimmering ambience we move within and through, distinct only when its absence jars us out of the well-being we take for granted.

The Development of Object Relationship

Balint's harmonious mix-up belongs to a world where differentiation barely exists. It is not until we reach the new world after birth that we encounter the hardness of objects and the emptiness of the space between them. We come to take this world of sharply separate entities for granted while the 'harmonious interpenetrating mix-up' recedes into the hinterland. It lingers on, barely acknowledged, in our relationship with air, earth, darkness, substance and space, in the transitional experience described by Winnicott and in the special relationship we expect mothers to have with their children.

Balint saw object relationship as an attempt to re-create the archaic harmonious mix-up, replaced after birth with a dual track of self-attachment and object-attachment. Balint suggests that narcissism, or self-love, reflects the baby's continuing attachment to the self-substance of the original mix-up, while object-attachment continues her bond with the other-substance. The baby's involvement with the harmonious mix-up thus continues in divided form after it has been torn apart. In time, the baby may transfer much of her self-attachment to the people around her; but if her world is too unrewarding she will be forced to keep her hopes turned inwards. It is the continuing substitution of self-love for object-love that constitutes the pathological narcissism which has been a focus of attention from Freud onwards.

In the post-birth world of objects and space, only scraps of the old harmony continue into personal relationships. The largest of these resides in the expectations the child has, or feels she should be able to have, of her mother. Mothers are routinely and uniquely expected to hold their children's happiness in the centre of their concern as a precondition of their own well-being, as in Winnicott's 'primary maternal preoccupation' which can be thought of as the mother's continuing harmonious mix-up with her baby. Alice Balint explores the 'naive egotism', which endures in attitudes towards mothers in 'Love of the Mother and Mother Love' (A. Balint 1939). This paper demonstrates how closely she and Balint must have worked together to develop a shared understanding.

In general, however, after the initial period of infancy it is unrealistic for the infant to go on expecting to be loved without doing anything in return. The child is compelled to move towards mutuality, which Balint envisages rather pessimistically as a kind of barter (Balint 1968: ch. 13). He suggests that what we really want is to be able to take someone else's love for granted, but the price is the hard work of loving them in return. In being loved, and most completely in mutual orgasm with a partner, transient echoes of the old blissful harmony make mature relationship worthwhile. Balint defines the building of relationship as 'the work of conquest' – winning someone's friendship – and the parallel 'adaptation to the object' – fitting in with the other's needs (Balint 1947). Thus two separate people, in search of their own experiences of harmony, construct a joint alliance.

Like Fairbairn, Balint thought that hate was a secondary phenomenon, a reaction to frustration rather than an aim in itself. It may be a cry of disappointment at a failed attempt at harmony, or a means of coercing others to maintain or improve their part in its provision. He suggests that amoral destructiveness, but not active hate, may be an intrinsic part of the interpenetrating mix-up. Self-interest, however, requires that this destructiveness give way to concern; otherwise our aggressiveness could backfire by driving away those who might provide us with an experience of harmony. The Balints saw fixed hate as a sign of not being able to move beyond early dependence: primitive attachment, as it were, 'with a negative sign' (A. Balint 1939; M. Balint 1951).

Ocnophils and Philobats

Post-birth relationships embody both the knowledge that the original harmony is lost, and also a denial of that knowledge. Reality forces upon us the fact of other people's equal and separate status, but true mutuality is fleeting: we rarely have more than moments when we care as much about another person's happiness as our own. In his attractive *Thrills and Regressions* (Balint 1959) Balint offers a quirky perspective on the compromise formations through which we express this contradiction. He called our contrasting reactions to the world of objects and space those of the 'ocnophil' and the 'philobat', indicating respectively timidity and recklessness.

In the ocnophilic reaction, we identify the substance of objects as safe and the space between them as threatening; we try to re-find harmony through attaching ourselves to the solid objects which we equate with primary matter. The old carefree harmony, however, has gone for ever with the caesura of birth, and fearing abandonment we cling to our emblem of safety. Balint suggests that Bowlby's Attachment Theory is a study of the ocnophilic tendency, our overriding need to keep hold of someone who induces a feeling of security.

Balint describes the adult ocnophil in humorously exaggerated terms. The ocnophil likes comfort and predictability. She hates swings, roundabouts and skiing, which make her feel afraid and sick; she prefers to be safe on the ground with her favoured person to hand, spending money on candy-floss rather than rides. She is happier driving in the nearside lane behind a protective lorry rather than out in the open with dizzy-making emptiness all around. As soon as she gets home she turns on the radio, and prefers it if someone else has got home first. The ocnophilic attitude to objects is pre-depressive. 'Her' person is highly important to her, but she feels no concern for that person. The ocnophil yearns to be held in perfect security so that she can forget all about the other person. Because of the traumatic separation of birth she lives in fear of being dropped and so she frantically and desperately clings. Touch is her favoured sense and physical closeness her optimum mode. She does not understand the philobat's way of life: she may admire it but she also abhors it.

The philobat, by contrast, finds enclosure claustrophobic. It is the expanse between objects that feels safe and trustable, while solid objects appear treacherous. The sense of harmony is recaptured in the skilful communion with space which echoes the limitlessness of primary substance. He (most typically 'he') feels most 'himself' when freed of encumbrances: piloting a plane, in mid ski-jump, seeking thrilling sensations through fast driving, drugs or the exhilaration of solitary creation or inner exploration. The philobat drives in the outermost lane, impelled to overtake any car which appears in the stretch of road ahead, irritated by any which encroach behind. He is space-seeking rather than object-seeking. While the ocnophil negotiates fearfully the 'horrid empty spaces' between comforting objects, the philobat relishes the 'wide friendly expanses' which are only marred by hazardous objects. The air through which he parachutes, or the abstract realms he swoops about in, are excitingly under his deft control; the dangers lie in rocks beneath the surface or in specific calculations or images which do not work and so spoil things.

However, as he is living in the real world the philobat has no option but to depend on certain objects, and this he does with characteristic nonchalance. The skier's skis, the pilot's controls, the artist's paintbrush, and whoever constitutes his 'ground control', are given exceptional status. He is highly dependent on them and feels them to be irreplaceable, but like the ocnophil, it does not occur to him that they may have needs or interests which could conflict with their usefulness. They are the allowable objects of the post-harmonious world. The philobat's favoured mode is vision in space; he feels contemptuous of the pathetically limited ocnophilic existence.

Balint sees the philobatic mode as coming together at a later stage than the ocnophilic. Space, independence and vision belong well after birth, and Balint suggests that philobatism has links with the phallic stage (Balint 1959: ch. 2). In a 'regression by progression', ancient security is sought through the development of new skills and powers (Balint 1959: ch. 10), whereas the ocnophilic mode is more obviously womb-like. It is also more fundamental, reflecting that our safety lies more in our connection with others than in independence.

Balint's playful division correlates with the hysterical mode on the one hand, where the other person is clung to and inner reality feared; and the schizoid on the other, where contact is feared and inner reality idealised. In Western society masculinity is seen as more schizoid or philobatic and femininity as more hysterical or ocnophilic, but Balint warned against overemphasising division by gender. These are ideal types rather than real people, and elements from each mode form shifting individual patterns.

Three-body, Two-body and One-body Modes

Balint focused particular attention on a group of patients who could not make use of the standard Freudian approach where problems are formulated in terms of Oedipal conflicts between love and hate. These are the borderline patients whose perceptions of the world are greatly distorted. Their relationships are fraught and puzzling, with the therapeutic alliance always threatening to break down. Their sense of self is fragile and shifting, their anxiety extreme; they often hear interpretations in ways that the therapist had not intended.

Balint pointed out that such patients are often intelligent, sensitive and unusually aware of their tormented internal world. This, together with their primitive mode of relating, can lead the therapist to become entangled in their suffering. He may attempt to mitigate their anxiety by changing the normal framework in a 'grand experiment' which only too often leads to 'a tragic or heroic finale'. Balint set out to discover why (Balint 1968: ch. 18).

The major difficulty for the therapist and patient working in this area arises from the breakdown of what Balint calls the three-body, or Oedipal level of functioning (Balint 1968: ch. 3). This is the level on which the smooth running of everyday life depends, and without which co-operation is extremely difficult.

In the Oedipal level, we can maintain our existence in a triangular situation: we accept that there is a partnership or situation – typically mother and father – of which we are not a part. Balint connects this Oedipal, three-body level to a three-term mode of functioning, with mother, father and child transposed to the three terms self, other and (separate) object, or alternatively self, object and symbol.

In this tripartite mode, the child experiences the word or the symbol as different from herself as the user of the word, and different from whatever it represents, although it is connected to both. This means that she can use language to communicate ideas, because there is an area which is separable from both the communicating parties. The therapist's interpretation or technical structure can thus be heard as a hypothesis, view or proposal which can be accepted or declined. This is the Kleinian depressive position, where we experience the other as separate from ourselves and where we can appreciate that symbols have a semi-independent relation to the thing or experience they symbolise on the one hand, and the symbolising self on the other.

The two-body or two-term mode is more primitive. There is little or no space for anything apart from the self and the other, and even these may be only vaguely differentiated as in the original harmonious mix-up. Symbolisation is not possible because symbolising assumes a reality outside the two participants; in the two-term mode there is no symbolic space, simply the two beings themselves. Words or symbols are experienced as the same as the objects to which they refer (Hanna Segal's 'symbolic equation'), and, when used by someone else, as an emanation or action of that person. There is thus no neutral zone; to the extent that the patient has regressed to a two-term mode, she experiences the therapist's words as the execution of an action rather than as the communication of an idea.

All kinds of misapprehensions can then occur. The patient may feel an articulation of her difficulty, however empathically expressed, as the ramming of her inadequacies down her throat; or conversely, a recognition of her strengths as a declaration of love or a quasi-physical gratification. In approaches such as Gestalt the client will not be able to use a cushion as a symbol of an absent person or an aspect of the client's self: it will either *be* the absent person, or else will bear no relation to that person. Touch can be dynamite, as Balint discusses in his differentiation between malignant and benign regression. The therapist may be drawn into the two-body mode and find himself feeling hounded or exposed by the patient or lured into believing the patient's idealisation rather than maintaining his usual perspective.

Balint refers to a paper of Ferenczi's which explores the muddle that can arise when the therapist's assumptions of adult communication meets the patient's regressed primitive communication. It also points out the bewilderment the patient may be faced with through her own conflicting infantile and relatively adult modes of being which result in feelings and reactions that seem incomprehensible (Ferenczi 1932).

Balint suggests that there is also a one-term mode of being which, intriguingly, he sees as arising from rather than preceding the basic two-term harmonious mix-up (Balint 1968: ch. 5). He calls it the 'area of creation', developing the concept from being with patients at times when externality did not seem to exist for them. The area of creation catches the experience of reverie and absorption, a state which is not defensively cut off and yet which does not involve the outside world. It is the process of creation of something out of oneself alone. The moment of creation, whether of a symptom, an idea, a move towards recovery or an understanding, cannot be shared with another. It connects with Winnicott's 'ego-relatedness', that internalisation of relationship which is manifested in the capacity to be alone without being isolated (Winnicott 1958). The special sensitivity Balint brought to his work led him to notice and value this state as something belonging entirely to the patient, which he as analyst could observe but in which he could not participate.

The Basic Fault

Balint's term 'the basic fault' describes a sense of brokenness that runs throughout one's being. It is the residue of trauma at the two-term stage when the harmonious mix-up was shattered too abruptly or finally, a mishap which may arise from a lack of attunement between the baby and her carer as well as from more overt trauma. Balint presents birth as the inevitable destruction of harmony, implying that birth always results in some degree of personal disruption. As with Winnicott's concept of privation, the basic fault has a more pervasive influence than would result from a later deprivation. Because the catastrophe happened before the establishment of the sense of self and other as distinct entities, the flaw encompasses the whole of subjective reality and one's very being feels tainted.

Balint's concept is a metaphor for a geological fault, a fissure embedded beneath the surface of a continuous structure. Even if the superficial layers appear intact, it is a weak point which particular stresses may expose as an obscure sense of disconnectedness or outbursts of desperate anxiety and primitive defences.

We normally try to live above the level of the basic fault and the frantic anxiety this involves, using whatever defensive strategies we can and intensifying them if the anguish threatens to break through. We may seek to avert a repeat of our forgotten catastrophe by seeing other people as dangerous and avoiding relationship. Alternatively, we identify others as saviours and attempt to attach ourselves, leech-like, to them. Philobatic or ocnophilic personal styles may thus become schizoid or hysterical patterns in the effort to cope with the breakdown of trust in oneself, the world and in being itself.

Psychotherapy involves the re-negotiation of the accommodation made to the breakdown of trust. When this entails serious unease at the level of the basic fault, and if therapist and client or patient feel able, a profound regression may follow on from more ordinary work. People express their 'basic fault' in terms of damage at the ground of their being: 'I'm not a proper person'; 'I'm only half a person'; 'The thing that's wrong is me'. Partial measures make little difference to the basic fault, though people may be helped to live above this level more constructively.

The patient comes to know that if her lifelong anxiety is to be reached, she has to enter into an exquisitely vulnerable dependency, living through the risk of disaster without any idea what the outcome will be. Balint called this dropping away of defences a 'new beginning'; it can emerge once or a number of times, briefly or as a phase, often as the completion of the therapy. It is a return to the harmonious trust which is neither an anxious clutching on to the therapist nor a pseudo-independence. Balint suggests the German word *arglos* to express the feeling of openness and rightness in simply being, which can be overlooked or misinterpreted by a therapist fixed on expression, insight or words (Balint 1968: ch. 21).

Balint warns that it is easy for the therapist to collude with the regressed patient's perception of him as big and powerful, whether as a threat or as security: therapists do not like being reminded of their basic fault, either. This collusion leads away from the quietly intimate rapport of the new beginning in which each can take the other for granted. Balint describes a fluid, ordinary, low-key being together which reduces the hierarchical distance between therapist and patient. Rather than looking for rescue or escape, the patient may then be able to experience simply being with another in vulnerability (Balint 1968: ch. 25). This is what Balint called 'primary love', and we can see how intangible the distinction is between loving and being loved. It is effortless for both people, though it easily slips off-course in a moment of inattention or fear. Balint reminds us that primary love cannot erase a person's history, but it can be part of a new beginning in object relating based on the repair of broken trust.

Malignant and Benign Regression

Balint's exploration of the hazards of the therapeutic relationship with the regressed patient makes a significant contribution to working with people in distress. He builds on Ferenczi's experience to distinguish 'benign regression', where a gently harmonious relationship leads to a 'new beginning', and 'malignant regression', where a spiral of demand sets in. Malignant regression is a frustrating and destructive process which most people in the helping professions will recognise. It arises from an extreme ocnophilic or hysterical reaction to anxiety and need.

It may develop, Balint suggests, through the therapist feeling that his normal working frame is too rigid and depriving for his acutely dependent and hysterically-inclined patient to bear. He may offer or agree to longer or more frequent sessions, contact between sessions, gifts, reassurance or touch. At first, these extras seem to help and the patient becomes calmer, which encourages the therapist to continue. Shortly, however, the demands increase, and an addiction-like spiral develops with both patient and therapist feeling that neither the patient nor the therapeutic relationship can survive without her increasingly disruptive demands being met. In this truly malignant escalation, the patient's frightened search for a powerfully gratifying figure to latch on to combines with the therapist's potential for grandiosity. Though few professionals speak openly about their ordeals with such patients, most will understand if not condone the position in which Ferenczi eventually found himself, offering sessions at weekends, during holidays and in the night.

Balint suggests that despite appearances the patient is afraid of emotional contact and is seeking not relationship but gratification; the therapist appears to be doing the same. Emotional maturation will therefore not develop, and any gratification will simply never be enough. Malignant regression illustrates Fairbairn's articulation of the hysterical process as the substituting of physical contact for emotional understanding. It would be interesting to research how frequently malignant regression, a creation of both therapist and patient, is a factor in the culminating omnipotence of sexual activity with a patient or client, where responsibility lies with the therapist.

Malignant regression of the kind Balint describes arises from a hysterical defence against emotional contact; the schizoid's frozen avoidance of relation, equally malignant, is the converse regressed mode. Both involve a regression to an early way of coping with trauma after the loss of the original harmony. The world of malignant regression is one of distinct objects or part-objects which may offer supreme bliss or threaten harrowing persecution, with physicality drastically separated from relationship. The regression does not go far enough to reach the primary sense of harmony which is undisturbed by extremes of fear or pleasure and undisrupted by instinctual drive.

Malignant regression may be a particular danger with more hysterical patients who are prone to these patterns of defence, especially those who have a sparse relational life. This may indicate that the patient has little capacity for the mature relating described by Balint as the ability to transform objects into co-operative partners. She may then be especially vulnerable to overwhelming neediness in conjunction with intense fear of relationship, as well as having to endure a real lack of physical gratification (touch and sex) which Balint saw as a factor in itself.

All therapies have their own pitfalls; malignant regression may be one in those approaches which, like Ferenczi's, assume that early deprivation leads directly to problems in living, and that the therapeutic task is to compensate for deprivation in order to unblock development. There are many versions of therapy as 'corrective emotional experience', articulated psychoanalytically by Balint's fellow-Hungarian Franz Alexander (1954). The implications of any change of frame are complex in such a perspective.

Humility is the main quality which helps practitioners avoid setting up a malignant spiral, through guarding against an easy falling-in with patients' assumptions of their powerfulness. The humble therapist will be more able to resist the responsibility for 'curing' the patient, whose experience will be seen as her own rather than something the therapist should give. He will put himself across as simply another person, without ultimate answers or solutions, who is willing to be alongside the client or patient without needing gratitude, attention or accommodation. Then tangles have a better chance of untangling, and being vulnerable does not mean losing autonomy. The patient can come to accept, perhaps with regret, that the therapist can never be more than a therapist to her. Like the child in the Oedipal drama, she becomes free to want only what is possible with him, turning to other people for a fuller life with them.

Regression may then be 'benign' rather than malignant, a step towards a new life rather than a perpetually vicious circle. Instead of the endless substitutive search for gratification which can only ever be partial, the patient can sink back into a relaxed being-with the therapist, experiencing him as 'someone like me' who will not judge or criticise, who easily tunes in, and whose failures can be tolerated because he does not expect to be perfect. The patient's need is not for instinctual gratification but for personal recognition. While this may involve some relaxing of the therapeutic frame, the purpose is not to allay suffering but to facilitate an atmosphere of openness and trust. Benign regression is the *modus operandi* of the new beginning.

Balint gives an example from his own practice of how a potentially malignant episode of regression gave way to a more benign form (Balint 1968: ch. 24). The patient felt he had got little from his session, the last before the weekend, and was fearful of the coming separation. He asked for an extra session, saying he could not manage without it. Balint had sometimes agreed to this request before; the extra sessions had seemed to give relief but nothing more. This time, rather than saying either yes or no, he simply acknowledged the patient's feelings and said he didn't think another session would be *powerful* enough to do what the patient wanted: it would be just another session. The patient left, none too pleased. Over the weekend he phoned Balint to say, rather disjointedly, that he was all right, he didn't want another session, he just wanted to say he was very near crying. That was all he needed to get through the weekend.

Touch

Balint's discussion on touch is immediately relevant to any practitioner who does not completely rule it out. While in the mature, three-term mode, touch can be perceived as a technical facilitator or a limited form of empathy, in the two-term mode it can be the entrance to a minefield. Many practitioners know from bitter experience how touch can induce or intensify a regression taking a malignant turn.

The patient's initially moderate demands for physical contact may escalate to desperate craving. The therapist appears as a god-like figure who with his magic touch can dispense ecstasy and redemption, or who by withholding it can doom the patient to wretched incompleteness. A frequent dénouement is the messy breakdown of the therapeutic relationship, leaving the patient with a sense of desperate grievance that can lead to complaints procedures, invasions of the therapist's privacy or suicidal threats or actions – all last-ditch attempts to hold on to the ocnophilic object which seems essential for survival. The therapist, meanwhile, may be left with a shameful sense of failure and a bitter hatred for the apparently manipulative and intrusive patient. Both feel their personal or professional survival to be in the malevolent hands of a powerful other. Balint suggests that the first recorded malignant regression occurred with the first psychoanalytic patient, 'Anna O.', when she was being treated by Freud and Breuer (Balint 1968: ch. 22; Breuer and Freud 1895, S.E. 2; Gay 1988: 63–9). Breuer fled in panic when she flung her arms round him and entered imaginary childbirth to give birth to their imaginary child. Freud was made of stronger stuff, and used the event to help develop his concept of transference; but it is small wonder he instituted the 'no touch' rule for classical psychoanalysis.

Yet Balint did not believe a fixed rule to be the answer. His response to the patient who wanted an extra session demonstrates his flexibility. His patient was able to telephone him briefly, but Balint differentiates this availability from a bestowal of a wish which would make the therapist the powerful one. In the same way, he suggests, the vulnerable patient in a benign regression may need a degree of touch in order to continue feeling: without it, a jarring sense of difference interrupts her 'going-on-being' and the basic fault is repeated rather than repaired (Balint 1968: ch. 21). If the therapist feels himself to be an enabler rather than a rescuer or provider, touch or other changes to the framework arise from his trying not to obstruct the patient's re-creation of harmonious mix-up with him, rather than from his own need to act. It will be low key rather than highly charged touch – holding the therapist's finger, for example. It is a way of reaching trust rather than defending against it and so does not lead to malignant regression. The patient is simply enabled to continue being open, feeling recognised by the therapist and thus more able to recognise and accept herself.

Balint's insightful analysis offers useful guidelines for the therapist as to when and how changes to the frame may enable the work to go further, and when they are more likely to lead to the blind alley of malignant regression.

Therapeutic Cultures

Balint was a stimulating early critic within psychoanalysis. He challenged the accepted view of the psychoanalytic setting as the perfect laboratory for the elucidation and treatment of psychological processes, suggesting rather that it is a 'peculiar, lop-sided two-person relationship' which sheds light on some areas while obscuring or distorting others (Balint 1957a). He suggested that like any situation, psychoanalysis cannot include the whole person. Since it offers opportunity for relationship but not physical gratification, it brings out the relational pole far more than the complementary instinctual pole. The one-term area of creation is also easy for the psychoanalyst to miss.

These remarks could apply to all psychotherapeutic approaches, and Balint suggested additionally that specific frameworks have a determining influence on what the patient or client experiences and how it is expressed. The therapist may take the material which emerges as confirmation of his theory in a self-fulfilling prophecy which prevents beliefs being questioned and reinforces rather than dissolves theoretical divides.

The title of his paper 'The Problem of Language in Upbringing and Psychoanalytic Treatment' (in Balint 1968) speaks for itself. His fluency in German, Hungarian and English supports an interesting discussion on the power of language to shape thought and experience. Different languages enable more or less subtle distinctions to be made within the same areas of experience, with some ideas being impossible to express in one language while easy in another. The 'cluster of associations' surrounding any word or expression makes translation a problematic task, and Balint highlights some of the differences between the English translation of Freud and the German original. The atmosphere surrounding a linguistic expression is particularly important in psychotherapy where intangible and semi-conscious processes mediate communication and understanding.

Balint points out that all schools of psychotherapy have emotional attachments to their particular language and the concepts that are central to it. The associations and atmospheres, even the history, of its essential terminology are likely to be lost on outsiders. Because practitioners 'learn' their psychotherapeutic language at a formative stage in their psychotherapeutic development, they may be unaware of using it. So while it is undisputed that therapists have to tune into the language, assumptions and world view of their patients, it is less acknowledged that patients have to do the same with their therapists. Each patient has no option but to take on the language, conventions and expressible content of her therapist's framework if communication is to be possible.

Balint suggests that classical psychoanalysis was based on interpretation leading to insight, rather than relationship leading to maturation. It was developed for those patients with an intact sense of self and an ability to make use of communications as ideas rather than experiencing them as actions (Balint 1968: ch. 2). The patient was assumed to live experientially as a separate, whole person in relationship with other separate, whole people, interacting reliably through words. This approach worked well with carefully selected patients, who confirmed the centrality of the Oedipus Complex and the usefulness of the interpretational approach. However, as Freud discovered, it stumbled with the narcissistic, borderline and psychotic patients for whom these assumptions were invalid because they could not function at the level the therapy required.

Balint's critique of Kleinian analysis (Balint 1968: ch. 17) suggests a similar induction of its own conceptual frame. The immediate interpretation of primitive impulses presents the analyst as a powerful and controversial figure. Idealisation, envy and hate become not only understandable but expected in the early Kleinian climate, possibly telling us more about the approach than about the patient or the primitive human being. The expression of pre-symbolic processes in adult communicational forms brings inevitable misunderstanding and confusion, and the specialised early Kleinian language sounded mad to outsiders. These drawbacks have reduced to some extent as Freudian and Kleinian theory and practice have developed.

Balint thus saw Freudian theory as leaning towards a philobatic bias; the emphasis on autonomous discovery and insight limited who could benefit from it and skewed what would emerge. Conversely, the Kleinian tendency to interpret all the patient's communications in terms of transference left little space for the patient's own creative discoveries; as an approach, its bias was towards ocnophilia.

Balint saw psychoanalysis becoming increasingly confined to the ocnophilic mode as the realm of transference and counter-transference expanded, reducing or even abolishing the conceptual area outside the therapists' influence. He saw this as an outcome of therapists' anxiety to control their patients. While psychoanalysts scrupulously avoided directing patients or making decisions for them, Balint suggests that they nevertheless influenced events covertly. Patients and clients usually pick up their therapists' views and values, and sometimes their unspoken thoughts, rather accurately. Where this is accentuated by the therapists' anxiety to feel personally effective, an over-reliance on transference interpretations or other explanations may develop which can constitute a force-feeding of the patient. Theory, Balint suggests, can provide a refuge for the therapist to hide from raw anxiety.

Many of Balint's ideas thus focus specifically on the effects on practice of the habitual conventions and assumptions, as well as the individual characters, of practitioners. Perhaps because he was not addressing his psychoanalytic colleagues directly, he expressed these ideas with particular forthrightness in his witty account of his 'research-cum-training groups' for general practitioners, much of which is directly relevant to all forms of psychotherapy and counselling and beyond (Balint 1957a). The groups started with the assertion that 'by far the most frequently used drug in general practice was the doctor himself' (Balint 1957a: 1) a drug which was barely recognised and whose effects were largely uncharted. 'Our chief aim was a reasonably thorough examination of the ever-changing doctor–patient relationship, i.e. the study of the pharmacology of the drug "doctor"' (Balint 1957a: 4). He thus treats the therapeutic relationship as the central issue.

Balint highlights the effects of the individual doctor's underlying beliefs and assumptions normally going under the guise of 'common sense', which he must induce the patient to share to a certain degree if they are to work together constructively: he terms this the doctor's 'apostolic function' (Balint 1957a: chs 16, 17). This can be related directly to the building of the therapeutic alliance in psychotherapy and counselling. His enquiry into the uses and misuses of advice and reassurance, summed up in the repeated question: 'Reassuring – but to whom?' is equally stimulating (Balint 1957a: 108). The chapters 'How to Start' and 'When to Stop' relate strategy to the particular circumstances of the therapeutic relationship. His exploration of the patient's relationship to her illness expands his concept of the basic fault to the bodily as well as the emotional sphere; and his discussion of training speaks to supervisors and trainers in all related fields.

Balint's prime message is that too much is lost through the isolation of different approaches and professions from each other. He suggests that as medicine can learn from psychoanalysis, so psychoanalysis can learn from medicine and other disciplines. Each approach, setting and profession has its own area of focus and expertise and can contribute unique insights. While different situations call for their own frameworks and techniques, Balint's plea is for a plurality of therapeutic approaches to be accepted in the co-operative development of a more complete understanding of human beings.

Commentary

Balint contributed theoretical and practical insights to Object Relations. His steady focus on how ideas translate into actions and atmospheres brought the dual aims of research and treatment into closer relation with each other. His ability to stand outside as well as inside psychoanalysis made him an imaginative advocate for cross-disciplinary co-operation and the integration of divided schools of thought. Throughout his work he puts forward a view of the whole person as a being who is both biological and psychological, pleasure-seeking and object-seeking.

Balint's original intention was to explore the development of the twin strands of object relations, or love, and sexual aims, or pleasure. His major insights follow the first of these two threads and he ends up giving little attention to instinctual development as such. However, he consistently maintains that although the psychoanalytic setting inhibits the study of the instinctual strand, it is nevertheless fundamental (Balint 1936). His criticism of Fairbairn's Object Relations theory rests on his view that it is valid only for what can be learned from psychoanalysis and does not necessarily cover the whole human being (Balint 1957b, in Fairbairn 1994a).

Intriguingly, he suggests that in the increasingly relational emphasis of current psychoanalytic practice, technique was forging ahead of theory (Balint 1949). This seems to raise a question of how thoroughgoing his dual-strand view really was: if relationship was not in some way prior to instinct, he would not have seen technique as in advance of theory, but as becoming one-sided. He ponders on the mysterious connection between the mental and the physical, but he does not develop an overall view. This may have been connected with his positioning of himself at the point of divergence between Freud and Ferenczi, his psychoanalytic heroes.

Freud's principal objective was to develop a coherent theory of the mind using psychoanalysis as a method of research. He was less concerned with the plight of individual patients, declaring 'I have never been a therapeutic enthusiast' (Freud 1933a, S.E. 22: 151). Although he did not ignore the relational factors in the human psyche or in the psychoanalytic situation, his personal creation of psychoanalysis underscores his reliance on insight as the agent of change. Freud's psychoanalysis offers a relational arena in which the patient can carry out research into herself.

Ferenczi, on the other hand, *was* a therapeutic enthusiast. He believed that patients came to him primarily for relief rather than knowledge, and he felt an obligation to try to help them. Because he saw emotional difficulty as a consequence of early deprivation, he believed the patient needed real new experience rather than simply to find a way of seeing herself more fully and truly. The result of this difference of view was the estrangement of its two protagonists and a taboo on further technical experimentation. It was in the centre of this conflict and this taboo that Balint placed himself.

Balint's eventual position on the insight-cure question was that relief became accessible almost by itself once the patient's situation was understood. However, the experience which must be understood only emerges if the atmosphere between therapist and patient allows it to do so. This means that the patient's 'situation' includes the general and immediate therapeutic relationship as well as her past and present world. It is therefore futile to hope for an understanding of the patient which does not include the therapist's individuality and the therapeutic relationship. The path towards a better way of living for the patient involves some degree of 'new beginning' which is real new experience: but it cannot be foreseen, manoeuvred, manipulated or given by the therapist, only experienced by the patient (and the therapist too). All the therapist can do is to try not to prevent the unfolding of experience. Thus Balint nudges the passivity of cure and the activity of insight a little nearer each other.

In his eagerness to bring oppositions together, Balint does not often acknowledge his lack of success in doing so. This is particularly evident in his attempt to hold a drive-based, pleasure-oriented view of the human being alongside a relational view resting on meaning. He presents his 'harmonious interpenetrating mix-up' as the most primitive form of relationship, without clarifying the place of instinct within it. We can surmise that in the pre-natal state the baby's instinctual needs are met and she does not therefore experience them, in the same way that Fairbairn's view of the unborn child precludes the experiencing of the need for contact. However, it is not clear why the distinction between self and other should be experienced in the relational but not the instinctual sphere: why should the foetus perceive the otherness of the maternal substance, albeit in harmony with herself, but not the thrust of instinctual life?

Balint's theory, like those of Klein and Fairbairn, supposes a radical break between pre-natal and post-natal life, with factors which are presented as fundamental having no discernible place before birth. For Balint, the place of instinct before birth is in question; for Fairbairn, the need for relationship; and for Klein, the status and activity of the instincts which she envisages being set into motion by birth. Winnicott's concepts of primary maternal pre-occupation and the environmental mother are close to Balint's harmonious mix-up, but Winnicott abhorred the idea of primary 'harmony'. He argued that such a term presupposes a situation which is too complex to be called primary (Rodman 1987: 127–9). Perhaps Balint was caught up in the same hunt for a theoretical end-point that he thought hampered others.

Like Klein, Balint places the experience of instinctual gratification and frustration after birth, as an aspect of relating to objects and part-objects. He implicitly sees instinctual experience as deriving essentially from separation; and love, quintessentially primary love, as a continuation of the harmony before separation. Malignant regression thus defends rather than dissolves a fixation to a trauma after birth, while benign regression goes beyond the fixation to an experience in which instinctual needs are presumably satisfied and therefore, subjectively, do not exist.

Balint's view of the one-term area of creation and the three-term Oedipal mode developing out of the original two-term harmony offers a fresh and imaginative perspective. Similarly, his harmonious mix-up and its manifestations in primary love, the new beginning and benign regression are clinical jewels. His enchanting depiction of these observations, however, links unconvincingly to his theoretical explanation of mature relationship as an almost cynical trade-off. He implicitly echoes Freud in an ultimately despairing view that human beings seek pleasure, not truth. If the value of human relationship lies solely in what is in it for the individual – for Balint, the sensation of primary harmony – the desire for contact with another which Balint holds as fundamental seems shallow indeed.

This extension of Balint's thinking jars with his overt humanity and optimism, whilst expressing the horrors in his life experience. It is surely the hidden underbelly of his thought and another indication of his drivenness to work in the centre of conflict. The lack of overall structure which results from this limits the theoretical significance of his inventive ideas. Perhaps he was sometimes simply unable to reach a resolution of the polarities he articulates; perhaps he felt implicated in the controversy between Freud and Ferenczi. As with his own father, he seems unable either to come down finally on one side or the other or to shift his standpoint so that the basis of his thought could be something other than irreconciled difference.

Balint offers us tantalising snippets based on acute clinical acumen which are crying out for development. The concept of harmonious mix-up, for example, leads straight to our relationship with the non-human world of objects, substance and space, the neglect of which gives force to Balint's view that psychoanalysis has many blind spots (see Searles 1960). His attempts to hold together pleasure-seeking and object-seeking, and cure and self-knowledge, articulate vital polarities. His critique of theory as artefact opens the door to a more rigorous psychotherapeutic attitude which regrettably has not on the whole been followed up. His contribution to medicine opens new possibilities in diversified fields, not least psychoanalysis, psychotherapy and counselling.

Because Balint did not develop a container for his profusion of ideas, his contributions offer more to practice than to theory. The aim he set himself by implication was to bring harmony between theory and practice, research and treatment, biology and psychology, Freud and Ferenczi; the task he achieved was to extend therapeutic thought and practice in lucid and imaginative ways that do justice to all his forebears.

6

HARRY GUNTRIP:
THE SCHIZOID EXPERIENCE

Guntrip was an early populariser of psychotherapy. He wrote directly and accessibly for social workers, ministers and the public, and even his theoretical studies are emotional rather than dry. His most memorable contribution to psychotherapy is the compassionate warmth that pervades his work, engendering understanding for the suffering of the neurotic person at a time when criticism was common. He is an effective though idiosyncratic ambassador for the work of Fairbairn and Winnicott, both of whom he was in analysis with. His aim was to bring together Fairbairn's theory and Winnicott's practice, which with his own specific contributions he believed could create a fully object-relational psychotherapy.

Guntrip lived a painful and driven life. He ministered to the practical as well as psychological needs of others, and his psychotherapeutic zeal was fuelled by his striving to resolve the personal difficulties that dogged him to his final years. Guntrip, Fairbairn, Winnicott and Balint represent the purest form of early Object Relations.

LIFE

Harry Guntrip was born in 1901, the elder son of an unhappy and ill-suited couple who both became estranged from their own families (see Hazell 1996). They came from fervently religious backgrounds: Guntrip's father, Henry, had begun his own Evangelical sect, The Ranters, and his mother, Harriet, admired Henry's fiery eloquence and Christian principles. She had spent her early years helping to look after her throng of younger siblings, four of whom had died. She was not allowed to continue her education, and when her father died she fell out with her brothers over the family business. Harriet had to start a business of her own to support the family members for whom she had been made responsible; her invalid sister Minnie lived with the Guntrips for the rest of her life.

Henry, in turn, was captivated by Harriet's forthrightness and capacity for hard work; they married after the death of his widowed mother, a dominant woman in whose sphere he had lingered. He gave up preaching for a safer job in the city, which he jeopardised by refusing to sign a petition in support of the Boer War at the turn of the century. Harriet, alarmed, set up a draper's shop which became the overriding focus of the family. She ran the business, Henry dealt with the book-keeping in the evenings, while Minnie and a home-help looked after baby Harry. He was born after an earlier miscarriage, and another son, Percy, was born in 1903. Guntrip was said to have been devoted to his baby brother, and the trauma of Percy's death when Guntrip was three became the symbol of his own psychological fragility for the rest of his life. He describes his desperate grief and subsequent collapse into illness after finding Percy dead on his mother's lap. This was the start of lifelong psychosomatic illness and emotional distress.

Guntrip's father lost his youthful dynamism, becoming a warm but ineffective father who largely gave up on a life of his own: Harriet's overbearing nature is often held responsible for Henry's inadequacy, as well as for Guntrip's difficulties. She seems to have given Guntrip intermittent and often insensitive care in his early years, taking him into the shop with her when he was unhappy, but using him to model girls' clothes until customers protested that this would not do. Hughes (1989) questions whether this made it difficult for Guntrip to grow out of a sense of himself as female, in identification with his mother and her treatment of him as an extension of herself. Perhaps all three members of this bereaved and unhappy family felt conglomerated into an indeterminate mass. It is noticeable that they all had versions of the same name, and both Henry and Guntrip seem to have accepted without protest their subservience in Harriet's troubled empire.

Guntrip was sickly and dreamy as a small child, rather like his father. His passivity provoked his mother to rage: she beat him, at times with little self-control. This changed as he began to have a life at school, away from home, when he threw himself into activity and a pattern of frantic drivenness developed. Harriet, relieved at his growing independence, readily supported his hobbies, and family life improved as the business began to do well. Throughout his childhood Guntrip was inseparable from his best friend Alf, even leaving school at fifteen to follow him into the Civil Service; Alf was the first of many 'brother-figures'. Guntrip was a fervent member of the Salvation Army throughout his adolescence; his anxious obsessionalism is evident in the 'Twenty-four rules for Life and Work' from his *Devotional Diary* (see Hazell 1996: 15) in which he exhorted himself to sleep little, practise self-denial and 'overcome sloth and fainting'. He eventually found the Salvation Army too authoritarian and moved on to train as a Congregational Minister.

Guntrip met his wife, Bertha Kind, as a student, and she did indeed surround him with kindness and support for the rest of his life. They settled in Leeds after a short period in Ipswich, and their daughter, Gwen, was born. Guntrip worked hard as a minister; he set up a project for the unemployed in Ipswich and a centre for refugees in Leeds, throwing himself into the pastoral work which eventually developed into psychotherapy.

His psychosomatic symptoms ranged from chronic constipation to insomnia and severe sinusitis, punctuated by periodic collapses when a 'brother-figure' disappeared or when he was in danger of being alone with his mother for too long. He turned to psychoanalysis in 1936, travelling to London intermittently for the next six years for analytic sessions with the first director of the Tavistock Clinic, Hugh Crichton-Miller, or his student Clifford Allen, attempting 'self-analysis' between sessions. Thorough as ever, he started the dream and analysis records which he hoped thirty-five years later to turn into a psychoanalytic autobiography; this task was eventually carried out with care and devotion by his analysand Jeremy Hazell (Hazell 1996).

Guntrip's father had died shortly before Guntrip and Bertha married, making his mother all the more antagonistic to them. Her bitter disappointment in life and her vitriolic attacks on Bertha increased over the years to the point of intermittent psychosis, and eventually it was clear that she could no longer live alone. From 1944 until her death in 1953 she lived with Guntrip, Bertha and Gwen, with most of the burden shouldered by Bertha. It is not surprising that Guntrip felt trapped, fraught and inadequate at this time. While he felt his analysis had been worthwhile, he still covered a sense of emptiness with anxious rationalisations. A 1948 diary entry reads: 'I must feel I haven't got enough resources of value inside myself, and that my life is slipping away in my late forties, and I haven't yet done anything worthwhile' (Hazell 1996: 67).

Guntrip must have yearned for something to live for, and also for some escape from his mother's presence. He found both in Fairbairn, whose early writings reflected the 'personal relations' philosophy of John Macmurray (1961) which had inspired him in his university days. By now he had stopped working as a minister to give his whole time to his psychotherapy practice and his part-time research into psychotherapy at Leeds University. He decided to embark on a full analysis with Fairbairn instead of undertaking formal psychoanalytic training.

His analysis dominated the family's life and finances for the next ten years: Guntrip spent two nights a week in Edinburgh and worked up to twelve hours a day on the remaining days of the week. He described his work with Fairbairn as ultimately disappointing, although current records showed a more mixed picture (in Hazell 1996). Guntrip felt that Fairbairn's therapeutic approach was more traditionally Freudian than was his theory, and he seems to have bombarded Fairbairn with criticism and corrections. He must have been a trying patient; in his frantic anxiety he could scarcely stop talking for long enough for Fairbairn to draw breath, let alone feel his way into subtlety or reflection. Guntrip felt that their most fruitful collaborations took place in post-session theoretical discussions, and in his own sympathetic and contactful expositions of Fairbairn's ideas.

The analysis dragged on inconclusively for years after Guntrip had overcome the worst of his psychosomatic symptoms, only ending when Fairbairn's health began to fail drastically. Both of them feared that Fairbairn's death could constitute a repetition of the trauma of Percy's death, which had become a symbol for Guntrip's lost self. Guntrip hoped that Winnicott, whose writing on therapeutic regression he had discussed with Fairbairn, might offer him the kind of therapeutic relationship that he felt Fairbairn had not. However, now that his mother had died, Guntrip felt that he needed time with Bertha more than further disruption to their life, and his sessions with Winnicott were periodic rather than regular. They extended over another ten years, until 1969 when Winnicott was also ageing and unwell.

Writing in retrospect, Guntrip was as enthusiastic about Winnicott as he was deprecating about Fairbairn (Guntrip 1975); but again, his view was not so clear-cut at the time. While he reached a new level of trust and relaxation, he was also terrified by Winnicott's view of the self as 'incommunicado' at its core. Guntrip hung on to his conviction that his problems arose from early deprivation and isolation and were symbolised by his inability to remember Percy's life or death. Winnicott, like Fairbairn, did not entirely agree. He sometimes suggested that Guntrip's endless preoccupation with Percy could represent jealousy as well as grief; these interpretations were never well received.

Guntrip's biographer, Jeremy Hazell, was an early worker for the Samaritans and was greatly attracted by the warmth of Guntrip's writing. In analysis with him, he found his actual presence very different: he was fidgety and impatient, coughing, talking and scribbling incessantly. However, Hazell found that during his analysis with Winnicott Guntrip became quieter and more peaceful, reaching correspondingly greater depths with his patients. He tells a moving story of a regressed patient whom Guntrip visited in hospital (Hazell 1991). The man was completely hidden by bedclothes; and Guntrip simply held his hand, in silence, for fifty minutes, which became a turning point for his despairing patient. Guntrip was becoming able to be as fully present in the flesh as in his writing.

Although Guntrip gained far greater inner peace, he remained restless and hardworking. His lifelong quest for a memory of Percy was fulfilled in a series of dreams which began when Winnicott died, culminating in two dreams (Guntrip 1975). In one, Percy was in a pram, with himself as a three-year-old close by; in the other, Percy appeared as an unhappy baby on the lap of a mother without a face, arms or breasts, and he was trying to make Percy smile. This seems to have been his journey's end: he took the dream as conclusive evidence of his lack of mothering as well as the finding of Percy. He may already have been suffering from the cancer that led to his death in 1974.

Despite his ill-health, Guntrip's final years were probably the happiest of his life because of the inner peace he had attained alongside his perpetual activity. He enjoyed time with Bertha and with Gwen and her husband and children. He was invited on lecture tours in America, continued to work with a few patients and was enthusiastically planning teaching and writing projects until a few weeks before he died. His son-in-law wrote a particularly affectionate obituary for him; inside and outside psychoanalysis, his work became increasingly respected and known.

Guntrip reveals himself as a generous, good-hearted man with a tormented inner world. He was painfully aware of the compulsive over-activity which he was convinced was a cover for his 'non-existent sense of basic being' (Hazell 1996: 259). Fairbairn, Winnicott and others have suggested that Guntrip's ultimate problem was rage at Percy's birth, rather than grief at his loss; rage which redoubled back on himself as his murderous fantasies were realised, and compounded by a deadly identification with an empty mother. Guntrip felt a missionary zeal to speak up for the essential goodness of the child, clinging to the certainty that his neurotic treadmill was simply a way of coping with fear and emptiness. Destructiveness, for Guntrip, is a sign of distress rather than a basic feature of humanity.

Guntrip's experience-based style is dismissed by some as sentimental and hopelessly lacking in rigour, while in other circles Guntrip is cherished as a theoretician who speaks directly from the heart. Both are true: he found that 'to care for people is more important than to care for ideas' (Guntrip 1977: Foreword), and the care he lavished on others seems real as well as at times compulsive. Surely both views of his personal difficulties were also true: there seems no reason why his vulnerability and his rage should be reduced to a single factor.

THEORY

Guntrip's contributions to psychoanalysis are twofold. Theoretically, he provided a wide-ranging historical survey of the development of Object Relations out of Freudian theory and American character analysis, and contributed a specific addition to Fairbairn's theoretical model. Practically, the vivid descriptions of the schizoid state and the corresponding psychotherapeutic approach he developed are moving testimony to the empathic involvement he brought to his work.

From Freud to Object Relations

Guntrip's first psychoanalytic book, *Personality Structure and Human Interaction* (Guntrip 1961), is an expansion of the doctoral thesis he wrote in 1953. He argues strongly against the reductionism which attempts to explain experience in terms of physical processes, whether in the medical approach of psychiatry or the 'psychobiology' of instinct theory. The subject matter of psychotherapy (which term, interestingly, he often uses rather than 'psychoanalysis') is the person, rather than the human mechanism. This requires a relational language and framework within an expanded understanding of what constitutes science and scientific method. With this in mind, he undertakes an overview of Freudian theory and psychoanalytic developments in America and Britain in a rather grandiose dialectic:

I.   Thesis. Dynamic Psychobiology.
II.   Antithesis. Dynamic Psychosociology.
III. Emerging Synthesis. The External-object and the Internal-object worlds. (Guntrip 1961: 53)

Guntrip points to Freud's initial hope that psychology could be reduced to physiology, obviating the need for psychoanalysis in the future since the balance of instinctual energies would be chemically regulated. Freud's roots in medicine meant that a biological approach to understanding the mind was inevitable; but he also developed a philosophical and personal strand to his theory, particularly in the concepts he developed through his self-analysis. Thus the Oedipus Complex and the super-ego are a different order of idea from those which arose from his earlier drive economy: they are created and sustained through relationship rather than bodily functioning. Guntrip argues that Freud never wholly abandoned his early hopes for a biological psychology, and that this resulted in theoretical inconsistencies such as the death instinct, which Guntrip makes short work of as groundless speculation. Guntrip suggests that Freud's move to a more truly psychological framework is held back by his retention of physiological 'thought-forms' (Guntrip 1961: 64).

Guntrip then turns to the American 'Culture Pattern School' of psychoanalysis. In a brief survey of the work of Erich Fromm, Karen Horney and Harry Stack Sullivan (Fromm 1942; Horney 1945; Sullivan 1953), he commends their recognition of social factors as influences in their own right, but criticises their comparatively superficial view of the person. He suggests that Sullivan has exchanged a biologically mechanistic base for one which is sociologically mechanistic, and that none of these theoreticians addresses the deeper unconscious levels of the psyche.

Moving to Kleinian theory, he argues strongly for its inclusion within psychoanalysis, pointing out that in diverging from instinct theory it takes further the personal strand in Freudian theory. He takes issue only with Klein's retention of the death instinct and the consequent primacy of aggression in relationship: the paranoid-schizoid and depressive anxieties she so vividly describes can be understood, he felt, as reactions to deprivation and frustration rather than as inevitable manifestations of instinctual conflict. However, Guntrip praises her focus on primitive processes, her theory of internal objects and unconscious phantasy and most of all her severance of psychology from biology, which help provide a framework for understanding human beings in psychological rather than biological or sociological terms. This was an understanding that Guntrip devoted his professional life to furthering, and which he felt was most accurately expounded in Fairbairn's Object Relations theory with its focus on the schizoid position as the primary division of the self.

Guntrip suggested that the concept of the schizoid position was a natural development from Freudian and Kleinian theory. Freud had focused on the Oedipal issues of sexuality, rivalry and the fear of retribution in the struggle to find a place as one amongst several in the family setting, and one amongst many in society. This struggle involves interpersonal conflict between whole individuals, presupposing clear roles and a functioning self, which can be an adequate basis for the psychoanalysis of less disturbed people. This was followed by what Guntrip saw as Klein's major conceptual innovation, the depressive position with its accompanying anxieties, which arise from the realisation that the personal universe is not divided into fragments of good and evil, but consists of a self and others who can experience and arouse both tender and hostile feelings. Kleinian theory focuses on intrapersonal as well as interpersonal conflict, enabling a more extensive analysis than was possible with early Freudian theory alone. Both the Oedipus Complex and the depressive position, however, rest on the assumption that psychological problems arise from the strength of asocial impulses, whether sexual or aggressive, and the corresponding difficulty in controlling or channelling them. In the pre-depressive schizoid position, a functioning self cannot be taken for granted; and problems cannot therefore be reduced to the instinctual content of coherent personal structures.

Guntrip, like Fairbairn, draws attention to cultural influences on individual psychology. He submits that the individual in twentieth-century Western society is less securely integrated into family and social structures than in previous times, increasing the likelihood of schizoid-related problems such as insecurity and disconnection from society and even from the self. This is in contrast to the guilt and overburdened depression which is more typical of a stable if rigid society. He suggests that weakness and fear, rather than badness and guilt, are the true foundations of a disordered personality, and that we find awareness of our weakness more threatening than a sense of moral badness. Guntrip sees Freudian and Kleinian theory as founded on the view that human problems arise from human destructiveness; he suggests that this prevents these theories from reaching further than the defensive structures shoring up the fragile self. 'Human beings prefer to feel "bad somebodies" rather than "weak nonentities"' (Guntrip 1968: 137).

Fairbairn's theory delineates the emergence of the schizoid position from primary trauma, leading to a concept of the schizoid person as withdrawn and riven. Winnicott, without focusing exclusively on this area, created the therapeutic response which Guntrip felt could meet the regressed schizoid person: an undemanding, quasi-parental acceptance which allows the patient's essential weakness and vulnerability to emerge and be supported in new personality development, in contrast to the classical neutrality which lays bare the patient's hidden impulses through interpretation. This is another version of the tension between psychotherapy as therapeutic intervention based on new experience in relationship, as against psychoanalysis as a path to self-knowledge, based on insight through interpretation. Guntrip comes down firmly on the side of psychotherapy as a healing relationship. He heavily endorses Fairbairn's and Winnicott's beliefs that the real relationship between therapist and patient, not the transference relationship, is the vehicle and facilitator of personal maturation which is the ultimate aim of psychotherapy.

The Schizoid and Depressive Positions

Guntrip offers a straightforward distinction between depressive and paranoid-schizoid anxieties (Guntrip 1968: 24–7). Depressive anxiety, he suggests, is 'love grown angry' through frustration or deprivation. Our anger has the aim of forcing the other person to become good again and give us what we need, but our fear is that we will drive them away in the process. We have enough sense of entitlement to make a demand, reflecting a confidence in ourselves and in the world which must derive from previous good-enough experience in relationship. Depressive anxiety rests on the ability to see that self and other are separate though related beings; and that the person we are angry with is also the person we need.

The schizoid state, by contrast, is 'love grown hungry'. Guntrip explains that in the earliest stages and most primitive layers of mental life, we do not have the strength to rage against the world. Frustration, loneliness or other trauma simply lead to increasing neediness, until the intensity of our craving becomes unbearable. We fear that our neediness rather than our anger will destroy the person we need, as though in our desperate craving we might swallow them up like a vacuum cleaner. He quotes an anorexic patient, who said: 'I can't make moderate demands on people so I don't make any at all' (Guntrip 1961: 37), a dilemma that most of us can relate to.

Fairbairn and Guntrip equate need with love at this early stage of development. Thus the focal terror of the schizoid state and the schizoid person is love itself, with its threat of subsuming him into another's system. What the schizoid person fears from the other's love he also fears to inflict through his own love. No links with others are safe, and it is this that leads to the cut-off schizoid state.

The Regressed Ego

Guntrip emphasises the conflicted vulnerability of the schizoid state: 'The schizoid person has renounced objects, even though he still needs them' (Guntrip 1968: 18). Fairbairn hypothesises that the schizoid person turns inwards towards himself while he turns away from others, creating an internal world of need, rage and frustration to compensate for his external disconnectedness. Guntrip, while agreeing with this, goes a step further. He suggests that the kernel of the traumatised person may withdraw even from internal relationship. He describes a sense of lying in suspended animation, as though at its heart the 'weak, needy and resourceless' self has made a symbolic return to the womb, away from activity, responsibility or even consciousness. Guntrip came to conceptualise this 'regressed ego' as both the aspect of the person that had recoiled in fear from the harshness of post-natal life, and also that element of the person which had never felt safe enough to emerge into relationship in the first place: Winnicott's 'undeveloped potential' and 'true self in cold storage'.

Guntrip suggests an amendment to Fairbairn's diagram, which as he jubilantly reports was endorsed by Fairbairn himself (Guntrip 1968: 77) (Figure 6.1).

He suggests that the libidinal ego, attached to the ever-elusive exciting object, is a post-natal oral ego which is always actively wanting, reaching out and trying to get its needs met. A further split results in another ego fragment, related to the libidinal ego but separate from it. This is the passive regressed ego, repressed by all other parts of the personality including the libidinal ego. It is attached to no inner object, because it has given up all relationship in a symbolic return to pre-natal life where there were no objects separate from the self. The regressed ego, deeply repressed and strenuously defended against, is consciously experienced as a pull to non-being, to passive giving up, even to suicide. He describes it much as the death instinct was described by Freud: they appear to be different explanations for similar phenomena.

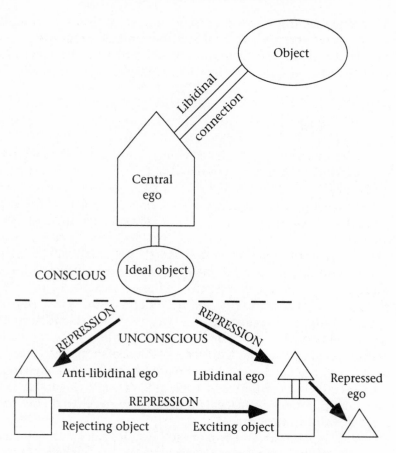

Figure 6.1: Guntrip's addition to Fairbairn's structure

Guntrip sees all neurotic and active psychotic processes ultimately as defences against the utter weakness and non-viability of the regressed ego. Anything is preferable to its deadly allure, and any other way of being, however conflicted, may be a way of trying to stay in life, in relationship, in the reality of the post-birth world. Internal agony and unsatisfying relationships may be ways of keeping afloat in the post-natal world of activity and separate objects. Aggressive relationships may feel safer than harmonious or supportive relationships because aggression allays the dread of being absorbed into another person's personality. Underlying all these exhausting vicious circles is a sense of despair and inadequacy, of not having the wherewithal to live as a person with oneself or in the world, and a longing to sink back into effortless oblivion.

Guntrip's regressed ego has withdrawn from the external and internal object relations of post-natal life to an imagined return to the womb and what Guntrip conceived as the most basic form of relationship: a vague sense of being 'safe inside' something indeterminate. This is very reminiscent of Balint's harmonious mix-up, though Guntrip emphasises a feeling of protected enclosure rather than expansive intermingling. Both, however, catch hold of an elusive sense of a dimmer and less total differentiation than that of post-birth relations with objects and part-objects. Guntrip suggests this clouded state is the primary identification of Fairbairn's full pre-natal infantile dependence, but in fact it is less total. Feeling safe inside something is not the same as being in a state of fusion with it, when there would be no sense whatsoever of any boundary. When Guntrip speaks of a total withdrawal from relationship, we must therefore understand this as a withdrawal only from post-natal relationship: he implies that the 'safe inside' feeling reaches back before birth, and endures beneath more ordinary experiences of being.

The state of the regressed ego is sometimes equated with the state of being dead. To the suicidal schizoid person, death may seem to promise the peace, rest and cessation of struggle and suffering which are already encapsulated within. But peace and rest are experiences and thus belong to living. Death is simply nothing unless religious belief gives form to the hope that being dead is indeed identical to Guntrip's picture of life in the womb. Guntrip captures the yearning of the suicidal for a twilight world of passive and timeless well-being, though he misses the murderousness of the suicidal act. He sees this kind of suicide as unconscious withdrawal to pre-natal safety, in which, tragically, the potential for rebirth is destroyed.

The person who has returned to the level of the regressed ego has thus retreated from present reality further than either the depressed or the schizoid person. The depressed person wants relationship but fears the destructiveness of his anger; the schizoid person fears but also needs relationship, and creates an inner relational world which is more controllable if more unsatisfying than relationships with other people. At the level of the regressed ego, we have given up on post-birth relationship as too painful, frightening and demanding, and we relinquish the capacity for active or differentiated relating.

Therapy

In Guntrip's view, the ultimate aim of psychotherapy is to enable those who need to do so to surrender to the pull of the regressed ego and allow total dependence on the therapist, returning gradually to relationship as a whole being under her protection and understanding. The therapist must be there as a reliable and undemanding 'good object' for the patient or client, as the womb is there for the unborn baby. With finely tuned empathy and relaxed acceptance, this weakest, most vulnerable core of the person may gradually recover confidence in being and relating. With the slow rebuilding of the self and the emotional world on a more secure footing, the patient may become less dominated by fear and insecurity and have less need for self-destructive defences.

This was an ideal, and Guntrip did not pretend it was easily or often reached. His own lifelong struggle demonstrates that he himself only managed glimpses of this fuller way of being in the last years of his life. No doubt with himself in mind, he suggests that the biggest blocks to giving in to the pull of the regressed ego are the patient's own desperation to keep going at all costs, and his terror of placing his trust in someone else. Regression to this level is a profound collapse which would be disastrous without someone there to provide the protection and support that were previously carried by the defences. Regression can only be fruitful 'if there is a real person to regress with and to' (Guntrip 1968: 56–7).

Guntrip's vision of therapeutic regression is very similar to Winnicott's, although he was working in this way with patients before his analysis with Winnicott. Like Winnicott's regressed patients, some of his patients needed a period in hospital where he visited them for sessions; others became profoundly dependent on support and protection at home; some were able to confine their collapses to sessions. However, the total breakdown potentially demanded by this approach may be too much for some people. Guntrip's own treadmill of resistance illuminates how unthinkable a willing de-integration may be. Guntrip's psychotherapy offers what may feel like the abandonment of life, which may lead to a new life through the reliving of utter dependency on the therapist: the chance to 'convert regression into rebirth and regrowth' (Guntrip 1968: 71) through the provision of an empathic and parental therapeutic relationship and, quite possibly, extra environmental care.

Comparatively few patients or clients would need or want to undertake this risky journey, which may also conflict irreconcilably with the responsibilities of everyday life. Therapists, too, will vary in their desire and their capacity to manage the extreme and unpredictable needs of a patient who has regressed to this level of dependency; and even those who are willing to work in this strenuous and hazardous area would not be able to manage the breakdown of more than the occasional person. What Guntrip describes, therefore, is at the extreme end of need, an experience of regression which some people may require in addition to the more usual approach which deals primarily with conflict and difficulty in the interpersonal and intrapsychic arenas. Even when this need cannot be fulfilled, Guntrip's emotional defence of human nature inspires a compassion and hope that reminds us of the vulnerability of the disturbed, aggressive or cut-off person.

Commentary

No one has written as passionately as Guntrip on behalf of the regressed patient and his need – almost his right – to the personal understanding and support through which he can gain or regain his wholeness. Yet various problems arise from the fact that he was a doer rather than a thinker, more concerned to offer help than to grapple with details of theory.

Guntrip's review of the development of psychoanalytic theory is broad-brush rather than exact. He offers an overview which, while interesting, is limited. He is largely uncritical of those ideas he favours, and dismisses in few words theorists whom he has already rejected, such as Jung or Adler. His objections to Freudian theory vary from the valid to the suspect. He makes the valuable point that human experience is of a different order from bodily mechanism and thus requires a different conceptual framework; yet at other times he suggests that viewing human beings in terms of drive is degrading and therefore invalid, as though theory should aim at comfort as well as truth. His theoretical contributions are built on personal resonance at the expense of conceptual rigour.

Similarly, Guntrip's exposition of Fairbairn's theory is a simplified version, using a warmer, more emotional tone than Fairbairn's measured precision. He fails to address what initially appears as a glaring incompatibility between Fairbairn's theory and his own addition to it. Fairbairn's basic assumption is that the ego is by definition always in relationship: it is for this reason that internal relationships are set up to the precise extent that external relationships are renounced. Guntrip's repeated assertion that the regressed ego is out of relationship is an impossibility in Fairbairn's framework. Although we have seen that this does not seem to be Guntrip's ultimate view, he does not make this crucial point at all clear. His reiterations that the regressed ego has withdrawn from all relationship suggest a lack of understanding of just how radical and far-reaching Fairbairn's object-relational theory was, and consequently of the importance of spelling out the status of his own concept.

Guntrip suggested that all states where the ego is actively struggling are defences against the passive regressed state. This can be turned around to give the idea that internal and external object relationships may have their roots not only in the primary need for relationship, but also in the need to escape being drawn into the regressed ego which seems always to exert a backwards pull. Guntrip implies that we seek relationship unless it is too painful, in which case we surrender to passivity in an illusory return which we simultaneously dread because it feels non-relational. He may thus be implying a complex object-relational theory with more than one aim: on the one hand, for relationship based on differentiation, and, on the other, for a prior state which is not unrelational but in which there is little differentiation or consciousness of need or desire. This resembles Balint's view that the aim of post-birth relationship is a return to the semi-fusion of the pre-birth harmonious intermingling; it also sounds like the internal conflict that the death instinct, in opposition to Eros, was supposed to account for. This reading of Guntrip leads him to the ranks of those who reject the death instinct with its primacy over the life instinct, yet who are unable to supply an alternative construct which deals as adequately with the problem of negativity.

It is surprising that Guntrip both expected and received Fairbairn's endorsement of his additional ego-part. Perhaps this is an example of Guntrip caring less for the conceptual adequacy of his ideas than for experientially vivid description, and of Fairbairn's uncomfortable need for Guntrip to communicate his ideas to a larger audience, even at the cost of theoretical precision.

Guntrip's regressed ego state is variously described as out of relationship, as moving out of relationship, as resisting a return to relationship or as a pre-natal form of relationship. This confusion illustrates Guntrip's carelessness in defining his terms: he was obviously thinking of particular patients in different kinds and degrees of regression, and did not bother to refine his thinking beyond what he saw. He describes an extreme form of the regressed ego state as a regression out of post-birth, differentiated relationship and into a pre-natal state in which there is simply a sense of being enclosed, together with a fearful sense of weakness and resourcelessness. The ultimate womb-state, however, sought in schizoid forms of suicide, appears to be simply a 'safe inside' feeling with no fear attached and without a sense of vulnerability or resourcelessness as there is no question of any demands being made. The fearful feelings must therefore be the fragments of resistance put up by the other ego-parts, giving rise to the need for an external person on whom to depend. Indeed if the enclosure were total, regression would have no way out because no external relational provision would make any difference: the only relation would be to the inner enclosing container. It may be the remnants of the person which are in more differentiated forms of relationship which make a therapeutic relationship in regression possible. However unable the regressed person may be to reach out, he nevertheless has some orientation towards what is outside his enclosure, and is receptive to its influence.

We are left with the regressed ego as a fragment of self in a protective enclosure, with enough of the other ego-parts available to make some external relationship viable. If the regressed ego is not out of relationship but in a primitive form of object relationship, different in quality and structure from post-natal relationship, Guntrip could indeed be extending Fairbairn's model. The regressed ego would be enclosed in, rather than attached to, a womb-like object from which it is only hazily differentiated: something which could be thought of as a providing object, accepting object or enclosing object or pre-object.

However, the question then arises whether this internalised structure also results from trauma, and if so, how that trauma is encapsulated in the inner world. The trauma would probably have been before birth, as the structure is one of pre-differentiation. This makes sense of the fearful regressed state of resourceless passivity, where the regressed ego seems to be pulling the central ego into absorption and annihilation. Pre-natal experiences of deprivation or persecution could be structured internally as rudimentary self- and object-fragments in the vague conglomerate we are terming the regressed ego in the enclosing pre-object. This structure would be repressed by all other ego structures but would be there to be regressed to when all else fails. If there were no inner structure of this kind, it is hard to see how the regressed person would have a clear place to withdraw to; Guntrip is specific in seeing the regressed ego as an encapsulation within which the therapist must reach, following Fairbairn's view of psychoanalysis as the breaching of a closed system. This begins to look very much like Fairbairn's exciting object/libidinal ego and rejecting object/anti-libidinal ego, lumped together rather than differentiated. It is possible that Guntrip did not employ sufficient observational and intellectual clarity to distinguish between these structures, and mistook the patient at the end of his tether for the patient in a totally different mode of being.

If, on the other hand, the regressed ego and its pre-object were internalised in the absence of trauma, as the benign 'safe inside' feeling suggests, Fairbairn's thesis that structural internalisation is by nature pathological is challenged. Guntrip does not offer another conception of internalisation that might be based on memory rather than trauma.

In his therapeutic fervour, Guntrip appears not to have thought about the implications of his new idea. He seems captivated by the idea of a regression out of object relationship, perhaps because it was the only way to express his own demoralisation and yet hope. He does not observe or consider the different ways in which regression can occur, nor the different forms of relationship that can arise between therapist and regressed patient or client. He gives no attention to malignant regression, or regression which turns out to be fruitless, and omits any alternative articulation of regression. For example, a Kleinian view of the passivity and resourcelessness characteristic of the regressed ego could be that an inner deadness had spread throughout the personality, as a consequence of massive projection out of the ego under the influence of the death instinct.

Guntrip addresses only that regression which he believed to underlie all regression. He postulates a purity of motive and an absence of defensiveness which he implies can be met simply by the therapist's attuned sensitivity and acceptance, giving little clue to working with the destructive, defensive and borderline processes through which many therapeutic relationships come to grief. Yet as we have seen, this absolute vulnerable purity is itself a muddled mix. If it is an inner structure taking over, it must be defensive and therefore secondary; if it is an undefensive return to a previous way of being, there is no provision for the retention of that experience in such a specific form. If Guntrip is suggesting that pre-natal experience can be encapsulated non-traumatically, he is challenging Fairbairn's premise that internal structure is secondary and pathological; if he is suggesting that the regressed ego is waiting inside without an inner object attached, ready to respond however passively to the right environment or pre-object, he is also overturning the assumption that the ego is by nature always in relationship. Guntrip's intellectual laxity prevents his theory matching up to his staunchly object-relational practice.

The assumption that the pre-natal state is one of blissful union has been challenged by research (Stern 1985). While the evidence and arguments are by no means conclusive, it is possible that concepts such as Guntrip's regressed ego, Balint's harmonious mix-up, Fairbairn's infantile dependence and Freud's primary narcissism derive from a later point in infancy than they assumed. Should this turn out to be the likely conclusion, psychoanalytic and Object Relations theory would need to be radically revised. What seems clear, however, is that whatever the timing, all these concepts address a phenomenon which is too powerfully resonant in human experience to be dismissed.

Guntrip assumes that the patient internalises a reasonably accurate picture of reality. With no concept of primary destructiveness, he could not utilise the Freudian explanation that inner objects are a reflection of inner aggression as well as the impact of the other. While Fairbairn emphasised that the inner personality structures use 'a maximum of aggression to subdue a maximum of need', and thereby have a regulatory function, Guntrip tends to presume that a patient's inner persecutory relationship is a copy of the persecution he underwent at the hands of his parents, and ultimately his mother (although he does concede that this may not have been the only or even the dominant experience). In his compulsive recording and mulling over of his dreams, he similarly assumes that they were straightforwardly representational. A dream is not a memory; yet his search for a clear memory of Percy was satisfied by the dreams in which Percy appeared. Fairbairn had suggested that dreams were pictures of inner reality rather than wish-fulfilling fantasies, but his view of inner reality was more complex than Guntrip's. Guntrip's direct correlation between early experiences in relationship and the nature of the inner world, in combination with his view of dreams, gives his overall psychology a lack of subtlety. There seems little space for true individuality: under his kindly but smothering gaze we appear as mechanical absorbers of experience resulting in traits and structures which are not our fault. A vision of inner life as a sparse and second-hand version of earlier external life emerges, which makes one wonder whether Guntrip's frantic extroversion arose in part from experiencing his inner life as desolate and depleted.

Guntrip is unequalled in his capacity to communicate warmth and empathy; but on the theoretical side, much of his work is repetitive and rambling, sometimes grandiose, often imprecise or partisan, and narrowly focused on the therapy of a specific regressed state. He does not discuss working with the defensive and destructive states he describes as an inevitable prelude to deep regression, nor does he explore subjects such as emotional development or the changing needs of the child or patient. Despite extensive experience of working with a wide variety of people in his role as minister, he shows no sign of appreciating different class or cultural backgrounds. He dismisses homosexuality, along with prostitution, as an evasion of commitment, although to do otherwise might be expecting too much from a man of his social context and time. The role of the therapist, like that of the mother, is reduced to that of a supportive nurturer, with the father's role viewed in stultifyingly similar terms. He does not question the reasons for failed analyses in any depth, assuming that the concept of the regressed ego equips an empathic and sensitive therapist to work with anyone. Most failures are put down to practical constraints or personal limitations: 'if the patient can face it, he will, and if he cannot, no amount of analysis will make him do so' (Guntrip 1968: 297).

All this adds up to more than a tinge of 'victim and rescuer' in his version of the therapeutic relationship, with the therapist portrayed as omnipotently benevolent. No real human being is like this for long, even in paid fifty-minute snatches. Counter-transference is not considered, there is little place for conflict or nastiness, and an anodyne view of the person as ultimately good but weak is an unconvincing counterpart to the Freudian 'bad but strong' view he rejects. His conviction that all destructiveness derives from distress and fear can border on sentimentality.

Yet none of these shortcomings detracts from Guntrip's fundamental achievements. He propelled an object-relational view of the person far into and beyond psychotherapy; he was a powerful advocate for the neurotic person as suffering rather than selfish; and he brought to psychotherapy an unrefuted insistence on the primacy of the therapeutic relationship.

There is scope for Guntrip's ideas to be developed. His inadequate conceptualisation of the regressed ego and its place in the personality teeters on the brink of a bold casting-back of psychotherapeutic theory to pre-natal life as a form as distinct from post-natal organisation as Oedipal or depressive-position functioning is from the primitive irrationality of the paranoid-schizoid position. Neville Symington (in Grotstein and Rinsley 1994) has suggested that Frances Tustin's work on autism (Tustin 1972) develops Fairbairn's work on the schizoid position. Thomas Ogden (1989) has postulated an autistic-contiguous position which precedes the Kleinian paranoid-schizoid position. If Guntrip's groping towards an articulation of the pre-natal state could be taken seriously rather than dismissed as syrupy vagueness, his ideas could perhaps be fruitfully brought together with those of Balint, Ogden and Tustin, amongst others. Whatever period of early life the states referred to turn out to be based in, both theory and practice would be advanced.

It is heartening that Guntrip's work is now being published and discussed more fully, thanks to the pioneering work of Jeremy Hazell (1994, 1996). Perhaps we can hope that the intuitive therapeutic gift which emerges with tender clarity from Guntrip's writing could lead to refinements and advances in theory as well as practice. We may also hope that his conviction that suffering underlies destructiveness can support a greater regard for human vulnerability, a regard which is in such jeopardy today.

7

JOHN BOWLBY:
ATTACHMENT THEORY

Bowlby's Attachment Theory was a new departure in Object Relations which went on to attain independent theoretical status. Attachment Theory is built on the Object Relations principles of the primacy of the need for relationship and the relational structure of the self, and goes some way to providing objective evidence for Object Relations concepts. Bowlby argued that psychoanalysis was losing its scientific roots; he turned to the new fields of ethology and systems theory to construct a theory of the person which drew on their methods and findings. As Fairbairn had used philosophy to update psychoanalysis, so Bowlby used current scientific developments to do the same, and like Fairbairn's, his contributions were viewed with suspicion within psychoanalysis. He realised the potential psychoanalysis held for preventative work in society as well as therapeutic work with individuals. Bowlby did more than any other psychoanalyst to change social policy and inform government thinking about the needs of children and families.

LIFE

John Bowlby's work is unusual in psychoanalysis. On the one hand he is external, exact, concerned with measurement and validation; on the other, he reveals an unexpected passion in his pleas for the suffering of children to be understood, devoting his professional life to making British society a better place for its children. These interwoven characteristics of objectivity and emotion reflect his divided early life (see Holmes 1993).

Bowlby was born in 1907, the fourth of six children. His was a well-known upper-class family: his father, Sir Anthony, was surgeon to the royal family. Bowlby had a close and competitive relationship with his older brother Tony, and was alternately teasing and protective towards his younger brother Jim. Jim was slow and awkward and was almost a contradiction in terms: an unsuccessful Bowlby.

The Bowlby lifestyle was split into ordinary life and summer holidays. In London, they lived the formal and restricted life typical of their social class. Sir Anthony was largely absent, particularly during the war years, and nurses and servants ran the household and cared for the children. Bowlby's sister Evelyn described the atmosphere as joyless. During the summer, however, the whole family spent six weeks in Scotland, and a livelier and warmer picture emerges of family activities, outings and far closer involvement, particularly between the children, their mother and her father. These summers engendered a lifelong love of nature in Bowlby, and he continued to holiday in Scotland throughout his life. Distance and closeness, formality and fun, seem to have developed as distinct strands within his personality.

Bowlby and his brother Tony were sent to boarding school at the outbreak of the First World War, ostensibly because of the danger of air raids, but primarily, Bowlby felt, in accordance with the educational traditions of the upper classes. Predictably, he did well at school and went on to join the Navy, which he disliked because of its intellectual limitations and because he suffered from sea-sickness. He persuaded his father to buy him out, offering to study medicine at Cambridge University in return. The death of his conventionally-minded father when Bowlby was twenty-one allowed him to do something unusual and radical between his university and hospital-based studies: he spent a year working in an unorthodox progressive school for disturbed children. He noticed that the emotional isolation and delinquency of a boy at the school were put down by the staff to his disrupted early life. Recognising his unusual ability to communicate with maladjusted youngsters, a colleague urged him to consider training in psychoanalysis. Thus his idiosyncratic professional focus emerged, bringing together his dry scientific rigour and his attunement to the hidden suffering of children.

Bowlby went on to combine medical and psychoanalytic training. His analyst was Joan Rivière. By 1937 he had qualified as a psychiatrist and psychoanalyst, and he began training with Melanie Klein in child analysis while working in the newly established London Child Guidance Clinic. It was here that he began to gather evidence for his conviction that environmental causes of neurosis were underrated. He considered the separation of a child from her mother in the early years of childhood, and the passing-on of parents' difficulties to their children, to be particularly significant. He was appointed an Army psychiatrist in 1940 and worked with psychoanalytically-minded psychiatrists and psychoanalytic colleagues, including Wilfred Bion and Jock Sutherland.

A gap was opening up between the tenets of Bowlby's Kleinian training and his own belief in the importance of external relationships and events. His views were treated as deviant by the Kleinians, and ignored by others who were uncomfortable with the drily objective tone of his papers and his lack of attention to internal dynamic processes. Nevertheless, he was useful to the British Psycho-Analytical Society as someone not clearly aligned with either the Kleinians or the Freudians, with considerable organisational efficiency and whose familial and medical credentials made him unusually acceptable to the British establishment. He pushed the Society into participating in discussions on the new National Health Service, speaking passionately for the inclusion of psychoanalytic methods and viewpoints.

In 1938 Bowlby married Ursula Longstaff, a quietly independent woman with a love of literature. Her sole involvement with the bulk of his work was in finding apt quotations; but touchingly, she worked closely with him on his last major project, a biography of Darwin which was published just before he died (Bowlby 1990). She and Bowlby were both middle children of large families; they had four children, and Bowlby seems to have replicated his father's distance. His unease in the role of father must have been exacerbated when his children showed unexpected academic difficulties which were eventually recognised as dyslexia – perplexing and troubling to someone with a top degree from Cambridge. His children also seem to have found him a puzzle. Perhaps he was a burglar, mused his seven-year-old son, since he always came home after dark and never talked about his work (Holmes 1993: 25). Again in his family tradition, however, Bowlby is said to have been a wonderful grandfather; and the country-loving Bowlbys spent long holidays in Scotland every year.

Bowlby may have been conscious of his own parental shortcomings, as well as alert to his research findings and his knowledge of the living patterns of other cultures. For many years the family shared their household with Bowlby's close friend, the Labour politician Evan Durbin and his family, and later Jock Sutherland and his family, an unconventional arrangement which expressed his dual nature.

At the end of the Second World War, Bowlby and several fellow Army psychiatrists defied the orders of Ernest Jones to avoid the Tavistock Clinic, a public psychotherapy clinic which was run along eclectic rather than purist lines. Sutherland was made Chairman of the Clinic, and Bowlby was his deputy; he remained at the Tavistock until 1972, setting up the Department for Children and Parents and, with the Kleinian Esther Bick, the child psychotherapy training. The majority of his time was spent on research; he developed Attachment Theory with James Robertson, Mary Ainsworth and Mary Boston and later worked with Colin Murray Parkes on the mourning process.

Bowlby struggled on in the British Psycho-Analytical Society through the 1940s and 1950s, convinced he had a contribution to make and dismayed by the widespread indifference and hostility he met with, particularly from the Kleinian group with whom he had trained. There was a temperamental and cultural chasm between the upper-class Englishman and the traumatised, European Jewish contingent who, together with the British Independents, were more at home with art, emotion and imagination than science, facts and statistics.

Although he maintained a small practice, Bowlby's professional focus was overwhelmingly on research and social policy. During the 1960s he withdrew from the Psycho-Analytical Society and concentrated on writing up his thirty years of investigations in the definitive trilogy, *Attachment, Separation* and *Loss,* published between 1969 and 1980. Attachment Theory became internationally known as a psychological approach linking psychoanalysis with developmental psychology, ethology and systems theory.

As an old man, Bowlby had his own circle of colleagues, friends and admirers. His eightieth birthday conference brought speakers from many countries. He spent more time at his Scottish home in Skye, where he died in 1990 after a stroke. He was an intriguing mixture of pompousness and sensitivity, shyness and arrogance, protocol and idiosyncrasy. More at home with procedures than patients, he nevertheless had an influence on psychotherapy that has grown over the years. External trauma and relationships are now given more weight in all kinds of therapy; early separations are recognised as inherently dangerous for children; the mourning process is accepted as necessary rather than self-indulgent. But his greatest influence is where he would have wished it to be, on the social arrangements that are made for children in Britain and beyond, in hospitals, in nursery schools, in care and where Bowlby so passionately felt they belonged, at home.

THEORY

Overview

Bowlby criticised psychoanalytic theory for placing too little emphasis on the environment and too much on the internal conflict that ultimately boiled down to constitutional differences. He stressed that while the early work of Freud had made full use of the scientific methods and ideas then available, this had ceased to be the case. Psychoanalysts were largely ignorant of current scientific developments and failed to recognise the necessity to continually revise theory in the light of new discoveries. Theories of child development were constructed retrospectively from impressions derived from patients, rather than from the direct observation of normal as well as disturbed children and parents. Bowlby was horrified that under the influence of non-scientists such as Anna Freud and Melanie Klein, psychoanalysis was tending towards becoming a philosophical discipline concerned with meaning and imagination rather than a body of validated knowledge (Bowlby 1988: 58).

Bowlby's strategy was to appeal to his colleagues by likening his own scientific outlook to Freud's physiological bias. His work, he felt, supplied proof for much of psychoanalytic theory; this validation could enhance the status of psychoanalysis as a science with links to other scientific disciplines. He was keen that advances in theory should lead to improved treatment for patients, and also to benefits to society at large through the development of social frameworks which took account of personal needs. He originally hoped that his Kleinian colleagues would accept his contributions as an addition to their own exploration of phantasy, leading towards a psychology both imaginative and factual, encompassing external events, internal processes and the relations between the two.

Bowlby's psychoanalytic influences included the early Object Relations practitioners, especially Balint, Ferenczi and Fairbairn, as well as Klein. He linked his emphasis on attachment to the later work of Freud, where the 'object' is seen as the target of the libidinal instincts, and weight is given to the child's real experiences as in the Oedipal period. Reading *King Solomon's Ring* (Lorenz 1952) introduced him to the new science of ethology, the biological study of animal behaviour from evolutionary and functional perspectives. This was the period of imprinting and critical periods. Separation experiments with monkeys showed that those deprived of a parent-figure were unable to mate or parent young; and offered the choice between a wire-frame 'mother' which dispensed milk and one which was more comforting, young monkeys overwhelmingly preferred the cloth-covered frame (Harlow and Zimmerman 1959, quoted in Bowlby 1969). These studies proved that contrary to Kleinian and Freudian assumptions, attachment was not a derivative of feeding and was essential for emotional maturation.

Bowlby holds a strange position in the polemic between psychoanalysis as drive-based or as relation-based theory. He proposed that relationship itself arises through autonomous biologically-based systems, honed by natural selection to specific behaviours, needs and capacities. The human species is not designed to live alone, and strong and permanent bonding is essential for the survival of all, especially the young and the vulnerable. These systems are in continual interaction with external factors: the actual experiences people have in relationship contribute to an 'internal working model' of the world which includes cognitive, emotional and behavioural representations of self and other and of the relationship which mediates their connection. Temporary or permanent separation from those people felt to be essential to survival is by definition a crisis, manifested in typical reactions to separation and culminating in the mourning process.

Much of Bowlby's writing provides the hard evidence for the social policies he advocates. These are mainly concerned with the overriding importance of young children remaining with their families whenever it is humanly possible, and with meeting their needs for comfort and re-attachment when separation is unavoidable. Glimpses of Bowlby's own suffering emerge in his sudden outbursts over the harm inflicted on children by traditions such as the routine separation of mothers from their new-born babies, and the rigid and repressive features of socially-condoned child-rearing practices. Most powerful of all are the films made by Bowlby's colleagues James and Joyce Robertson (1952, 1976), unrepeatable historical documents which graphically record the agony young children go through when ripped away from home and family. Even those children whom the Robertsons fostered with loving care found separation a difficult and painful experience, while those without substitute attachment figures were profoundly traumatised. These films bring Bowlby's influence to bear with unfailing effect and continue to be widely shown in social work, childcare and psychotherapy and counselling training.

Attachment Theory

Attachment Theory takes as its premise that human beings are born with inbuilt patterns of behaviour which promote and maintain relationship, unfolding in an orderly sequence in interaction with the environment. The basic human unit is a mother with her children, with men who may include the mother's father, brothers and/or sexual partner or partners being either part of this unit or remaining on its periphery. No human social group is smaller than two families or larger than about two hundred people. Atachment behaviour is designed to form and maintain this kind of stable community. Different cultures create their own variations on this universal theme.

Human development is seen as a process of creating and maintaining attachments towards the primary attachment figure and other significant people. The growing child goes on to form bonds beyond her immediate circle with people in the wider community, and the upheavals of Western adolescence are the fall-out of the crucial transfer of attachment from family to a sexual partner, often via the peer group. Our primary attachment figures constitute the 'secure base' from which we can sally forth into the world, knowing we have a refuge to which we will return. 'All of us, from the cradle to the grave, are happiest when life is organised as a series of excursions, long or short, from the secure base provided by our attachment figures' (Bowlby 1988: 62).

Without a sufficiently secure base, we feel anxious; without the opportunity to explore, life is boring. Our experiences of relationship and exploration are encoded in an 'inner working model', an internal base which reflects the security or insecurity of our attachments and incorporates the modes of relating and exploring we have learned. This internal representation should ideally remain consistent yet open to change; but difficult relationships lead to a disjointed or distorted model, with dissociated areas which remain frozen and out of awareness.

Developmental Stages

The first attachment is almost always to the mother, although Bowlby's theory holds for any primary carer, male or female, related or unrelated to the baby. Baby and mother both contribute to the building and maintaining of attachment through the experience and enactment of attachment behavioural systems which are triggered to different degrees at different times in different ways.

The baby is born with a preference for human voices and a fascination for the human face. She has an ability to track moving objects with her eyes, and a capacity to be soothed by voice, touch and the slow, rhythmic rocking which derives from or simulates being carried by a walking adult. She is pre-equipped to experience and manifest distress when she feels out of human contact for too long, in ways which are designed to bring about the presence of her carer and the loving behaviours she finds comforting. Crying, sucking, smiling, clinging and following are all instinctive rather than learned behaviours: even blind babies smile. During the first few months, the baby's crying, sucking and smiling alternately coerce and entice the mother to respond to her and invest in her emotionally. The baby is not a passive recipient of care, although the mother, or other primary carer, has her own agenda of attachment, mediated through her own internal working model. Thus the mother and the young baby are powerfully motivated to remain close to each other physically and emotionally; both become anxious if separated for too long.

There is an initial period when specific bonds are being built: babies younger than four to six months usually show a general rather than an individual attachment, and although they may recognise their mother or main carer they may not be distressed if another responsive, loving carer takes over. During early infancy, the mother (or mothering person) is the one who is inwardly impelled to make sure she is close to her baby: the baby actively relates to a responding other, rather than insisting on a particular person. The comforting actions of the caring adult are the baby's secure base, while interactive games involving movement, babbling and eye contact are her excursions into the world, together with her interest in objects and the excitement of practising her developing skills.

After about six months the baby has normally developed an intense attachment to her main carer, together with secondary attachments to specific others. This is the time of 'stranger anxiety', when an unknown face is neither pleasurable nor exciting to a baby, but constitutes danger because it is not mother's. Intriguingly, this matches the stage at which the baby is likely to become mobile, and could crawl off from her mother unless she is internally prevented from doing so. She now has an inner need to keep mother preferably in view, but certainly to hand. Her sucking, crying and clinging systems may not be triggered as easily as before provided her carer is close, reflecting her less dependent state, her growing ability to infer information from what she can see and hear, and the development of an inner secure base. However, her following and proximity-maintaining systems are very sensitive at this time, as parents of young toddlers can attest to. Bowlby describes an observation of two-year-old children in a park, where practically all stayed within a two-hundred-feet radius of their mother, who remained in one place. They were using her as the secure base from which they could venture forth: but only to a certain distance (Bowlby 1969: 306).

From six months to three years, children have a strong need to remain physically close to their primary carer; they can tolerate separation for limited periods only, preferably with another familiar person. Prolonged separation during these years is a major trauma and is exacerbated if the child cannot build a new attachment. The pattern and security of the child's relationships are intensively encoded in the inner representation of her relational world. It is as though the years up to the age of about four constitute the human 'critical period' for laying down how and how much we relate to others, patterns which are not easy to change later, as all psychotherapy patients and clients know.

A second threshold occurs at about three years. Sometimes with surprising suddenness, the child becomes able to tolerate not actually seeing mother, provided she knows where she is or when she will return. She can now comprehend that other people are separate from herself and have their own thoughts, perceptions and desires, and that her existence is independent of theirs. She is beginning to engage in reciprocal rather than egocentric relationships, mediated through language and with an appreciation of space and time. For all these reasons, Bowlby suggests, three years is the age at which children become able to benefit from regular periods as one of a group of children, such as at nursery school. Before this time, while they may enjoy an opportunity to play in the company of known and trusted others, they need an individual relationship with the subsidiary carer. Unless they have ready access to the substitute carer, they cannot easily cope with being one of a larger group. They are often distressed, however briefly, when the parent leaves.

The child's area of potential exploration enlarges insofar as her internal model allows, depending both on the maturity of her attachment behavioural systems and the security of her external, and therefore internal, base. Typically, the school life, clubs and friendship groups which are of such importance for schoolchildren provide the opportunity for this exploration. In adolescence, the peer group may seem even more important than the parents, and certainly may appear more influential as the Western teenager struggles to overcome her childhood dependency on her parents and creates new dependencies with her peers. However, home and family, whether the parental home or one's own adult home, remain fundamentally important throughout life, enabling rather than restricting exploration and direction. While there are many different kinds of attachment and living arrangements, most people feel the need for a few people on whom they can depend, to whom they matter and who matter to them. Without this secure base, our internal resources – the secure base we are able to supply for ourselves to some extent – may be over-strained and become depleted.

Even in large households, and across cultures, children tend to develop attachments of varying intensities to different people, but with a principal figure, usually the mother, to whom they are most strongly attached (Bowlby 1969: ch. 15). It is the quality of relationship rather than the quantity of time spent together which is the decisive factor in who becomes the child's primary attachment figure. Bowlby gives examples of babies who were predominantly attached to fathers or other relatives who did not have prolonged daily contact with them but who were more responsive to them than those who did. Similarly, children brought up in kibbutzim have stronger attachments to their parents than to the nurses who care for them most of the time, because of the importance parents allot to their children's daily visits and therefore the intensity of the contact between them. It is interesting that a child with several subsidiary attachment figures rather than just one or two is more, rather than less, attached to her main figure: a consequence, no doubt, of her friendly internal working model and her freedom to explore her relational world.

The Strange Situation

Bowlby's Tavistock colleague Mary Ainsworth is seen as the co-founder of Attachment Theory. She designed an observational procedure which she carried out on one-year-old babies and their mothers, known as 'The Strange Situation' (see Holmes 1993: 104–6; Ainsworth et al. 1978). Mother, baby and experimenter settle into a playroom, and mother then leaves the room for a few minutes. The baby's reaction to this separation and mother's and baby's responses when mother returns are noted. After a few more minutes, both mother and experimenter leave the room for a further three minutes, and the baby's behaviour is recorded both when she is alone and when the adults return. The whole videotaped procedure is used to assess and examine the mother–baby relationship and the baby's ways of coping with separation. This reveals the baby's internal model of relationship which can then be related to the mother's behaviour and responsiveness.

The relationships thus revealed were classed in three main categories, ranging from secure to insecure attachment. The secure group of infants, while usually upset by the separation, demanded and received care from mother when she returned and then continued happily with their explorative play. The less secure children showed avoidance or ambivalence towards their mothers. The insecure-avoidant group were not overtly upset when mother left and ignored her on her return, but watched her acutely and were unable to play freely. The insecure-ambivalent group were panicked by the separation and simultaneously clung to mother and fought her off when she returned: they were also unable to return to their own activity. Most disturbed of all were the insecure-disorganised children, a fourth categorisation that was made later. These children were confused and chaotic, with bizarre patterns of repetitive movements or frozen paralysis expressing their bewilderment (Bowlby 1988: 125).

Interestingly, but not surprisingly, Ainsworth and others went on to establish that the kind of attachment shown by the babies was linked closely with their mothers' responsiveness to them during their first year (Bowlby 1988: 45–50; Holmes 1993: 107). The mothers of the secure group were the most attuned to their babies, interacting with them freely and with enjoyment, picking up their signals accurately and responding to their distress promptly. The insecure-avoidant babies were likely to have mothers who interacted with them less and held a practical rather than personal attitude towards them. The mothers of the insecure-ambivalent group tended to respond unpredictably and were rather insensitive to their babies' signals; while the insecure-disorganised children generally came from profoundly disturbed backgrounds involving abuse, severe neglect or psychosis. The importance of these correlations lies in the differentiating of environmental and constitutional influences. It is clear that the mother's expressed attitude towards her baby is the overwhelming deciding factor in how secure the baby will be at one year, a pattern which holds true even for infants who are very easily upset in their first few months.

Bowlby's thesis that the environment is as potent a cause of neurosis as genetics has been confirmed repeatedly (Bowlby 1988; Holmes 1993: 109–14). There are studies which show that if the mother receives help in changing her feelings and behaviour towards her baby, the baby can develop a secure attachment from an insecure starting point. Some babies even show different patterns of attachment behaviour towards mother and father, although the mother pattern tends to become the main pattern over time. Moreover, the attachment shown by the one-year-old child predicts future development. Securely-attached children are more likely to relate better to others, to have more capacity for concentration and co-operation and to be more confident and resilient at age six. Four years later, they are also more able to make sense of their own lives and encompass difficult experiences without blocking them off or becoming confused. Even adult neurotic behaviour has been correlated with the pictures shown by insecurely-attached babies and children.

The 'strange situation' observes the relationship as manifested in both child's and mother's behaviour rather than something which belongs only to the mother or only to the child. The child's internal working model reflects the nature and structure of this relationship and the kind of care she has received. The secure child has an inner representation of a lovable self and responsive other, with enjoyable interactions alternating with exciting explorations in an interesting world. The insecure-ambivalent child, on the other hand, has a picture of a self which is not lovable and an unpredictable other who has to be manipulated or coerced into caring. The insecure-avoidant child has an internal model of a self which is not worthy of care and an other who does not care, forcing the child to repress her longing and her anger in order not to drive the other even further away. In this pattern of detachment the child disowns her anger, need and anxiety and the awareness of her carer's rejection in what Bowlby termed 'defensive exclusion'. Those systems of perception, feeling and incipient behaviour which involve unbearable pain are 'deactivated' into dissociated frozen blocks of cognition and emotion. As long as they remain deactivated, these systems cannot be revised or integrated and so lead to a partial, distorted or fragmented internal working model of relationship. Wholesale defensive exclusion occurs in the emotional paralysis that follows acute physical or emotional shock. Usually the numbness gives way gradually when the traumatised person reaches safety and support; but where the situation which gave rise to the process continues, the exclusion becomes permanently encoded in the internal working model.

Where much is excluded, gaps in the inner model show up as emotional detachment and a difficulty in giving a clear and integrated account of experience, revealing a fragmented and incoherent sense of self. Where there is little defensive exclusion, the secure child or adult relates to others easily and can articulate a coherent and continuous account of her life. Since these capacities are largely derived from the child's first relationship, early orientation towards external reality must be greater than either Kleinian or Freudian theories assumed.

Reactions to Separation

Until Bowlby's work had become known, children were thought to be unable to mourn an emotional loss as adults did. Both Freudian and Kleinian schools presumed that if they mourned at all, it was for the services provided by the lost person rather than for the relationship. Bowlby's work on the reactions of young children to separation, especially prolonged separation, from parents, led him also to turn his attention to the mourning process of adults. He was able to clarify that the loss of an attachment figure is a truly emotional disaster for the young child, who reacts like a bereaved older child or adult.

Lengthy separation is particularly damaging for a child between six months and three years, when strong and specific attachments have developed but before the child is able to understand that the parent's absence is temporary. Typical reactions to separation in this age group can be divided into three phases.

The first phase is protest. When the child has come to the end of her capacity to tolerate separation, she will do everything in her power to bring her attachment figure back. Younger children cry in angry distress, looking for the parents where they last saw them; older children demand the parents' return, cry and search for them. The protest stage can last up to a week; if the separation then ends, they are likely to greet the parents with anger, relief and anxious clinging.

After protest comes despair: the child gradually loses hope that her lost person will return. She may cry inconsolably or withdraw into apathy and grief. This withdrawal may mistakenly be seen as 'settling down', as an angry and unhappy child becomes quiet and amenable. In one- to three-year-olds, the stage of despair may continue for up to nine or ten days.

This phase is followed by an apparent recovery which Bowlby describes as detachment. The child emerges from her withdrawal and begins to take an interest in her surroundings again. She represses or disinvests in her relationship with the lost person and begins to attach herself to an alternative figure. This can lead to considerable difficulties if the child is then reunited with her parents. Bowlby recounts heartrending stories of children who, after prolonged separation, remained politely aloof from the parents they had missed so much, or even failed to recognise them. Rebuilding the relationship is a painful process, as the child retraces her emotional steps through grief and despair to anger and outrage, often remaining clingy and insecure for a prolonged period and vulnerable to further separation in the longer term. Bowlby found that some degree of detachment occurs when a child is separated from her main attachment figure for a week or more in this critical early period, although the degree and reversibility of detachment vary with the quality of substitute care and the situation to which the child returns.

If a child experiences a series of separations from attachment figures, particularly during the vulnerable early years, her capacity to relate may be permanently stunted. The child with no consistent mothering person, or who is moved repeatedly to different settings, becomes detached from all relationship. She invests in things rather than people – sweets, toys and money – and ceases to discriminate between those who care for her. She thus becomes well-adapted to the kind of care she has received, cheerfully accepting whoever is on duty and showing no distress if nurses or childcare workers change rota or leave their jobs.

The inability to form close bonds makes it difficult for such children to return home or settle into the familial intimacy of foster care. Foster parents find them heartless and exploitative. The destructiveness which may accompany their detachment does not help, although paradoxically it is a hopeful sign: a spark of protest in the shreds of their capacity for attachment. Destructiveness is more extreme in those children who lost attachment figures, and less of a feature in children who never developed attachments in the first place. Bowlby's early study of 'Forty-four Juvenile Thieves' (Bowlby 1944) correlates adolescent delinquency with separation in childhood, showing how the glassy detachment of the 'affectionless psychopath' develops from childhood trauma when the grieving child was driven to the defensive exclusion of almost all attachment processes.

The sequence of protest, despair and detachment may be clear-cut and sequential but is more likely to be intermingled. The intensity of feeling will depend largely on whether the child is supported during the separation by a consistent and responsive substitute attachment figure, especially one who is already familiar to the child, or whether she is left with unresponsive or impersonal care. A shorter separation is less damaging than a longer period, and older children cope better than younger ones. Other mitigating factors include the presence of someone known, even a younger sibling, and having some possessions from home.

Mourning

Bowlby studied mourning in both adults and children, and has been influential in the social acceptance of mourning as a healthy rather than pathological process unless it becomes suppressed, delayed or distorted (Bowlby 1980). As soon as children are old enough to have developed a specific attachment, their reactions to separation correlate with the mourning process. Only the initial phase of numbness differs, a phase which young children perhaps cannot afford: the younger the child, the more their survival and well-being depend on their giving immediate and effective signals of distress.

Bowlby outlines the stages of mourning as numbness, yearning and searching, disorganisation and despair, and reorganisation. The disbelief which almost always accompanies the news of death is an emotional shutdown comparable to the physical shutdown which enables badly-injured people to reach safety without being incapacitated by pain. The initial numbness may last hours or days, until the bereaved person feels able to give way to their feelings as the truth of the situation sinks in; the numbness may then alternate with eruptions of anger and distress.

Intense sadness follows. Waves of longing and yearning may be overwhelming in their intensity, often accompanied by fury at the doctors or any others who could conceivably be blamed for the death. The bereaved person may also vent her anger on the person she has lost; on anyone trying to comfort her, particularly if they try to get her to accept the reality of the situation; and on herself for not preventing her loved one from dying or not being good enough while he was alive. Guilt and anger are particularly intense where the relationship between the bereaved and the dead person was conflictual and ambivalent, and when the bereaved person's internal model of relationship is one of anxious, ambivalent, insecure attachment.

The bereaved person may feel irritable and restless, unable to settle to anything, continually wandering from room to room. This may be due to the searching systems becoming activated in an instinctive attempt to find the lost person. Similarly, she may hear the lost person's voice or feel his presence, reliving the past in a fantasy of undoing death. The yearning and searching phase may last for months, or sometimes years if it is particularly difficult for the bereaved person to accept her loss.

The stages of numbness and of yearning and searching are analogous to the initial protest stage of separation. The reality and permanence of loss are not immediately accepted, even when the cause is death; and anger, yearning and searching are predicated on the hope of finding or having restored the lost person and preventing him leaving again.

The next stage of mourning is disorganisation and despair. The bereaved person feels an increasing sense of meaninglessness and fragmentation, and life may seem not worth living. Her internal working model has broken with the loss of a crucial figure, and a new working model has not yet formed. It is a time when suicide may be a temptation, particularly if there are few or no people to care for or comfort her. It is perhaps the most painful phase of bereavement and may be exacerbated by expectations that she should by now be beginning to recover. It matches the despair phase of separation, after the reality of the loss has become starkly clear and before new attachments have begun.

The final phase is reorganisation, when the new situation becomes reflected in the internal representation of the relational world. Old routines rendered meaningless give way to new habits. Memories become a comfort, and it becomes possible for fresh relationships to be sought. Reorganisation parallels the detachment phase of separation, with the acceptance of loss and the seeking of new attachments. In healthy reorganisation new attachments remain possible, and the old attachment does not have to be excluded from consciousness. Less successful reorganisation involves a diminution in the capacity to relate.

Any of these phases can become prolonged or distorted, with one phase clung to in a desperate attempt to ward off the next. Depression and anxiety may indicate chronic yearning and searching; comparative detachment may denote continued numbness or a failure in reorganisation. Bowlby's lucid account makes self-evident the need of the bereaved person for contactful care with no expectation of immediate recovery. The mourning process is facilitated if feelings of guilt and anger as well as loss, anxiety and sadness can be accepted by the bereaved person and those around her. Full information and the opportunity to see and touch the dead person enable her to take in the reality of his death. Mourning ceremonies give structure in a time of crisis, drawing the community together and ensuring support for those on whom the impact of the death is most acute.

Disordered mourning is a particular danger for those who already relate to others in anxious and ambivalent ways or who derive their identity and self-esteem from the compulsive caring for others. Thoroughgoing detachment protects against the pain of mourning through pre-empting the development of attachment; but superficial detachment can cover a catastrophic build-up of anxiety, sadness and anger which may explode unpredictably or implode in depression and thoughts of suicide. Bowlby points to the difficulties arising from sudden death, and suicide in particular, where shock, guilt and anger are especially excruciating and difficult to resolve.

Bowlby's study of mourning translates into specific recommendations for the care of children who have lost a parent. Apart from the age-dependent phase of numbness, the differences between the mourning of adults and that of children lie predominantly in children's lesser experience and knowledge of what death means, and their lack of control over what they are told and how they are treated. They live more in the present than do adults, and so their mourning is more frequently interspersed with activities and moods which arise from other aspects of their lives. Because children are still in the process of building up their internal models, and because they have a constant need for their main attachment figures, they are particularly vulnerable to distortions in their development arising from inadequate care following bereavement.

Bowlby emphasises that children are in absolute need of information in order to make sense of their loss, and that this must be given sensitively and at the level of their understanding. They must be enabled to understand that death is permanent and that the lost parent is never coming back; they should be told what has been done with the body, and that dead people do not breathe, eat or feel. Comforting fictions engender bewilderment and make it impossible for the child to come to terms with the true situation. When an adult with no religious belief suggests that mummy has gone to heaven or is 'at rest', the child can only feel confusion at the inauthenticity she senses: children accept the view of death that the adult believes and clearly tells them. Full information is especially difficult to give after a parent has committed suicide. Well-meaning or self-protective attempts to shield the child from what has really happened clash with the child's perceived impressions and inculcate a lack of trust in the adult world.

Children, as well as adults, need to take part in mourning rituals and to be able to talk about their loss as they express and work through their feelings. They need to be able to remain children rather than having to take on the responsibility of supporting the remaining parent. Children who lose a parent may come through their mourning process unscathed, especially if the original relationship was good and they are fully supported afterwards. However, this is usually the most difficult time for relatives to give full attention to children, preoccupied as they are with their own grief and the practical crises which accompany untimely death. Thus family relationships may deteriorate through a combination of emotional stress, financial constraint and the isolation which so often follows bereavement. It is not surprising that most bereaved children remain vulnerable to further loss, and that the loss of a parent in early childhood is significantly associated with depression in adult life. Bowlby gives a timely reminder that mourning may be a sequel of divorce or separation as well as death; the breakdown of the parents' relationship can lead to permanent loss for their children.

Emotional Deprivation

Bowlby is often criticised for stressing the effects of physical separation at the expense of emotional unresponsiveness. However, he does give attention to the less tangible forms of deprivation which occur without physical separation (Bowlby 1988). He found parental threats to abandon a child or even to commit suicide to be not uncommon; they are as damaging to the child's security as actual separations, and may lead to an inverted relationship where the parent seeks care from the child. Such children are afraid to leave home, to go to school for example, in case the parent is not there when they return; they may develop a pattern of compulsive care-giving which can persist through all their relationships as a cover for anxiety and anger.

Bowlby writes with passion of the injustice done to children when their feelings or perceptions are denied. Assertions that a certain event did not happen, or that they do not or should not have the feelings that they do, confuse and isolate the child. These contradictions of reality can only be resolved by containing them within in the form of incompatible inner working models, or by excluding certain feelings and perceptions as part of the 'bad' self. At an extreme, defensive exclusion gives rise to multiple personality disorder, a state in which autonomous systems of thought, feeling and behaviour are activated without reference to each other.

Bowlby's later papers (Bowlby 1988) cover the effects on children of family violence, abuse and neglect. His focus is always on the re-enactment of internal models built up in the parents' childhood, demonstrating how patterns of feeling and behaviour endure through generations, rather than on the attribution of blame. Encouragingly, he also makes the point that those who have had traumatic and unhappy experiences in childhood are not destined to inflict similar suffering on their children. Because we have inbuilt potential for systems of behaviour and feeling that include responsive care to others, especially children, negative patterns need not dominate if we have been able to come to terms with what has happened to us. The integration of past experience and the resolution of conflicting and painful emotions makes defensive exclusion unnecessary. If we can bear our past, we can see it in perspective; present experience can be new experience rather than a rehashing of old trauma, and old patterns can be revised.

Therapy

While Bowlby's major contribution was in the field of social policy, he maintained a small psychoanalytic practice and developed his own approach to psychotherapy (Bowlby 1988). His suggestions must be seen in the context of psychoanalysis before Object Relations, when dependency was viewed as essentially infantile and attachment as based on the gratification of physical needs. Both Kleinian and Freudian approaches laid a greater emphasis on intrapsychic factors than on external events and influences in the causation of neurosis; internal processes were therefore the main area of focus in psychotherapy.

Bowlby's main message, like Fairbairn's, is that human beings are contact-seeking: our well-being depends largely on the state of our relationships. Attachment is not something we grow out of, although our modes of relating develop and attachment patterns may change. The purposes of psychotherapy are to diagnose the attachment pattern of patient or client, largely through monitoring the ways in which she relates to the therapist, to discover what were the major events and influences which gave rise to her particular internal working model, and to revise and modify patterns which are now limiting or self-defeating. These aims can only be achieved if the therapeutic relationship itself is one of security and trust. The role of the therapist has much in common with the role of the mother towards the child, from the earliest stages of relationship through to separation.

A primary task in psychotherapy and counselling is the creation of a secure base in the reliability and consistency of the therapeutic relationship. Only when the client or patient feels some confidence in the therapist's responsiveness and empathy will she feel able to make excursions into risky areas. With the therapist's understanding and support, however, she will begin to explore her internal and external world in the past and in the present in her efforts to express herself and understand herself.

An attachment-oriented therapist will pay particular attention to the client's relationships in the past and the present, including of course the therapeutic relationship. Bowlby underlined that the quality and consistency of relationships are as important or more important than events, even traumatic ones, in the formation of the expectations, assumptions and capacities structured into the internal working model. The therapist should therefore be alert to the quality of the patient's relationships: whether they show secure, ambivalent, avoidant or disorganised patterns of attachment and how these patterns are experienced and enacted. It will also be taken for granted that a limited capacity for relationship indicates disturbance and profound unhappiness.

Together with the focus on relationship, there will also be attention to events, particularly those with a direct bearing on attachment. Childhood separations from home and family are naturally significant, as are the kind of threats to the child's security that may have been made by the parents, implicitly or explicitly, directly or as overheard by the child. In the same way, breaks in the therapy or absences of other present-day attachment figures are treated as important and as likely to cause some difficulty until the patient or client has a sufficiently secure internal base to manage such separations.

Bowlby suggests that psychotherapy should be an equal rather than hierarchical partnership between client and therapist. He underlines that the client has a natural capacity for growth and development. As the parent's task is to constantly adapt to the needs and maturity of the child, so the therapist's attitude to the client should be flexibly relational rather than arbitrarily authoritarian. 'The psychotherapist's job ... is to provide the conditions in which self-healing can best take place' (Bowlby 1988: 152). Because attachment is an essential part of life, the therapeutic relationship is important in its own right rather than predominantly as an indicator of transference issues.

The ending of psychotherapy can be compared with adolescence. When a sufficiently secure internal base has been established, with the capacity to develop rich and rewarding relationships that this implies, the therapist can be left though not forgotten. After successful therapy, the patient or client will understand and accept herself more, relate to others more fully and realistically and withstand difficulties more easily. She will have developed a more coherent and continuous understanding and experience of herself and what has happened to her, encompassing both positive and negative events and influences.

Bowlby's recommendations for psychotherapy are non-prescriptive and non-controversial; they amount essentially to a plea to allot attachment an overriding importance in human life. He shares the view, common to Object Relations practitioners, that the new experience gained is crucial in facilitating growth and development; insight alone is by no means sufficient. Bowlby's neutral language and comparatively simple frame of reference make his theory widely accessible. His multidisciplinary base expresses the hope that different schools and professions can overcome competition and prejudice to work together.

Commentary

Bowlby had a more direct effect on British society than any psychoanalyst except Freud. However, this influence was only possible because of the rigorous limitation of his area of enquiry. Bowlby studies the person as a human mechanism rather than a human subject. His emphasis is on events and external life, the measurable and behavioural effects of the mainly physical absence of important figures, rather than internal phenomena. Phantasies and their effects on relating have little space in Bowlby's internal models, which are seen as photographic impressions of external reality meeting genetically-fixed systems of behaviour and feeling-tone. 'Protest' and 'detachment' are tame words beside Kleinian greed and envy, and the experiencing of the emotional states to which Bowlby does refer is barely elaborated. This emotional emptiness is probably what enraged his colleagues, leading Winnicott to speak of 'a kind of revulsion' that Bowlby's work aroused in him, and Guntrip to exclaim sarcastically that Bowlby has managed to 'explain everything in human behaviour except what is of vital importance for psychoanalysis' (Holmes 1993: 28).

Bowlby raises the trauma of maternal deprivation above all other trauma, simply because it is the only factor he really explores. The father has no intrinsic value or role other than as an additional attachment figure. All possible shades of experience, of relational expectations and emotional modes, are reduced to one or other variety of attachment pattern, offering a meagre framework for understanding the myriad neurotic and psychotic processes and patterns of human beings.

In a sense, Bowlby's work would have been more cohesive and solid had he remained within his main area of research into the effects of physical events of childhood, such as separation and the specific actions of parents. Those events which can be measured and recorded, such as the mother's responsiveness to her baby's crying and the amount of time she spends interacting with her, find a logical place in the internal model of the baby as a straightforward representation of what has happened to her. The effects of what is not said or not felt in relation to the child find a far less easy home in his theory, because too long a string of deductions has to be made. While similarities in family patterns can be readily found – analogous to the feelings and perceptions that are placed behind the family's metaphorical screen in Skynner and Cleese (1983) – the subtler shades of atmosphere creating and mediating these dynamics require a more meaning-based approach. Bowlby's theoretical frame is too behaviour-oriented to do justice to the subjective world. This would not be a criticism had he acknowledged a limit to the area his approach could encompass.

Bowlby was perspicacious in his selection of a focus for research which was clear, specific and of current social relevance. The topicality of his area of interest initially fostered, but later blocked, the acceptance of his message.

Separation was an experience common to many during the war years, with men wrenched away from their families for extended periods, city children evacuated to the country, women in many cases deprived of both partners and children. The trauma sustained by soldiers was investigated by Bion, Sutherland and Fairbairn; Winnicott focused on the needs of evacuated children who could not be easily fostered.

Women's distress, however, was barely touched on except in passing by Winnicott and Bowlby. This paralleled a cavalier political attitude in which women were sidelined into invisibility while men were more overtly exploited as fighters. When women were required for factory work, for example, nurseries were built and their benefits for young children extolled: day care would make children more independent and sociable and offer them space and stimulation.

After the war, as the jobs were required for the returning men, nurseries were closed down. Now a woman's place was said to be in the home, and children who were not cared for full-time by their mothers were said to be in danger of irrevocable damage. 'Maternal deprivation' became a watchword striking a chill into the hearts of women who failed the total-care standard of mothering, and false complacency in those who stayed at home full time, however resentfully. That socially-induced guilt was used as an agent of control is betrayed by policies in hospitals and institutions where children were routinely separated from their parents and viewed as 'spoiled' if they complained. It is only in recent years that a more objective, less simplistic attitude has been taken towards the needs of young children, resulting in a more sophisticated and flexible approach which can take into account the situations of individual families.

Thus Bowlby's area of work was and is particularly vulnerable to distortion and exploitation. It is partly because of this that the feminist protest against him has been strong. However, when his work is read with his social context in mind, he comes across as moderate rather than fanatic, although he clearly favours conventional arrangements for the care of young children. He extols the extended family system of most cultures as one which naturally promotes relationships which are secure, enjoyable and relaxed, and deplores the isolation of the nuclear family of twentieth-century Western society. Here he practised what he preached in the shared households which were extraordinarily unusual for a man of his social class. He considered that the sole care of young children was too demanding and isolating a task for any single adult, emphasising that 'if a community values its children it must cherish their parents' (Bowlby 1953: 100); also pointing out that attachment was strengthened rather than diluted by attachment to figures additional to the child's main carer (Bowlby 1969: 249–50). He was an early advocate for financial help to prevent children being taken into care and to enable mothers of young children not to have to work; but he also records that there is no evidence of children of working mothers suffering when they have good alternative care (Bowlby 1953: 91).

Bowlby's own childhood experience of relative deprivation must have been the wellspring sustaining his decades of focused study, and the vehemence arising from this emotional root must have contributed to his insistence on maternal care for children. Perhaps at this point we can remember the seven-year-old who must have yearned for his nurse, if not his mother, at boarding school. However, he seems to have tried to prevent his personal views prejudicing the objectivity of his work. His harsh words for mothers who do not want to care for their children full-time are tempered by his perspective on intergenerational familial dynamics and matched by his outrage at social policy which removed even new-born babies from their mothers' care (Bowlby 1988). While he suggested that children under three should ideally be cared for by a willing and happy mother, he envisaged her having frequent breaks from their care. He encouraged nursery school care for the over-threes and found the idea of working mothers unpalatable but not unthinkable.

Bowlby's vision is therefore limited but precise, his style largely devoid of the passion which is such an attractive feature of theorists such as Winnicott and Guntrip. If we can accept these constraints as necessary to the task in hand, Bowlby opens doors which are not even noticed by other theorists. His aim was to restore scientific rigour to psychoanalysis, forge links with other relevant disciplines and focus on the external events and influences which lead to emotional disturbance. In these areas he built a solid foundation.

Bowlby is often overlooked in Object Relations overviews, in the same way that his colleagues dismissed his work as behavioural and external rather than truly psychological. However, he always saw himself as making his own contribution to Object Relations: 'I am with the object relations school', he said, 'but I have reformulated it in terms of modern biological concepts. It is my own independent vision' (Grosskurth 1986: 404). Despite its non-conformism, Attachment Theory holds closely to the tenets of Object Relations. It is thoroughgoing in its insistence of the primacy of relationship, and is the only theory to prove this point conclusively. The 'working model' concept is a practical though blunt-edged version of the internal world, complete with inner relational structures. It is to the detriment of mainstream psychoanalysis that the more philosophically-inclined have not risen to Bowlby's challenge to become scientifically literate.

Attachment Theory is thus both essential groundwork in the study of psychobiological determinants of behaviour and emotion, and also a framework which can be used across theoretical and professional orientations. Bowlby's approach correlates with the more observational American psychoanalytical tradition; Otto Kernberg writes of his hope to bring together aspects of Bowlby's and Fairbairn's theories with those of Margaret Mahler, Edith Jacobson and others (in Grotstein and Rinsley 1994). Bowlby offers a basis for integrating diversity both inside and outside psychoanalysis.

Perhaps Bowlby found safety as well as satisfaction in the disciplined, detailed study of a demarcated area of life. He aspired to be objective rather than charismatic, and it was surely no accident that he excelled in deputy posts. Yet his leaps backwards to Freud's hopes for a scientifically respectable psychology, and forwards to the vanguard of research, were in their way as revolutionary as were the ideas of Klein and Fairbairn. The methodological rigour of his work makes it hard going for those who prefer a more emotionally indulgent style; but his writing is fluent and clear rather than dry and abstract. Odd shards of pain surface unexpectedly in some of the case histories illustrating his theoretical points, in the apt and beautiful poems and quotations he dots throughout his work, in outbursts of indignation at the damage wreaked by society on the individual, and in his dedication to changing common social régimes which lead to untold anguish.

Part II
Application

The focus of our study now moves from theory to application. The first chapter of this second part discusses the practice of Object Relations in the helping professions, particularly counselling and psychotherapy. It is followed by a chapter on working with difference and diversity, reflecting the widening range of people whose experience must be encompassed if Object Relations is to remain of value in today's world. The final chapter explores some of the questions and pitfalls which are revealed in the process of examining the ideas and assumptions of Object Relations and integrating them with other points of view.

8

OBJECT RELATIONS IN PRACTICE

The clash of ideas running throughout the development of Object Relations invites flexible and creative application. The concepts, skills and attitudes which derive from its perspectives can be applied directly in psychoanalysis, psychotherapy and counselling. The intelligent appreciation of the therapeutic relationship as a primary medium of change enhances work throughout the helping professions.

Object Relations frameworks and constructs help us to better understand our interactions with others. We may assimilate them in individual form into a personal philosophy of living which is relationally sensitive. Practitioners who espouse other theoretical approaches may turn specifically to Object Relations when making an assessment of a client and his needs, in more difficult phases in the therapeutic relationship and in the potentially baffling experience of working with someone who is more than usually disturbed. The focus on the process of relationship enables the exploration of the dominant or current relational mode in depth and detail.

A RELATIONAL FRAMEWORK

Balint (1968: ch. 15) pointed out that the language, assumptions and concepts of any psychotherapeutic or counselling approach define the area that can be thought about and organise the terms in which thinking can happen. Practitioners who train in Object Relations approaches may automatically evolve a relational frame for their work, but this is far more difficult for practitioners with a different form of training to develop. While the application of theory to practice is seldom straightforward, it is to practitioners of approaches other than Object Relations that this section is primarily addressed; it may also be of particular interest to trainers and supervisors. The intention is not to offer a guide to practice, but to relate the ideas discussed in previous chapters to direct experience and foster sensitivity towards relational processes.

Since many practitioners who have trained in other approaches use the word 'client' rather than 'patient', it is used in this chapter. These different terms signal the ferocious rivalry within the psychotherapy and counselling world, and are often imbued with emotion and judgement. One of the primary aims of this book is to further communication and tolerance across theoretical orientations, and 'patient' and 'client' are used as simple alternatives.

A basic framework for observing and analysing therapeutic interaction can be derived from the three stages of development worked out by Freud and Abraham (Freud 1905b, S.E. 7; Abraham 1927; Jacobs 1986). These stages were expanded by Erik Erikson (1950) into eight life-stages, from infancy to old age. Each stage has its central issues and challenges, from the first-stage balance of trust and mistrust to the final-stage weighing of integrity versus despair. Erikson's extension of the Freudian developmental stages helps us tune in to the tasks and hazards which a client is likely to be confronting in his particular phase of life. However, it is the successful negotiation of the first three phases which provides a basic stock of trust in oneself and the ability to relate enjoyably and effectively to others. When these are problematic life is inevitably troubled, and the issues which lead people to seek therapeutic help usually centre on or arise from difficulties in these areas. Similarly, when people regress significantly in therapy, it is to one of these three early ways of being and relating; regressions to the later stages are less problematic, easier to understand and usually more fleeting.

The relational framework is articulated in terms of oral, anal and Oedipal dynamics. These terms are not overtly relational, except perhaps the last; but they reflect the Freudian base from which Object Relations developed, and offer a viable container for relational dynamics, modes and defences. Object Relations theories are overwhelmingly concerned with the oral stage in their extension backwards from Freud's focus on the Oedipal stage. However, the two subsequent stages are taken for granted rather than seen as superfluous. Including all three stages in an observational frame helps practitioners keep in mind the later psychological developments which are also highly influential in personal development and which are often reflected in practice. Object Relations theories from Freud onwards, with their shifting conjunctions of relational and physiological premises, can all be subsumed within these broad metaphorical divisions.

Oral Stage

The oral stage covers roughly the first year, divided into early oral and late oral periods. The predominant issue is how much trust the baby develops that the world will love and care for him, and thus how far he can take his own existence and survival for granted. Because need and dependency are the crucial factors, help, goodness and power seem either to be outside the self, or in a repudiation of the world, to reside solely within. This can lead to an idealising or alternatively a paranoid feel to the interaction, and the counsellor or psychotherapist can easily get caught up in trying to disprove her badness or prove her goodness by filling the client up or attempting to gratify his urgent needs. The mouth itself may be a focus in oral-stage dynamics. Smoking, drinking, drug use and eating disorders frequently incorporate anxiety about whether or not one will be rescued from desperate need by the substance in question, imbued with magical maternal powers.

Oral-stage dynamics are the most problematic to work with, and their more extreme forms constitute borderline and psychotic states. Even in the forms which are common in any counselling or psycho-therapeutic practice, our own primitive anxieties are powerfully reverberated. This can bring us closer to the client's experience, but it can also pull us into his urgent desire for an instant solution. The challenges of the oral stage are to build a sense of self which can endure through difficult circumstances; to come to terms with living in a world which is real rather than a product of our own wishes; and to reach an acceptance of and responsibility for ourselves and our feelings, together with an appreciation of the separateness of others and their own subjective selfhood.

Early oral dynamics revolve around the schizoid anxieties of the loss of the integrity of the self through engulfment, disappearing boundaries, atrophy or persecution, all areas discussed in detail by Object Relations theorists, especially Klein and Fairbairn. Defences used at this stage are aimed at changing not what is actually happening, but rather the perception of what is happening, in a primitive attempt to bypass anxiety.

Denial is one such defence: if I close my eyes, the situation which gives me the bad feeling will not be there. This was the method used by Daniel, who had been seeing a therapist for several months. An occasion arose when a change in his work pattern meant he had to come to his session from home rather than from his workplace, which he disliked as something new and therefore unpredictable. Daniel arrived forty minutes late, disoriented and panicky, with ten minutes left of his session to go; in this time his therapist helped him to understand what had happened. Daniel had dealt with his anxiety about the unfamiliar journey, and his anger with the therapist to whom the journey was to be made, in two ways: he left home at the identical time that he would have left work; and he did not bring his map of the town and its transport system with him. His denial that the journey would need any special planning saved him from an anxious day, but at the price of terrible bewilderment during the actual journey, despairing rage at being 'robbed' of his time and, of course, losing most of the session itself.

Projective defences are also a feature of this stage, because of the baby's absolute need for another to be part of his intense emotions. The client relating through early oral dynamics may unconsciously but effectively force into the therapist or counsellor the internal malignancy which would otherwise eat away at him; or conversely, he may make his world seem safer through the projective creation of a powerful saviour. The splitting characteristic of this stage means that projections are extreme and unrealistic, and the pressure to take them on through projective identification may be backed up by an implicit threat of primitive persecution if one does not do so. It is in this kind of situation that normally competent and well-bounded practitioners can find themselves giving way, extending the time, disclosing too much personal information or spending inordinate time between sessions worrying about the client: all danger signs for malignant regression. To add injury to insult, the practitioner is then likely to find that the excessive efforts she has made have escalated the client's anxiety rather than lessened it: the blurring of the therapeutic frame and the anxiety which may have led to it can give the client the message that the practitioner cannot manage the client's overwhelming feelings any better than he can himself.

Rosemary had fought her way to middle-age through deprivation, violence and loss, and had found a sympathetic student therapist who had also experienced turmoil and crisis in his life. He was impressed by her courage, while her anxiety and despair resonated within him. During one particularly intense session, which she dreaded coming to an end, he offered her the possibility of an extra session each week. While this was not in itself a bad idea, its timing arose from the therapist's anxiety about primitive neediness, stimulated through projective identification as well as his own difficult experiences. This led Rosemary into a process of disintegration in which she lost her accommodation and her only friend through panicky acting-out of her inner chaos. She had heard the therapist's offer as a vote of no confidence in her ability to cope with her volatile feelings and her lonely life; and without the conviction that he believed in her, she could not maintain her belief in herself.

The negative of dependency may appear as forced self-sufficiency or an apparent indifference to other people. This denotes particular difficulties in the early oral stage, with the person concluding that the world cannot meet his needs or sustain his being. His disowned neediness may be expressed in a rejection of everything associated with personal vulnerability, including the fragile body with its physical limitation and craving. His ambition to attain abstraction and thus invulnerability, and his preoccupation with himself rather than others, are matched by a contempt for those upon whom he projects his own carnal nature and emotional hunger. His dependency is as acute as that of any infant, but he cannot afford to acknowledge it.

Early oral modes of relating thus include the schizoid, where the person attempts to cut off from his need for others, focusing instead on a complex internal world; the hysteric, where he clings ferociously to the designated needed person with little concern for that person's needs or wishes; paranoid dynamics, where painful realities are projected out into the other person rather than being held inside; and addictive processes of all kinds, where a substance, taking the place of a human relationship, is treated as the answer to all personal needs without the requirement for reciprocity. Borderline and psychotic processes make overt the lack of a coherent sense of self and confusion between reality and fantasy; the psychotic creation of an illusory world is an extreme example of the primitive strategy of manoeuvring perception to keep at bay the sense of an overwhelmingly dangerous reality. Regression to the early oral stage involves the most fundamental disturbances in the formation of the self in relation to another. Because of the intensity of focus on perceived survival, with truth often becoming a casualty, it is all too easy for the counsellor or therapist to be drawn into the fractured, tormented world view of the patient or client, losing sight of her own mature and measured perspective.

The late oral stage may still focus on need for the other or the denial of need, but in a less out-of-touch manner. By this stage, the worst anxieties about the cohesion and continuity of the self and the other have lessened, and there is correspondingly less need to mask reality. However, this leaves an intense fear of losing the needed person: the baby has realised his lack of power and his dependency, but has as yet few internal resources.

The depressive position with its anxieties about anger and destructiveness is a rock on which many founder. The turning of anger inwards rather than outwards is a hallmark of depression, resulting in painful guilt and sometimes savage inner persecution when paranoid-schizoid anxieties remain unresolved. At the same time, the depressed person presents others with a placating exterior which seems to exude a hidden reproach: 'Why won't you help me?', or envious attack: 'It's all right for you, of course.'

The strategy of depression is to internalise anger so that other people are not hurt by it overtly. The undermining of the self which this leads to is manifested in a lack of self-confidence, an inability to say no to others and continual, low-grade feelings of guilt, resentment and despair. This may increase to the more severe clinical depression with the physical corollaries of early waking and loss of appetite and energy. The acutely depressed person may suffer from a heavy, brooding sense of paralysis in the face of any demand for action, with suicidal thoughts, feelings and actions being sometimes the first signs of returning energy. Psychologically, all are essentially the result of the internal enactment of rage and need rather than using them in direct relationship to others or containing them within benign internal structures.

The main defences of this later oral stage involve attempts to meet the situation by changing oneself rather than doctoring one's perceptions. Feelings may be consciously suppressed and unconsciously repressed. A depressed person who is keen to appear kind and pleasant, who constantly placates others and does nothing which could justify criticism, is likely to have repressed feelings of rage, disappointment and demand which he considers would be unacceptable, and which he fears may be disastrously destructive to those on whom he depends. While not offering resolution, repression is a less self-defeating defence than those used in the early oral stage because there is some attempt to deal with the actual situation.

Difficulties relating to the late oral stage are predominantly depressive attempts to internalise an often 'biting' anger and demand, and also its opposite, the turning outwards of destructiveness which feels intolerable when trapped inside. Winnicott (1984) describes this as the compulsive destructiveness of the delinquent, who demonstrates his inner state of turmoil, rage, persecution and need in a form which ensures a response from society. Abraham and Klein saw manic depression as a depressive psychosis, the manic defence operating as a total denial of overwhelming depression (Klein 1935, 1940).

Anal Stage

The anal stage succeeds the oral stage, peaking between two and four years. With some resolution of oral-stage anxieties, the child is more able to take for granted the existence and cohesion of the self and the reliability of the other. He has found that conflict and anger can be overcome and that he is not 'too much' for his parents or carers. Of course, there is great individual difference in how far these questions have been satisfactorily resolved, depending largely on the constancy and quality of the child's most important relationships as he has experienced them. While the adult contributions to these relationships are important, additional factors include any special difficulties the child and his parents have had to contend with, such as a disability, loss or deprivation which hampers his development, or a trauma which has disrupted his security.

Power is the issue of the anal stage: not so much mature, co-operative empowerment, but power over others or others' power over you. The burning question is who is in control of whom. It is as though, having settled his doubts about his personal existence and well-being in relationship, the child now moves on to ask how worthwhile he is in relation to his immediate others. As the later oral-stage issues are culturally embodied in weaning, so are anal-stage dynamics enacted in Western-style toilet-training. This may be the first arena in which child and parent encounter each other's will and wilfulness, and is probably the first circumstance in which the child is expected to use his new capacities for bodily control for the apparent benefit of his parents rather than himself.

Battles with the 'terrible twos' are graphic everyday examples of the anal stage in action. 'Holding on' and 'letting go' become weapons the child can deliberately employ, from holding his breath in tantrums to shutting his mouth against food to refusing to use the toilet. They are often met with similar parental behaviour: reactions arising from the parents' own unresolved anal-stage feelings include forced feeding and physical punishment, which often starts at this stage.

In the therapeutic setting, anal-stage dynamics can be as frustrating for the therapist or counsellor as for the parent. Defiance, refusal to 'co-operate' and passive resistance can seem maddeningly self-defeating. Commonly, especially in therapeutic approaches which are built around emotional expression, the client may protest how much he would like to express his feelings, but be quite unable to 'let go'. In a group setting, the whole group can become involved in cajoling and provoking one member to explode or evacuate his feelings, often anger, with the apparently helpless object of their attention caught up in a more or less unconscious conviction that to 'give in' would constitute defeat, humiliation, loss of self. Battles of wills which centre on the product (whether expression of feeling, or faeces in the right place) usually lead to impasse; the real issue is not the product but the relationship which is concerned with the negotiation of power and control. The therapist or counsellor, like the parent, can easily become as stubborn as the client, determined to keep the upper hand at all costs. This simply ensures that the encounter will be as unproductive as the squabbles of two toddlers.

It is important to remember that the child in the anal stage, or the adult who has regressed to it, is relating through conflict and opposition in order to firm up his boundaries and establish his autonomy; otherwise he would simply feel an extension of the will of the parent or the therapist. This is why to say 'yes' can feel a betrayal of the self: it is only saying 'no' that brings the reassurance that he has boundaries and that they are in place.

What is needed from the therapist or counsellor is neither retaliation nor compliance, but rather a firm and strong encounter in which she is seeking neither to win nor to humiliate the client, but to maintain the boundaries of the therapeutic framework and to refuse to allow herself to be walked over. If she can remain firm without descending into attack or withdrawal, there is the possibility of a genuine meeting between two distinct people, each with their own power. The client is likely to feel relieved rather than disappointed that the therapist does not crumble before him, and he gains the opportunity to discover that one can have power *with* another, rather than simply power over people.

The obverse of the defiant anal-stage stance is the equally provocative submissive position. The client who has internalised a sadistic or controlling relationship may make a virtue of necessity by becoming masochistically attached to being on its receiving end. He may only feel safe if he is under the control of an other who shows dominance by treating him badly. Projecting his own anger and wish for power into the other allows him to safely inhabit the submissive counterpart. The passive-aggressive person can thus indirectly express a degree of sadism and extort control out of others effectively.

When these dynamics are played out in the therapeutic relationship, the challenge for the therapist or counsellor is to find a way of stepping out of this kind of collusive battle. Respecting the client means refusing to take as partial and demeaning a view of him as he would appear to wish, but to keep hold of the fact that he has his own capacities for decision making, assertiveness and anger.

While these are the most common forms of anal-stage relating, there is also the equivalent of the child who refuses to be toilet trained. Rather than compulsively holding on, the regressed or immature client will compulsively let go, 'leaking' his feelings impulsively and inappropriately. To the extent that this is a refusal to be controlled or to follow society's rules, the underlying dynamics are similar; the client may also have an underlay of anxiety about containing and being contained from earlier stages of development, and Abraham correspondingly saw this expulsive stage as earlier than the retentive anal stage.

Sadistic and masochistic elements are therefore common, and there may also be obsessive-compulsive patterns. Preoccupations such as whether the lights have been turned off or whether they will cause a fire, or tormenting thoughts that one may be about to injure someone or swear inappropriately, may betray a struggle to control anger which seems frighteningly destructive, or need, including sexual need, which seems dirty and shameful. Obsessive preoccupations may act as distractions from the feelings which might otherwise burst forth.

The major defence of the anal stage is repression. It is often backed up by reaction-formation, which is simply a going to the opposite extreme. Ironically, reaction-formation fools no-one, though it may confuse many: the too-nice, too-tidy person is merely avoided as irritating, inauthentic and boring.

Oedipal Stage

The third stage includes the Freudian phallic and early genital stages and relates particularly to the years between three and six, when Oedipal dynamics are at their height. It is the transition between the infantile way of relating with a single other person, where any intruder is seen largely as a threat or a rival, and being part of a group. With a reasonable foundation of trust and self-esteem, the opportunities that come from moving into a wider personal sphere enable the growing child to accept the concomitant deprivations. Towards the end of this stage, children have become junior citizens of their society, identifying strongly with its particular values and culture. While still highly dependent on their primary attachment figures, they are strongly drawn to their peers and to adults beyond their immediate circle.

In the therapeutic relationship, Oedipal issues appear in the spheres of sexuality, status and competition. Most obvious is the kind of transference where the client longs for an equal, perhaps sexual, but certainly gratifying relationship with the therapist or counsellor, with anything less felt as a humiliating rejection. To be 'only a client' feels unbearable; the thought of other clients, or worse still, those people whom the therapist or counsellor sees because she wants to, not because she is 'paid' to, may arouse fury and mortification. Regression to the Oedipal stage may be complicated by earlier disturbance.

Maria had grown up as the only child of an invalid mother and an overbearing father whose family had suffered political persecution during his childhood. In her late twenties she was still trying to gain his elusive approval. Her difficulty in maintaining relationships with men led her to see the male counsellor at her general practitioner's practice. They arranged a series of sessions, and about half-way through these a meeting at work made attending the next session problematic for her. Maria felt outraged and uncomprehending that the counsellor did not make a special arrangement to see her outside his normal working hours. She felt that he was gloating over his superior and invulnerable position, while she, humble and dependent, was 'just a patient'. If he had been truly concerned, he would have seen her at his home, or at least stayed late at the surgery. He felt helpless and strangely guilty in the face of her unhesitating condemnation. This made sense to him when he located an uncomfortable memory of his brothers jeering at him that he was their mother's favourite. He was then more able to empathise with the internal predicament colouring Maria's experience without taking responsibility for her feelings.

As this example shows, the person who has regressed to the Oedipal stage will not have resolved all its issues, and will still tend to view others as agents of his convenience. He will have few qualms about using heavy pressure, manipulation or seductiveness in the pursuit of his goals because of the strength of his conviction that his status and future satisfaction are at stake, together with his comparative inability to see the other person's point of view. All these factors will be exacerbated by the earlier stage preoccupations with identity, need and power which are likely to be only shakily resolved in an Oedipal regression.

The therapist or counsellor may be cast in the role of the powerful, desirable, glamorous parent in an idealised Oedipal transference; or conversely as dowdy, embarrassing or repulsive. She may be the frightening judge condemning the client's forbidden wishes, or the killjoy pouring cold water on his excitement. Other Oedipal transference options include the older brother or sister against whom the client must either compete at all costs or against whom competition is useless, or the sibling he feels guilty towards because of his apparent Oedipal triumph.

Therapists and counsellors will frequently see Oedipal dynamics in the relational and fantasy lives of their clients (and themselves). Falling in love with people who are unavailable is a common and painful re-run of Oedipal defeat which may hold the unconscious hope of rewriting childhood history while covering a fear of sexuality and intimacy. Love may only be safe when it does not bear relational consequences; and what is being sought may be the always-elusive exciting object, rather than a real person out in the world who reverberates an inner responsive other.

While the oral-stage client is looking for trust in himself and others, and the anal-stage client is grappling with power, control and self-worth, the client involved with Oedipal issues is trying to assess whether he still counts even if he is not the centre of the universe. The successfully negotiated or re-negotiated Oedipal stage brings the capacity to form co-operative relationships which can involve intimacy, self-exposure and sexuality.

Whatever the developmental stage, the therapeutic task includes relating to the client in a thoughtful, authentic and non-collusive way which is empowering to both people. This involves the therapist's or counsellor's relational capacities in their most mature forms, coupled with a readiness to recognise and remedy her inevitable relapses into immaturity. The practitioner has to bear the loneliness of keeping hold of her own perceptions and capacities, tuning into but not succumbing to the terms on which the client unconsciously feels he has to relate. If the practitioner can resist these pressures from her own and the client's emotional worlds, the client may discover, rediscover or regrow his lost, distorted and undeveloped capacities, encountering a real other person who tries not to abandon, humiliate or attack him.

Example

Sessions can be analysed by going through the interactions (on tape or written down after the session) and noting the dynamics, language, issues and modes of relating in terms of the oral, anal and Oedipal stages.

Most sessions do not fall neatly into stages and dynamics, although the issues of one stage often predominate for a while. The example below is taken from an exercise which students undertake at the beginning of their counselling or psychotherapy training. Two volunteers, taking the roles of counsellor and client, carry out in front of the group a short session which enables the observing students to practise relating live interactions to the framework. This exercise is only possible where an atmosphere of trust has built up in the group, and where students can exercise their own responsibility for what they expose in this relatively public setting.

On this occasion both students who volunteered were lesbians, from white working-class backgrounds. The exercise began with a lengthy silence.

Counsellor: 'We have seventeen minutes left.'

Client: 'I don't know what to say: I feel angry with bosses. With rude managers. I have one at work at the moment. When she's around, she doesn't even have to say anything, I seem to lose all my initiative. I feel automatically criticised and worthless.'

Perhaps the public arena, backed up by the therapist's rather pressurising and anxious opening remark, crystallised the idea of oppressive others. The fact that both women belong to groups subject to discrimination and prejudice may also emphasise the concerns with power and authority which are triggered by power differentials. The session has started with issues belonging to the anal stage.

Counsellor: 'Why do you think you feel that way?'

Client: 'I think my boss is jealous of me. She always dismisses any ideas I have or any views I express. It's really getting to me. In one way of course I know it's all the government's fault, the Health Service is just getting eaten away, we're all under tremendous pressure.'

The counsellor responded by taking the client's subject matter at face value: this could be to gather further information, or it could suggest that she is not considering whether the client's issue may have a connection with her own statement about time. The client's perception of jealousy in the boss could be a projection of her own envy of the boss's power (which could of course exist alongside the boss's possible envy or jealousy of her). The powerful metaphor of the National Health Service getting 'eaten away' has overtones of persecutory anxiety. Dimensions of envy and persecution (early oral stage) are beginning to appear beyond the anal-stage issues of power and authority.

Counsellor: 'So you feel it might not be all your boss – that she might be under pressure herself.'
Client: 'I suppose so. But I still hate having to have dealings with her. I find myself trying to avoid talking to her, and if I have to be in a meeting with her, I hate it. I feel a nobody, diminished. I always take anything difficult that happens in meetings personally – it's always my fault.'

Here, the counsellor reveals an anxiety about the boss being blamed: perhaps she is unconsciously aware that in this situation, she is the boss who is also 'under pressure herself'. The client continues to elaborate the paranoid and schizoid basis to her problem; her existence is at risk (feeling a 'nobody') and while her assumption of blame sounds like a touch of depressive anxiety (late oral stage) it is with a very persecutory tinge. The session is moving to oral-stage issues and dynamics.

Counsellor: 'Can you say a bit more how that feels?'
Client: 'It's like feeling invaded. I feel filled up with all her scorn and contempt. I can't stop thinking about whatever she said and whether it's true or not.'
Counsellor: 'How could you change that feeling?'
Client: 'I suppose I could focus on me rather than on the event, on whatever just happened.'
Counsellor: 'If you focus on yourself now, how are you feeling?'
Client: 'Well, I'm not feeling completely empty, not full either. The question is whether I feel I'm worth anything. When my boss speaks I feel totally worthless, like a piece of shit.'

The client feels in danger of being invaded by total badness, showing projective processes at work – early oral stage. She is preoccupied with emptiness and fullness, in a metaphor reminiscent of faeces as weapon and the bad breast. The counsellor has by now become embroiled in the client's vicious and persecutory inner world. Her unconscious awareness of the transference may also have played a part in her adopting the early oral defence of denial: she attempts to change the client's feelings rather than explore them. Her challenge to the client is also, at a conscious level, an appeal to her strength and autonomy. The client responds momentarily by defining herself as more separate. However, she quickly relapses back into the persecution/authority issue on the cusp between the oral and anal stages, expressed as feeling 'not empty but not full' and 'like a piece of shit'.

> *Counsellor*: 'That sounds like an awful feeling. How do you usually cope with it?'
> *Client*: 'Usually I cut off from the person who makes me feel it, walk away from them, write them off. I don't really want to go on doing that. I've lost a lot of friendships that way. And I can't really walk out of my job. I'm trapped. It's so humiliating.'
> *Counsellor*: 'This has been happening for quite a time in your life.'
> *Client*: 'Really, it goes back to how we all felt as a family whenever my father lost his job. He'd come home defeated, angry, humiliated, and we'd all feel the same. Except then he would take it out on us.'
> *Counsellor*: 'What was that like?'
> *Client*: 'Frightening. He'd shout and find fault with everything I did, we'd all wait for the day he'd find work again so he wouldn't be at home. I suppose I just learned to shut up, keep quiet and keep out of his way.'

Client and counsellor create a working alliance which enables some constructive exploration to take place. The counsellor has regained her perspective and realised that the client is not going to snap out of feeling humiliated and got at: her feelings have got to be addressed. Her first, empathic remark in this section allows the client to reflect on her (oral-stage) tendency to cut off those who cause her anxiety. She realises that she has lost 'friendships', indicating that she has grasped some depressive position ambivalence (people are both good and bad) and a capacity to deal with the situation as it is, rather than simply changing her perceptions (walking away from the trigger for her feelings). When the counsellor remains accepting and interested, the client reaches deeper, relating present reality to her past experience.

> *Counsellor*: 'What would you like to have said to him?'
> *Client*: 'What I'd really like to say is: "You're crap". I'd like to say that to my boss too: "You're crap".'
> *Counsellor*: 'How does it feel to say that?'
> *Client*: 'Well, rather useless really. If I really said that, I'd lose my job and then I'd be no better off than my father. We're all just pawns in the same system – powerless. I can't say what I want any

more than he could – that was why he was a bully at home. It wasn't really his fault, it's the system's. But it makes me want to destroy people like that.'
Counsellor: 'We have to finish now.'

The counsellor was perhaps feeling under (anal-stage) pressure to produce a resolution in the client in order to demonstrate her worth as a counsellor. She leaves her position of simply being alongside the client, pushing her into an action which may well express the counsellor's feelings as well as the client's. While the client does indeed find her early anal anger, the situation is not resolved. She portrays her father as a victim as well as a bully, and her oral-stage anxieties about her own existence, her confusion about where she ends and other people begin, underlie her difficulty in standing up for herself. She is identified with her father, and immediately she attacks him she collapses. The counsellor, in trying to side with her against him, over-simplified the situation (splitting); she was perhaps tempted by her own anger at the effects on her of the patriarchal nature of society, mediated at this moment by the potential judgement from me and the rest of the group.

The client reveals how powerfully destructive she feels her anger to be. Perhaps she felt it as an unexploded bomb which could have destroyed her father, her family and thereby herself. In the transference, she may fear that her anger might similarly endanger not only herself and the counsellor but the whole group.

The counsellor's abrupt ending mirrors the anxious beginning. Had she at some level heard the threat in the client's comment about wanting to destroy? Perhaps she also felt angry and demoralised that her attempt to finish the exercise on an up-beat was frustrated.

Reviewing the exercise afterwards, the client was surprised to hear that the counsellor had felt 'on trial', in relation to her as well as the group. The persecutory dynamics started from the situation itself, and the counsellor's unconscious perception of me as an oral- or anal-stage ogre made her anxious to keep control of the session and, above all, its boundaries ('We have seventeen minutes'; 'We have to finish now'). No doubt her own persecutory anxiety also supplied her with her own reasons for wanting to steer away from more dangerous areas, such as her fear of the client's anger. However, she was probably also experiencing the client's anxious inner world through projective identification.

We can see that the oral- and anal-stage problems at issue were relational, rather than belonging to any one person. Both students, and beyond them quite possibly the group as a whole, were engaged in the question of how to use power constructively: was it destructive or could it be channelled? Both students had good reason to experience others as oppressively powerful, because of the reality of the prejudice they met; yet they also felt empty and disempowered, indicating that there was some degree of projection in addition. Oral dynamics and deficits were hampering the resolution of anal-stage issues.

The client experienced the counsellor as supportive but passive. She would have welcomed a more challenging presence to help her address the aggression under the surface, although she realised she would also have been annoyed by having to confront her mode of relating and its impact on others. It is clear that this particular relationship held the potential, over time, to explore need, anger, power and disempowerment.

We can glimpse the complexity of the transferred relationships between counsellor and client. With hindsight, the client thought that she may have heard the counsellor's peremptory opening as though she were the father of her childhood. She became quick to supply the counsellor with plentiful material, while 'shutting up' about her feelings towards the counsellor. Her anger leaked out, however, in both the content (the rude manager and critical father) and the process. She seldom answered the counsellor's questions directly, did not give her the reward of a clear resolution, and constantly hints about her (unconscious) dissatisfaction. The observing group makes an appearance as the cruel system which renders its members powerless and humiliated, with me as the heartless manager/father.

The counsellor had her own counter-transference: she was already expecting to be judged negatively – after all, this was a training session, although the purpose was not to judge her as a counsellor. She had her own history of vulnerability to judgement, to feeling diminished and being under the power and control of others. The sharpness of some of the client's remarks were not lost on her, although she had not had enough experience or training to know what to do with them. Working in front of the group reverberated both students' experiences of social oppression, as lesbians and coming from working-class backgrounds.

There is no way, of course, to use this whole wealth of material directly in a session. It would be impossible to hold all the factors consciously in mind, and trying to do so would block most of our sensitivity. It is more a question of retaining as open a mind as possible, with the 'free-floating attention' advocated by Freud. The feelings, sensations, thoughts and hunches we shrug off in everyday life can then be used for the benefit of the therapeutic or counselling work.

Tolerating our own experience as therapist or counsellor, rather than trying to get away from it, enables us to maintain a fuller connection with the client. We can monitor how our remarks might be heard, and whether our own feelings may match those of the client in a process of 'trial identification' (Casement 1985). While we should always question how far our feelings are our own, and how far we can attribute them to the client, those which seem to be the result of projective identification often have a subtly different flavour; we may realise, 'I'm feeling sad (or anxious, or angry), but it's not my kind of sadness'. This makes the feelings easier to manage and use. We can subliminally say to ourselves: 'I'm feeling criticised, inadequate and redundant: how interesting! I wonder what this phenomenon means, and why I am feeling it right now? What are the subtle details of this experience? What has it to do with me and my client?'

We cannot tell what turn our practice session might have taken if the counsellor had felt able to manage and use her own feelings, the reality of the current situation and her common background with the client. We can see, however, that while simple attention was of benefit to the client, close attention to the therapeutic relationship as it is experienced by both participants, its setting and the social and personal context of both therapist and client has enormous potential to enrich therapeutic opportunities. This attention is the essence of using Object Relations in practice.

We have only been able to touch on a few possible associations to this brief example. Concepts such as projection, splitting, denial, repression, transference and the relational framework help us focus in detail on relational processes. So too do Klein's concepts of the paranoid-schizoid and depressive positions; Fairbairn's exciting, rejecting and ideal inner objects and associated ego parts; Winnicott's concepts of transitional phenomena, therapy as play, the true and false self; Balint's one-body, two-body and three-body modes, the yearning for the harmonious interpenetrating mix-up, our variable success in creating co-operative partnerships with other people, his analysis of malignant and benign regression; Guntrip's evocation of the suffering and the need of the schizoid client, defended against by anger, paranoia, obsessions; and Bowlby's inclusion of the real happenings in people's lives and his secure, ambivalent and avoidant patterns of attachment. All these ideas can help us develop a personal framework as we assimilate them in our own way.

OBJECT RELATIONS AND OTHER APPROACHES

Few techniques or therapeutic approaches clash irrevocably with an Object Relations perspective, although there will be differences in emphasis. Winnicott, Klein and Balint have shown that it is quite possible to hold relational premises alongside other assumptions of what a person is and how therapeutic work can be useful, although how satisfactory such a dual basis is remains an individual question.

In approaches such as Gestalt, Transactional Analysis and body-oriented therapies, the meaning to client and therapist of a technical structure, or of touch or the lack of it, can be borne in mind or explored. Does a suggested technical structure come over as a helpful framework, a peremptory order or a dehumanising dismissal? Does touch feel like a fusion with the universe, a seduction, does it promise more than will be delivered, or is the experience of touch reassuring, grounding or guiding? Object Relations as attitude rather than dogma can help therapists and counsellors become more sensitive to their clients and to themselves, and more able to use their relational awareness to enhance their work.

An example from the early days of my own practice illustrates the extra dimension a relational perspective can add to other therapeutic frames.

Suzanne was in her early thirties, white, an adult entrant into the middle class. She had driven herself from an early age to achieve the educational success which would enable her to escape from the dreary, limited life she saw around her in her country of origin. Although successful in this, her relationships felt unfulfilling and her work lacking in meaning. She was thin, driven, tense, and appeared on the surface competent and even intimidating. As she talked she seemed hardly to notice my presence. She found what she discovered about herself interesting, but made little apparent emotional contact with either herself or me.

I frequently felt redundant or inferior, but did not bring this into the sessions for some time, partly because there was always a sense of movement and direction. During the first year and a half, Suzanne's work situation improved through her efforts to carve out an area of relative autonomy; and towards the end of this period she found, to her surprise, that she had left one of her two sexual partners, the one she saw as intriguing but self-centred. She was embarrassed to find herself moving towards her other partner, whom she described as warm but dull; she worried that she would no longer be able to play down this relationship to her friends.

As her physical tension gave way, Suzanne was disquieted to find herself becoming less thin. She let me know, in asides and by implication, that although she found the new developments in her life difficult and shameful, she knew that the sessions and her relationship with me were important. I also felt they were important, despite her lack of expression of either attachment or anger towards me, although I seemed to be implicated in her change and discomfiture.

Suzanne began to have strange sensations during her sessions. They started as soon as she sat down, and gradually took her over. Her mind emptied and her body took on a paralysed feel as though she were heavily drugged. Pulsing spread from her head down her spine. She had the sense that the front of her body was being broken, and that her left arm was being dragged from its socket. This gave her no pain or distress; she simply observed it. Her eyes remained closed throughout, and she reported her strange experiences to me clearly and without anxiety. I told her when the last part of the session was approaching so that she had time to orient herself again. She was able to do this without difficulty, and was always ready to leave at the end of the session. These sensations never occurred at any other time.

Like Suzanne, I felt unmoved, though intrigued, by what was happening. As usual it seemed to be something she was going through in my presence but without my involvement. Yet although I seemed superfluous, I clearly was not: these experiences only occurred with me, and were therefore part of our shared world rather than something that was within Suzanne alone. My general hypothesis was that Suzanne had begun to loosen her internal grip on herself through developing some degree of reliance on me and on the predictable therapeutic setting. This had allowed a bubble of dissociated experience to break surface in a form which held both past and present meaning.

Some of the past meaning emerged when Suzanne told me that her premature birth had taken place when her mother was very young, in a remote rural hospital where medical care was basic. It had been a prolonged and difficult labour, and because her mother was heavily sedated she was unable to take an active part in the birth process. Finally dragged out with forceps, Suzanne's breastbone had been broken and her left shoulder dislocated in the rush to save her own life and her mother's. Her mother remained barely conscious for several days, while Suzanne was in a precarious state in the hospital nursery. The correlation between these events and Suzanne's sensations was remarkable: Suzanne had no previous experience and little knowledge of psychotherapy, and had never heard of people re-experiencing birth or early infancy. Many questions remained, however. Did Suzanne's unusual states reflect a primary state of non-differentiation or her post-birth isolation? Did they symbolise the lack of emotional contact with her mother which continued to the present day? In what way did they relate to the continuing apparent dissociation of her need for contact? What did they have to say about the way she and I related in the present?

Different theoretical approaches would see Suzanne's experience in different ways. Humanistic regressive or bodywork approaches, without an added Object Relations perspective, might view Suzanne's experience as the reliving of a dissociated traumatic memory on a bodily level. This viewpoint implies that a person can be seen as a discrete unit; to be whole, as much of one's past living as possible should be potentially available. The repudiation of intolerable experience involves the cramping of the whole organism. With a relaxed body and mind, no experience is disallowed and we live more fully with ourselves and in the world (see Keleman 1985; Lowen 1975).

Many psychotherapeutic views of infant development suggest an initial autistic or merged state out of which the baby gradually individuates. Freud and Mahler (Mahler et al. 1975), Fairbairn, Winnicott and Balint, and the humanistic theorists Lake (1966) and Grof (1975), all postulate a greater or lesser degree of early symbiosis with the mother which may be preceded by autistic encapsulation. The details and extent of these cut-off states or experiences of limitlessness differ, and all are placed under question by more recent research. Suzanne had no awareness in these episodes of even the possible existence of another person. Could this be explained as a return to a merged or encapsulated state?

An early Freudian approach might highlight the emotionless quality of Suzanne's state, seeing it as an hysterical reliving of a traumatic memory which had been split off from the personality as a whole, and which could be re-integrated through finding and expressing the missing emotions. A later Freudian approach might additionally focus on Suzanne's regression to a less active and individuated state. Her awareness of the world or of any other person was curtailed, and even her ability to move was temporarily submerged. Yet there was something Suzanne sought in this state: she did not struggle to get out of it, and found it a relief to 'let go' into it. Her experience could be framed as a conflict between her wish to create or destroy, move forwards or move backwards, embrace life or retreat from it; these episodes could manifest a temporary dominance of the death instinct with its aim of returning to simpler, less active, earlier states of being, epitomised in total non-being, ultimately death.

A Kleinian viewpoint might focus on the emptiness of Suzanne's experienced state, noting that at least by association it was connected with a traumatic birth followed by isolation. The Kleinian death instinct is stimulated by birth, and has as its aim the abolition of the perceived reality of birth and separateness and an illusory return to the pre-natal state. The life instinct, in the form of attachment to the world and to life after birth, is awakened by being fed, held and comforted. Suzanne's mother was unable to give her this contact after a dreadful birth process, which could have left Suzanne's death drives highly sensitised and comparatively unmitigated by feeling loved and protected. Suzanne might have taken in a deathly inner object through her experience of her unresponding mother, and would then have been forced to project large parts of her death-dominated inner world. This in turn would have given rise to intense paranoid-schizoid fears through the projected fragments rebounding back on her emptiness.

A Kleinian view would go beyond the historical meaning in Suzanne's experience; as well as reliving an early infantile state, it would hold a specific transferential significance. It is this connecting of past association with the current therapeutic relationship that Object Relations particularly addresses. With or without the concept of the death instinct, Object Relations facilitates the exploration of events as relational happenings in a shared world.

As my own awareness of this dimension grew, the meaning of Suzanne's unconscious communication emerged more clearly. The contrast between her subjective self-sufficiency and her actual vulnerability as she lay, eyes closed, open to any impingement, seemed more and more striking. Her regressed states seemed to convey a message both of rejection and its opposite, trapped in the closed system described by Fairbairn as the sequel of trauma.

We thus began to understand Suzanne's detachment, epitomised in these special states, as intra- and interpersonal communications about dependency. Suzanne did not welcome this idea, but addressing it helped her become more able to take in her partner's love and care. As she did so, he seemed less boring and stupid, and she began to feel more simply loving towards him. Eventually they had a child, which at first gave Suzanne anguish. Attachment meant pain, weakness and loss, yet she could not bear the thought of staying aloof from her own child. During the pregnancy and birth she gave in, accepting new joy and terrible fear. Yet with me, her need was inferred rather than acknowledged, a dangerous secret which she wanted me to know but hated me to articulate.

As her son's babyhood passed, Suzanne gradually collapsed. As an active toddler he no longer embodied the helpless, needy infant within her whom she could care for vicariously; perhaps their psychological separation reverberated the traumatic separation of her birth. Suzanne became fearful and fragile, unable to cope with shops, work or friends, able only to come to sessions, look after her child and stay under the protection of her partner. The closed system was increasingly giving way.

In sessions, the regressed states returned in a different form. Suzanne now felt as though she was leaving her body and floating off in endless space, again without emotion or awareness of any other person. Unlike the earlier phase, when I had felt as numb as Suzanne, I began to feel indignant at being excluded. It was as though, before, I had taken in the emotional paralysis that Suzanne was experiencing and could not see that we were both captured by her unresponsiveness. The underlying need, fear and rage which she and her mother (and I) must have felt had remained split off and unresolved, contributing powerfully to the distant and detached nature of both Suzanne's and her mother's relationships. These feelings were gradually coming into the picture between us.

The freeze progressively thawed, and I began to enter Suzanne's enclosed states more resolutely. Her strenuous efforts to deny all dependency came to a peak when I said that she was trying to pretend that even as a baby, she had had no need of her mother. 'I can give birth to myself', she rejoined.

The delusion thus laid bare could no longer be sustained; and slowly Suzanne began to get the feeling that someone, somewhere was suffering while she was off on her pain-free, emotion-free trips. One day the realisation hit her that her split-off states were a way of escaping from dreadful isolation. She felt unbearable grief and longing through her whole body: a vacuum was where another person should be, and she realised she had wanted to die. She understood that although this vacuum was originally visited upon her, she now created and even sought it. Her lifelong dread of death and darkness eased as she faced the non-being she had sought as a mitigation of her torment. This marked the 'new beginning' described so movingly by Balint.

Suzanne was now far more accepting of her dependency in relation to everyone except her mother: she was the bad figure, while I was all good. This splitting gave way when I finally exploded at the passivity which she seemed to be dangling in front of me infuriatingly. The fact of my expostulation was due to my failure to contain and reflect on my feelings, a mixture of frustration, envy and impotent anger; but the feelings I experienced were Suzanne's as well as mine. It seemed that she had transmitted in direct emotional form the unbearableness of being in an inescapable relationship with someone utterly unresponsive and apparently self-sufficient. I felt with her as she had felt with her mother. This rage could now be endured and expressed, constructively by Suzanne as well as by default by me. She was furious with me for suddenly attacking her: I was no longer the perfect person but someone she hated as well as loved. However, in realising that I was imperfect and fallible, she could reclaim some of the power she had projected on to me, albeit perhaps less fully than if I had managed my feelings better.

As Suzanne thus gathered her strength, she did not lose her softness. Her family life gave her rich struggles and satisfaction, and she developed work which gave her more freedom, though still not enough fulfilment. A new separation loomed as her son became ready to start school; but instead of collapsing, she prepared for the new opportunities this would bring. In a beautiful parallel with her child, Suzanne decided that this was the time for her to leave therapy. The ending period was as rich as the beginning had seemed barren. She felt and shared a searing grief at our parting, without losing sight of the rightness of her decision. Both of us were rewarded with the opening up of Suzanne's life through the truly joint discoveries that emerged and the depth of contact that we eventually reached.

9

WORKING WITH DIFFERENCE AND DIVERSITY

Object Relations theorists and practitioners hold in common a belief in the centrality of relationship between people and within people. Relationship is conceived not as an easy process, but as an ambivalent expression of both our incompleteness and our autonomy. We are drawn by our need for affiliation to connect with others in the elusive shared phenomenon we call rapport, while the equal imperative to preserve our individuality fosters distance, conflict and estrangement. The fact of our separateness ensures misapprehension and mortality means certain anguish.

It is the same within ourselves. We cherish the impermanent sense of self that reveals us to ourselves and touches off the inner harmony which flees as we grasp at it. Being at war with ourselves, feeling barren or alienated from the springs of our selfhood are painful aspects of everyone's lives.

Any society must achieve its own balance between fusion and separateness, dependency and autonomy, if it is not to collapse or disappear; any society that has endured over time must therefore have a viable structure, although it probably depends on the creation of scapegoats to maintain its equilibrium. Object Relations offers an insight into the dynamics of prejudice in terms of Klein's bad object, Fairbairn's exciting and rejecting objects and Bowlby's insecure or avoidant attachment patterns. Demons are easily made when we identify with one side of a split: women for chauvinists, men for separatist feminists; foreigners and black people for extreme Western nationalist groups, racists for white liberals; encounter groups for some psychoanalysts, psychoanalysts for some humanistic practitioners. Groups and individuals are scapegoated in all societies, and under any status quo, people suffer injustice; under any revolution or upheaval people also suffer, though not necessarily the same group; under the next status quo, suffering continues.

Working against prejudice can thus be a self-proliferating activity to a depressing degree, because prejudice involves splitting and projection at its most raw and unconscious. There seems to be no real resolution other than to attempt to hold in mind as consciously as possible the full range of our own potentialities for love, hate and destructiveness. This is excruciatingly difficult, as we grasp at any opportunity to externalise what we cannot bear within, terrified of seeing ourselves like the groups we repudiate. While the difference this may make will be minuscule, it is still the only difference that can lead to real progress. It leans more towards working for justice, equality and the overall good rather than against the perpetrators of injustice, oppression and deprivation. Even this solution will not cover all eventualities: there will always be acts or attitudes that we feel compelled to oppose totally and fight against fully, and others that we as fully espouse. All we can then do is try to resist denying that hostile opposition breeds a counter-force, however inescapable our own position may be to us.

Object Relations cannot and should not take the place of social and political involvement; its theories can, however, inform our thinking and our actions. While relationship is not the whole of life, Object Relations reminds us to honour the internal and external relational background which sets much of the tone for experience, whether for the individual or society. It articulates the attention, discomfort and work which relationships take, including the one with ourselves, if they are to survive and grow through impasse, disappointment and loss.

The context from which psychoanalysis arose limited its initial application to the middle-class neurotic person within the social, cultural and family structures of central and northern Europe in the late nineteenth and early twentieth centuries. Object Relations has played a major though erratic part in enlarging the scope of psychoanalysis, most significantly in the development of work with clients in borderline states, and in increasing understanding of the psychology of psychotic states. A male-centred, heterosexually-biased account of the human being is inherent in Freudian theory, but his deliberate involvement of women in psychoanalysis contributed to the early attention given to gender difference. Klein, Deutsch and Horney (see Sayers 1991), were followed by feminist contributors (Eichenbaum and Orbach 1982; Chodorow 1989) in fruitfully addressing the experience of women.

In other areas, however, advances have been slower. Though theorists in the feminist tradition have led the way in addressing personal diversity, we have only a sketchy understanding of the personal and relational dynamics and needs of other minority groups in Western society. Class, sexual orientation and ethnicity are areas in which further work is urgently needed, together with the particular needs of disabled people, older people, and those with learning disabilities. This lack is exacerbated through the diminished social power which makes it difficult for these groups to develop a voice which will be listened to, and the obstacles hampering members of these groups from contributing directly to psychological theory whether as practitioners, patients or clients. Given the human propensity to create insiders and outsiders, there will be an enduring need for psychotherapists and counsellors to bring rigorous thought, honest feeling and fresh relationship to the diversity of human experience.

BORDERLINE AND PSYCHOTIC STATES

The widespread closure of psychiatric hospitals is leading more people in borderline or psychotic states to seek psychotherapeutic help, especially from practitioners working in the public sphere. Those working privately may see fewer unless they offer places at low fees, perhaps because they are completing their training or are newly qualified. It is crucial for all practitioners to make accurate assessments of potential clients, to know when and how to refer people on to specialised provision, and to develop the capacity to work with those whose sense of reality may be fragile. This section is addressed particularly to practitioners whose initial training did not address these issues from a relational perspective, but it does not substitute for training in assessment, psychiatry and practice.

Borderline and psychotic states are modes of being in which the sense of self and other, of what arises from within the person and what from outside, is fragile, distorted or fractured. This is to some extent a subjective assessment on the part of the assessor: the person in a psychotic or borderline state can seldom assess her disturbance for herself. As the diagnosing of psychotic or borderline states is a relational process, it is therefore nebulous and open to misjudgement as a result of the assessor's limited viewpoint or the confusion that arises through projective identification. Psychiatric diagnosis has been used in some parts of the world as an agent of social control; and cultural differences have been wrongly construed as mental illness.

Apart from diagnostic pitfalls and the intrapsychic particularities of people in borderline or psychotic states, the practitioner has difficulties of his own to contend with when working with people he perceives as odd or different. Personal conceptions of madness carry projections from the most murky corners of our inner worlds. The mad person brings to life our dread of losing a sense of personhood and the boundaries of identity; our fear of not managing or making sense of what we experience; the isolation that arises from the failure of others to validate and confirm our perceptions; and our terror of losing control. The borderline person may evoke overt or subterranean rage and panic by her failure to offer the basic empathy on which everyday communication relies, by her apparent refusal to allot us the status of a full human being, and by her consistent misinterpreting of what we do and say, while her evident lack of psychosis may make her way of relating seem particularly intolerable. It is therefore easy to dismiss the experience of the psychotic or borderline person in a fearful or antagonistic rejection of relationship which may be backed up by projective identification. We may deny the reality of her mental state, avoid engaging with her, denude her experience of meaning or focus on her pathology rather than her personhood. When we add the inherent difficulties arising from borderline and psychotic modes of relating, we can see that where intense reactions or fear of madness are aroused in the practitioner, special attention should always follow.

The person in a borderline state may be in a transient or relatively permanent state of disturbance. Most of us have experienced a temporary or fleeting borderline experience, with the faltering of the boundary between rational knowledge and emotional conviction, perhaps under the impact of psychotherapeutic work which takes us to the edge of our ordinary ability to cope. When extreme anxiety and vulnerability break through our usual defences, more primitive ways of managing feelings are revealed, based on the manipulation of perception rather than the recognition of reality. Thus we may 'know' in the absence of evidence that people at work are gossiping about us, and even be convinced of who is saying what, because the intensity of our paranoid fears has overwhelmed our ability to differentiate between feeling and fact. The borderline area of the personality can be the growing edge of maturation; even a small advance in our ability to contain and manage our feelings represents the reclaiming of experience from the rule of infantile processes.

Where the borderline state is more permanent, it may show itself either as extreme instability or unchanging rigidity. The person in a borderline state may be in a perpetual flux in which her moods, the way she sees the world and experiences other people, her own sense of self, change continually, giving rise to constant confusion and anxiety. While she may be briefly psychotic, even this will be unstable; she is more likely to distort her perception of reality than completely change it. A comment such as 'That must have been difficult for you' may be experienced as deeply gratifying ('You're the only person who's ever understood me') or as a vicious attack ('You're always undermining me'). This kind of borderline state has been described in terms of Balint's two-person mode, Guntrip's in-and-out régime and other descriptions of a rapid oscillation between hysterical and schizoid processes.

Alternatively, a systematic set of defences may prevent even an ordinary degree of emotional flexibility. Cut-off states such as Fairbairn's schizoid state, Winnicott's false self, the narcissistic disturbances described by the American theorists Heinz Kohut (Kohut and Wolf 1978) and Otto Kernberg (1975), and the neo-Kleinian concept of 'pathological organisation' (Steiner 1993) are examples of this kind of fixed borderline state. Whether unstable or rigid, the borderline condition rests on a disturbed, but not destroyed, relation to reality, and a difficulty in seeing other people as full individuals in their own right.

'Borderline Personality Disorder' (American Psychiatric Association 1995) is the psychiatric diagnosis given to those showing borderline states of the unstable kind, when it is a way of life rather than a passing response to stress. A personality disorder implies that the disturbed mode runs throughout the personality rather than being confined to a bubble or a strand within a more functional whole. The disturbed mode may be unstable borderline, schizoid, paranoid, narcissistic or other, and there are thus a range of overlapping personality disorders falling within the broadly defined borderline state. Building a therapeutic rather than a collusive or simply superficial relationship will be difficult; and where the client has little mature functioning, change may be limited and slow. In practice, a relationship which is supportive rather than challenging may be more beneficial. For those who really wish to change (and who are therefore more likely to have a nugget of hope and trust in themselves and others), suffering will be intense, involving rage, anxiety and raw dread, perhaps progressing to grief, guilt and regret as they become more able to tolerate depressive anxieties.

The borderline state may thus be a passing and potentially creative phase or a more established and painful way of being and relating. Similarly, conditions such as eating disorders, drug or alcohol abuse and other destructive or self-destructive patterns of behaviour may be anything between a brief response to intolerable pressure and a permanent substitute for more satisfying modes of being.

Psychosis which is relatively fixed and which does not arise purely from physical trauma falls into two inexact and poorly understood categories: affective psychoses such as manic depression, and schizophrenic disorders. These categories cover a wide range of behaviour, merging into each other and into borderline or more normal modes of being. These psychoses often arise in adolescence or early adulthood, probably through a combination of psychological and physiological upheaval. A detailed description is not possible here: but the affective psychoses are more related to mood disturbance, while schizophrenia is characterised by disturbed perception and thought. People may suffer from a single psychotic episode or from more continuous, intermittent or chronic psychotic states.

Other psychotic or severe confusional states arise in brief reactive psychoses following overwhelming trauma; from drug or alcohol use or withdrawal; or from an organic disorder such as brain damage or disease, or the dementia that arises from the deterioration of old age. While Object Relations has addressed the first of these, the others are more often seen as of physical rather than psychological significance.

A practitioner working with someone in a psychotic or borderline state will need to judge the kind of approach and relationship which will be of benefit, and whether a specialised setting is needed. The same relational principles apply as with any other client; it is only the therapeutic mode which may be different. A relationship can be therapeutic to the extent that the intrapsychic and external worlds of practitioner and client are encompassed, including their personal and practical limits, with the purpose of facilitating or supporting the client's maturity.

Nature and Nurture

The causes and therefore the treatment of the psychoses in particular is a subject of controversy. An extreme medical view is that psychosis is an inevitable manifestation of biological abnormality requiring physiological treatment; psychological aspects are seen as largely irrelevant. An extreme psychotherapeutic view sees psychosis solely as a fixation at or regression to early disturbance. Medication is seen as irrelevant or even oppressive: while it may lessen suffering, it does so through stealing the client's humanity (Winnicott 1949b; Laing 1960).

Both views are built on a one-sided view of the person, rather than a recognition that we are subject to both biological and environmental impact and that we actively and idiosyncratically construct personal meaning in relation to these impacts. Psychoanalytic theory, research and our own experience suggest that the organisation of experience into inner and outer, self and other, truth and fantasy is a definite achievement which remains more or less fragile but for which we are genetically pre-equipped. It could not happen without sensory and perceptual input, a mind to interpret and maintain coherence and an environment to support development. Our different sensitivities must influence our vulnerability to stress in general and to the various stresses which arise from our biological inheritance, our social and relational world and its inner counterpart, and the physical environment with its chemical pollutants and other dangers. These individual differences are themselves a function of the complex interplay of all these factors with each other and our own agency of perception and interpretation: the 'I'.

All experienced conditions, from broken legs to psychotic states to senile dementia, involve psychological meaning as well as genetic or biological particularity. Freud and Klein made matter-of-fact assumptions of individual variations in sensitivity through their concepts of the life and death instincts and the relative balance between them, seeing external factors as playing a supportive rather than a leading role in the development of disturbance. This did not stop either theorist from investigating the psychology of what they conceptualised as ultimately biological differences. They worked from the belief that there is a spark, an originality, a source in the human being which enables her to develop her own ways of managing difficulties of whatever origin, to some extent. Although current views of psychosis are beginning to include biological, cultural and psychological perspectives, the terms on which these factors meet remain mysterious.

Object Relations offers varied psychological perspectives on psychosis, with some theorists, such as Klein, Winnicott and even early Laing (1960), including biological predisposition as a background assumption. Internal reality is seen as overwhelming the distinction between externally and internally derived perceptions, sometimes blotting out perceptions of external reality as well. Fairbairn viewed psychosis as the internal objects taking all the perceptual space and experienced therefore as external. Winnicott suggests the psychotic person is in a developmentally early state of fusion with the world, while Klein emphasised the fragmentation that arises from extreme splitting and massive projection. The loss of the capacity for symbolisation leads to the schizophrenic experience of a shattered self or selves in a shattered world, where the destruction of meaning gives rise to concrete dread and emptiness.

These frameworks help us to stay in relation without denying either the circularity and defensive misconception of much psychotic thinking, or the possible contribution of physiological factors. However, we are still a long way from an approach which could be called integrated. We do not have a theory of the person in which the division between the physical and the mental is transcended, or even one which does justice to both perspectives. The theoretical bases on which combined approaches rest are largely pragmatic. The philosophical centrality of issues such as meaning, free will and suffering ensure that individual views of psychosis and severe disturbance must inevitably differ, depending on circumstances, client and practitioner; they should rightly remain the subject of uncertainty and debate.

It is a matter for personal and professional judgement as to the kind of relationship client and therapist feel able to embark on when psychosis and borderline modes are significant. The therapeutic relationship may take the form of a psychotherapeutic journey which in searching for contact and meaning brings forth pain; or therapeutic counselling in which the focus is on relational support to cope with practicalities (which, of course, carry their own meaning); or a partial or total living situation which offers consistent rather than fleeting structure, relation and activity; or a mixture, or different emphases at different times.

The question of medication and psychotherapy reflects the tensions arising from our uneasy distinction between mental and physical causes, and medical and psychotherapeutic values. While drugs cannot create meaning, they can either alleviate or increase suffering through the chemical diminishment of extreme emotions and psychotic processes. This may be experienced as a clearing away of the fog which obscures personal meaning and capacity; as the merciful mitigation of unbearable pain; as the confirmation of the suspicion that one's suffering is unbearable to the therapist; as the ripping away of a personal creation, leaving an intolerable reality or a sense of impotent futility; or as evidence of one's own freakish difference from common humanity. Practitioners will have their own philosophies of the value of medication in psychotherapy, and they will be as influential as their clients in the creation of the meaning of medical intervention. Medication enables many thousands of sufferers, whether depressed or psychotic, to live more meaningful lives, and to withhold or discourage the use of medication can lead to stasis and increase the risk of suicide; but to force or even encourage the taking of medication can also lead to suicidal despair in people whose psychosis or whose anguish involves necessary defence or a high degree of personal meaning, when meaning and autonomy are deeply cherished.

There are no easy answers, nor the prospect of any; too often, a lack of resources makes a mockery of the careful consideration of individual needs. Where this is possible, we are left with the responsibility for thoughtfully and responsively encompassing the personal and interpersonal realities of each practitioner and each client; a responsibility for which we may feel ill-equipped, but which is none the less real.

Differences Involving Social Power

Psychoanalysis does not have a particularly good track record in working with the whole community. People subject to racial prejudice have at times been judged as unsuitable for therapy because their problems are external rather than internal, older people because of their supposed rigidity and inability to change. Homosexuals, lesbians and bisexuals were pathologised as fixated at an immature stage of development, while the disabled and learning-disabled were barely mentioned. The ideal psychoanalytic patient was the white, heterosexual, middle-class, articulate, young or middle-aged person, inhibited rather than impulsive and able to pay private fees.

Despite these limitations, Object Relations and other branches of psychoanalysis share a tradition of concern to reach beyond what constrictions could be seen. Analysts from Freud and Ferenczi onwards have worked with patients who were unable to pay for treatment as well as those whose prognosis was poor and for whom the conceptual and methodological frame needed modification. Klein saw children younger than any whom analysts had worked with before, including psychotic children and those who would now be called autistic. Fairbairn allotted a good proportion of his time to hospital and clinic work, working with psychotic patients and traumatised children. Winnicott's area of work spanned vast numbers of ordinary families, as well as children in care and delinquents; he gave advice to parents and foster parents and worked creatively with psychotic and borderline patients. Guntrip's patients included manic-depressive patients and others in breakdown; and Bowlby had a powerful impact on social policy in relation to young children.

Psychotherapy can no longer ignore the multicultural society of today. Racism and other forms of prejudice have been effectively deconstructed as a process of extreme and unconscious splitting and projection (Kovel 1988; Rustin 1991). White psychoanalysts and psychotherapists were and are not exempt from the ingrained prejudice of Western society, and one result is that our theoretical understanding of difference is at an early stage.

Roland's study of the transposition of psychoanalysis to Indian and Japanese contexts (Roland 1988) reflects on culturally-dependent variation in the inner world. A central difference is the degree of differentiation between subject and object which in Western cultures is taken to an extreme degree, while other cultural modes may engender more flowing connections both interpersonally and intrapsychically. Working with people from non-Western cultures involves different expectations of what constitutes development and personal maturity, and different modes of understanding and communicating: differences which can easily be missed or pathologised by the white Western practitioner. Cultural difference is fundamental, yet often remains unacknowledged. While practitioners expect to read up on areas such as eating disorders or borderline states, few see the necessity to acquire some knowledge of their clients' cultural backgrounds, perhaps through novels and films, and historical, geographical and sociological sources. Without some sense of this, communication at any depth seems impossible (see d'Ardenne and Mahtani 1989).

Where prejudice is a factor, cultural difference acquires additional meaning and splitting is at its most unknowing extreme. Most practitioners would agree that for the dominant groupings in Western society, prejudice can be monitored and perhaps limited, but not eradicated. Similarly, those subject to prejudice from their earliest years cannot remain unaffected. Sinason's compassionate study (Sinason 1992) offers a graphic portrayal of the painful internal conjunction of social prejudice and individual psychological processes in learning-disabled and multiply-disabled people. She reveals the characteristics commonly associated with the disabled as often constructed rather than authentic, the manifestation of the projections of mainstream society on to these groups of outsiders, who internalize them defensively.

What gets split off and projected in prejudice is what is feared or envied by the majority culture. Thus rampant sexuality is ascribed to homosexuals and lesbians. Disabled people are treated as helpless and pre-sexual, while those with learning disabilities are even more overtly equated with children or animals. Even the lower classes are expected to share the labels of lesser intelligence, reckless physicality and stunted subjectivity. Black people have all these feared and desired qualities projected on to them with an anal tinge of dirt and smell; while less black people, such as Asians and Jews, are attacked enviously as greedy and conspiratorial.

Personal factors such as ethnicity, disability, class or sexual orientation may become confluent with injustice or trauma in the inner world. A child may view sexual or physical abuse and her despised ethnicity as one factor rather than two; or her low educational achievement as an intrinsic aspect of the disability which reduces her social worth.

The traditional pathologising of non-heterosexual orientation illustrates how prejudice of any kind obstructs both perception and thought. Freud, in advance of his day, asserted that a change to heterosexuality should not and could not be an aim of psychoanalytic treatment and that heterosexuality is not a 'self-evident fact' (Freud 1905b, S.E. 7, footnote 1915). He overturned Jones' recommendation that homosexuals be barred from membership of the Psycho-Analytic Societies (see Stubrin 1994: 90–1). But his various statements implying that non-heterosexual orientations were immature, pathological or perverse provided a hook on which later analysts could hang their prejudice, allowing them to see non-heterosexuality as intrinsically inferior.

Differentiation between gender identity and sexual orientation is often partial. With heterosexuality as the only paradigm, lesbians and homosexuals are seen either as stuck in a pre-genital sexuality, as narcissistically relating to mirror images of themselves, or as identified with the opposite sex (O'Connor and Ryan 1993). Nor have the particularities of homosexual, bisexual and lesbian internal structuring been separated out from the impact of prejudice. It is difficult to ascertain what arises from social invalidation and what from sexual orientation, and the individually variable impacts of biology, early relationship and culture are not yet understood (Stoller 1968, 1985; Chodorow 1994). Despite our ignorance, prejudice remains significant in psychotherapeutic circles; as recently as 1994, some of the major psychoanalytic training organisations in Britain were shown to be covertly discriminating against non-heterosexuals (Ellis 1994).

Although intentional discrimination on the grounds of race, class, disability or sexual orientation is now usually abhorred, at least officially, in mainstream organisations, the movements to promote equality of opportunity and the respectful acknowledgement of difference have only partially ameliorated the situation. The fear of being seen as bigoted or insensitive acts as a mental straitjacket which is equally effective as were earlier assumptions, blocking thought and free-ranging discussion in a similar way. The result of all these factors is that we understand very little of how any sexual orientation develops (Stubrin 1994), comparatively little about the details of class, age and cultural differences and not enough about the psychology of power differentials.

10

THE PREMISES OF OBJECT RELATIONS

All theories are built on foundations which limit and organise their concepts. The assumptions which underlie psychotherapeutic theories are seldom articulated, making them all the more powerful in their invisibility.

This chapter touches briefly on some of the premises of human nature on which Object Relations theories rest. The purpose is not to offer a definitive view, but to raise similar questions for others. The usability of any theory of the person resides largely in how far it has been assimilated into personal thinking and practice, and readers will, I hope, use this book to uncover and explore their own philosophies of human life and psychotherapeutic change.

THE INDIVIDUAL AND THE GROUP

Paradoxically, Object Relations focuses its attention on individual experience while defining the essence of this experience as beyond the individual. Our completeness is identified with our incompleteness; our unity with our disjointed nature.

Some biologists suggest that insects such as ants and bees may be best understood by treating the whole colony as a single organism. Each insect can be perceived as a tiny sub-unit with its own differentiated functions like the parts of a single body. A body part, ant or human being cannot survive alone; to view individual experience as autonomous is a convention comparable to defining an arm or a foot as a viable entity.

The interdependence which lies at the heart of Object Relations views of the person therefore raises questions about its overwhelmingly individual focus. Object Relations texts do not usually make clear that the psychology of a person is a deliberately isolated part of a larger system. Despite the avowed centrality of relational needs and capacities, Object Relations still treats the individual as finite.

Adding paradox to paradox, the self itself is understood in terms of subdivisions which derive from those others who form the group of which the individual is a part. The Object Relations self, or ego as the experienced or structured self, reflects our social nature; it can neither develop nor long survive outside a relational context. The autistic person, shut out of full relationship, is stuck in an asocial, rigid treadmill which seems lacking in meaning; we view such people as missing some essential part of what it is to be human. Without a felt other, there can be no I; without an object, no subject.

To have a subjective sense of self, we import the other, and otherness metaphorically resides within us. Without this otherness within, there is nothing from which to distinguish ourselves. We cannot be aware of ourselves, pleased with ourselves, frustrated with ourselves. We can experience neither conflict nor harmony, nor even the oneness that contrasts with our usual state of dissonance. We all harbour delusions of inner division to a psychotic degree, as when we say, 'I don't know what came over me. I was not myself yesterday.' Who was I then? What was it that came over me, like a storm over countryside?

The I, then, is object and subject together. The individual as subcomponent of the group is an inner group of objects and subjects continually defining and creating itself. The external group in turn requires an object to define as other in order to bolster its subjective unity. The persistence of war in human life suggests that perhaps we should view not one group but at least two groups as the basic human unit. The potential single group of humanity seems forced to subdivide in order for its subgroups to experience a cohesive identity. Separateness and unity thus only exist as the tension between divided parts which cannot exist without each other, whether at the level of the individual, the group, the society or a group of societies.

Discussing the complexity of the social human being gives a rather strange idea of the 'I' or the self. Object Relations conceptions of 'the other within the self' see self and other in spatial terms, like little boxes that can be put inside bigger boxes and that can (magically) take other boxes inside them as well. One of the criticisms made by Klein's contemporaries (King and Steiner 1991) was that the early Kleinians spoke as though people had real inner objects – penis, breast, combined parental couple – inside them, all to be unwrapped like separate little parcels in the giant pass-the-parcel of psychoanalysis. They felt the metaphorical status of these concepts was beginning to fall away. We must allow their criticism, which is reflected in the similarly spatial language of such terms as 'schizoid emptiness' and the 'cutting off' and 'repression' of parts of the self.

Klein's reply was that, while of course these concepts are metaphors, at the level of unconscious phantasy we do indeed experience our internal objects as physical things which we can suck in or spew out, resulting in a sensation of fullness or emptiness, toxicity or benignity. Her language is an attempt to speak directly to the original experience which forms the ground of all our later sophistication. Like the foundations of buildings, while the surface structures may look very different from those underground, the deepest structures define, organise and delimit what can be built upon them.

Much of the language of Object Relations thus suggests that we experience ourselves in fundamentally physical terms, without differentiation between the abstract self and the material body. We hope to 'have' a 'solid sense of self', or to 'build' or 'support' 'ego-structures' in others. How far does this really accord with experience, and how far is it a convention deriving from the biological basis of early Freudian thinking? Is it valid, even, to say that experience is based in physical existence? If so, where does this leave the move away from biology towards psychology, championed by Object Relations? Or does the subjectivity of experience automatically disconnect it from physiology?

Winnicott, in contrasting the fluidity of the 'true self' with the aridity of the 'false self', characterises it simply as the 'experience of aliveness' (Winnicott 1960b). Elsewhere, he returns to a spatial metaphor, a view of the self as a thing, when he describes the self as having an innermost core which remains 'incommunicado' (Winnicott 1963b). Kohut, the originator of Self Psychology, writes of the self as natural 'vigour' which tends to persist, but also as ideally 'a firm and healthy structure' with 'various constituents' (Kohut and Wolf 1978). Object Relations concepts such as whole-object as against part-object relating, the depressive position as against the paranoid-schizoid, and mature dependence as against infantile dependence, point towards but do not reach a vision of the person that transcends the inertness of their constituent terms.

All these ideas suggest that at least at times we experience our actuality as a process rather than a possession; as happening, rather than as taking up space; a verb rather than a noun. From this perspective, however, articulating our social nature becomes even more problematic. While I as fluid flow of subjectivity could conceivably be described as incoherent or continuous, fraught or smooth, it is less straightforward to imagine this I-process incorporating other people in its stream, even if we similarly imagine other people, or aspects of them, or experiences of them, in the same fluid terms. Would that not bring us straight back to the inside–outside spatial view that now seems questionable? Is it even true that we experience others as processes rather than as things?

While the idea of the I-as-process is tenable, even evocative, the times when we attribute such open continuity to others are few and far between. How much more usual is it for us to envisage another person as a block or an asset to ourselves and our plans, or as warm, boring, funny, good at music? All these attributes are more redolent of unchanging objects than of the river-like motion of life.

Similarly, it is seldom that we even wish to experience ourselves in fluid rather than static terms. We yearn to be in possession of a self which is solid, clear and deep; to be 'seen' by others who thus confirm our existence; to not have to worry any more about our essential reality and identity for ourselves and other people.

The thing-based view of the self which prevails in Object Relations language, though not wholly in its thought, may thus reflect an easy way out of living. It is safer to cling to the illusion that we 'have' a self which can be defined and summed up and which we therefore fear less to lose. It is frightening to realise that above all life is uncertainty and change: the self we have we have already lost by clinging on to it. Perhaps the timidity shown in this respect by psychoanalytic language is connected with the fact that it is created by people, both patients and therapists, who find their relational and emotional lives difficult and painful, who search perhaps more than others for certainty and solidness, and for whom the idea of the thing-self may be an especially comforting refuge. While many Object Relations concepts betray a sense of frustration with the limitations of the theoretical constructs available, a psychological language with broader expressive potential has not yet been forged.

Conceptions of self are highly culturally relative; the twentieth-century Western personal identity is an outcome of historical and cultural currents and traditions of thought which have allotted increasing significance to a view of the self as an autonomous, essentially inward personal structure which holds intrinsic dignity and value (see Taylor 1989). Modern Western culture places a uniquely high value on individuation, separateness and self-sufficiency, all of which suggest that the self should be an item which can be divided off clearly from other items or selves. This Western self is object-ive and unrelational; for Marxists it reflects the fetishism of commodities within capitalism. To lack a sense of self is thus like being penniless in a shopping mall.

The characteristics of the Western self are highlighted through considering the self-concepts of other cultures, where the pinnacle of achievement is not self-sufficiency and where there may be more intermingling between people, both concretely and metaphorically. Roland (1988) refers to the 'we-self', where personal identity includes the encircling group. This expresses a more realistic sense of humanity; it acknowledges, rather than denies, the group of which all individuals are a part and on which all individuals depend.

Eastern thought has long been recognised as offering a different view of the self, less finite and less solid, and has been explored with devotion by Westerners who feel boxed-in by their social conditioning. Perhaps the self they hope to transcend is the thing-self, which we can now conjecture as a defence against uncertainty which shields us from the fullness of experience.

The Object Relations focus on the single individual is therefore incongruent with its basic premise of the social origins and nature of individual subjectivity. Conceptions of the ego with its inner and outer 'objects' can be overly material; and with the partial exception of Fairbairn, Guntrip and Bowlby, individuation is often given very positive value, in contrast to less highly delineated states which are usually seen as immature.

Despite these drawbacks, Object Relations has moved beyond the insight-orientation of Freudian theory, where the patient was treated as a discrete unit who only needed information through interpretation rather than also a shared living process. Klein, Winnicott, Fairbairn and others built on the parallel relational orientation of Freudian psychoanalysis where community with others is seen as the vehicle of change. Object Relations took up the need for meaning, relationship, and relative fluidity in a growing appreciation of qualities that Freud described as maternal and regressive rather than paternal and progressive. It is unreasonable to demand that Object Relations should totally emancipate itself from its roots; but it is not too much to hope for the continual examination of theory in the quest for a more inclusive and self-aware conception of humanity.

On a personal level, each individual will have his own sense of separateness and shared humanity, of individuation and merger, a sense which will embrace both defence and simple perception. While we can scrutinise our own underlying assumptions for their comfort value as opposed to their experienced truth, we will hardly overcome in any definitive way our tendency to create consoling fictions, and will thus continue to spread partial and misleading accounts of what is of most importance to us.

Fortunately, however, we are not alone. The increasing communication between cultures offers new opportunities to recognise and acknowledge the limits of any single cultural framework. We can thus more easily move towards a greater appreciation of both our crucial sociability and our partial autonomy. More varied paths can open up to us in our search for a life with the meaning which comes from a sense of being part of something larger than ourselves, whether we define this in religious or humanist terms. Such exploration involves challenging, changing, relinquishing the treasured certainties we cling to in our fear, as questions of who we are, what we are, where we are, tip us out of the rut of complacency we so readily inhabit.

In this developmental process, concepts and frameworks crumble and grow as language proves inadequate for the reality we experience. It is up to each of us to go further than the people in this book.

WHAT DO PEOPLE SEEK?

Drive and Relationship

Object Relations has moved towards a more unitary view of human nature than did Freudian theory, with its silently overarching drive towards non-being conflicting irrevocably with creativity and love. With the progressive abandonment of the instincts, what has taken their place? What does Object Relations see as the aims of human life?

Klein developed her own subjectively-based version of the Freudian tenet that the urges towards both creativity and destructiveness are built into the human constitution, making conflict and depredation unavoidable. In contrast, later Object Relations theorists saw the human being as having the wish and the capacity to live in greater harmony both internally and externally. Fairbairn goes the furthest in this, suggesting that inner conflict and the destructiveness this leads to arise solely though the failure of the good relationship which is our only true psychological need. Guntrip and Bowlby endorse this view, while Winnicott and Balint retain a more ambiguous stance. They suggest that we are both sensation-dominated and relation-oriented, implying that the duality of our pleasure-seeking and object-seeking aims gives rise to inner and outer discord almost incidentally.

Their duality is a continuation of Freud's alternative conceptions that the mind is an offshoot of the body (the physiological view), and that the inner world is a subjective entity (the psychological view). His oscillations reflect his aspirations towards overcoming the mind–body division which has governed Western thought for centuries. He hoped that psychoanalysis would bridge the gap between the brain and the mind through psycho-physiological concepts such as the drives and mental structures (Freud 1938a, S.E. 23).

However, such distinctions are not easily overcome. The Freudian 'drive' bears different meanings when it is conceptualised in material terms and when it is imbued with psychological intent. Phantasy may not be experienced consciously, but nevertheless belongs to the realm of subjectivity and abstraction rather than objective physicality. The accompanying physiological processes can be measured and seen, but cannot translate into experience without changing the arena of discourse. Alluding to experience of any kind, conscious or unconscious, brings us out of materiality into the subjectivity of representation and interpretation.

Freud's drive theory is therefore dualistic both in its view of human aims and in the theoretical status of these aims. Eros and the death instinct express a duality which he embraced with fervour; but despite his hopes and intentions, he could not bridge the biological and experiential concepts of mind between which his theories move. His bold attempt at a psycho-physiological thought-form masked rather than joined the break between psychology and biology, and Object Relations has for the most part built on this confusion rather than elucidated it.

Winnicott's version of this duality is a case in point. He abhorred the death instinct as unbiological and overly pessimistic, preferring a less conflicted foundation to human development; yet he was left with the dualism of bodily-based urges and subjective experience which he expressed as 'id experience' versus 'ego-relatedness'. This does nothing to address the disjuncture between biology and psychology, but rather evokes a disjuncture in our (psychological) experience of being. He is suggesting that we find ourselves wanting different things in different ways, each arising from one aspect of our nature.

Fairbairn and Guntrip, despite their apparently unitary psychological framework, are also forced to contend with the duality inherent in psychoanalytic thought. For them, instinct is the physical potentiality through which relational aims are enacted, and instinctual pathways are the instruments through which we reach our goal, rather than ends in themselves. However, they also saw instinct as providing a fall-back position in the alternative aim of instinct gratification when relational goals prove unattainable. Fairbairn and

Guntrip thus propose a secondary dualism in the aims of human beings, while seeing relational needs as primary.

Klein, Fairbairn and Balint express psychological duality in developmental terms. Klein's unconscious phantasy and paranoid-schizoid position, Fairbairn's infantile dependence and Balint's two-body mode all refer to primitive ways of being in which there is little or no conceptual space between the bodily self and whatever impacts upon it. Emotion and sensation, interpretation and actuality are experienced as one in a concrete and sensation-dominated symbolic equation. This contrasts with more mature modes in which perception and actuality are not so collapsed into each other, and there is space for a thought, image, gap, to exist in semi-independence from the self and the other who is now perceived as separate. Symbolisation has grown out of symbolic equation, bringing meaning and a heightened subjectivity to experience. Klein envisages both modes existing together from birth with the depressive mode gradually taking over relative predominance from the paranoid-schizoid position, their shifting fluctuations composing the ebb and flow of psychological life.

All these versions of duality are related to the physical and mental bases of our lives, without directly addressing this duality. Our physicality drives us towards food, shelter, sex; our subjectivity yearns for relationship, for art, for meaning. While the Western mind–body distinction forces us to differentiate between these aspects of ourselves, empirically they lie together in a single humanity. The subjective experience of our physicality renders it psychological; yet our split self-concept stands in the way of unitary language.

We thus seem to live in a psycho-physiological world in which we both search for meaning and thrust towards gratification; but the division between desire and drive, emotion and appetite, is partial, hazy and culturally relative. Supposedly physiological drives such as lust and hunger do not exist in a psychological vacuum: passion and need are universal experiences, although how and when we experience them and our attitudes towards them vary enormously. The diverse values and meanings with which we invest potential foods or sexual 'objects' affect both physical and psychological manifestations of hunger and sexuality. Foods which readily arouse appetite in one culture arouse disgust in another; and how many more people would experience a greater fluidity of sexual feelings towards others if different sexual orientations were equally validated?

The idea arises of a spectrum of experience with one pole more weighted with physiological processes, which we experience as drive for satisfaction in sensation, and the other more weighted with perception, interpretation and emotion: except that the idea of these polarities is itself a cultural artefact based on limited forms of conceptualisation. In 'reality', the poles intermingle: any phenomenon can be seen from the drive perspective or the meaning perspective. A psychology without the body seems thin and precious, while a physiology without the mind is irrelevant to the dilemmas people face.

Object Relations concepts thus constitute an uneasy bridging of what is not in fact divided: mind and body, psychology and biology, and their respective aims. A more satisfactory account awaits new ways of organising thought, perhaps through contributions from cultures which do not have the same tradition of mind–body distinction.

Relationship and Meaning

We are left with the constructed yet real experience of subjective as against material existence, and emotional as against physical needs. This leads us to ask if a life without the primary emotional need for contact is still a human life. Does human status depend on the capacity to experience relationship? In developmental terms, this question can be reformulated as: is there something psychologically human before object relationship?

Freud says yes, by grafting the mind on to the body: 'psychoanalysis ... explains the supposedly somatic concomitant phenomena as being what is truly psychical' (Freud 1938a, S.E. 23). He saw our ultimate desire as narciccistic or auto-erotic: an urge for bodily pleasure without reference to anything external to itself. He concluded that meaning, thought and object relationship arise through the forced accommodation to the reality principle in the service of the primary and more profound pleasure principle.

Fairbairn, Klein and Winnicott say no: the beginning of human life, as opposed to biological life, is the beginning of object-relatedness. While early relationship looks self-centred and pleasure-oriented, they suggest that this is due to the infant's lack of experience: he has not yet seen far enough outside himself to value others as people in their own right, and can experience only in relation to himself. Our fundamental aim, in Fairbairn's view, is contact with the other. If pleasure-in-sensation becomes the primary aim, it is a perversion of living.

In bringing object relationship to the start of human life, Klein and the early Object Relations theorists also brought meaning to the start of human life. Meaning derives from perceiving both a connection and a difference between entities, which are thereby related yet distinguished. This may involve imbuing things and experiences with different degrees of value, as well as spatial and temporal organisations which differentiate between up and down, in and out, now and then, shallower and deeper and, critically, me and you. Symbolising of any kind, including Segal's symbolic equations, thus involves experiencing one thing in relation to something else. It is the construction of meaning that raises phantasy to the level of creation rather than reflex. This seems to be the root of the object-relational conviction that the human beginning is the beginning of the experiencing subject. Without the possibility of otherness, there can be neither self nor meaning: before the I, there was simply a pre-human being.

Neither Freud nor the Object Relations theorists we have discussed give a coherent account of the genesis of the ego or psychological self. Freud suggested either that it was always there or that it developed out of the id. Winnicott simply says that the start is when the ego starts. An account that does attempt such a conceptualisation comes from Francis Mott's eccentric epic *The Universal Design of Creation* (1964). It is a comprehensive enquiry into the world of the foetus in the womb and its staged translation into post-natal life, seen as the reflection of a larger cosmology and based on the painstaking analysis of dreams and myths. Mott traces how pre-natal sensations might coalesce into conceptual configurations. He links the pulse and flow of blood and electrical charge between the skin, the placenta and the umbilical cord with subjective relational experiences of nucleus and periphery, and point, line and plane. While much of his presentation seems as obsessional and as difficult to argue with as a delusion, patchily brilliant intuition and startlingly luminous insight periodically leap from the pages.

Individual convictions as to where human life begins and ends will vary with the influences of culture and personal resonance; our responses will be expressed in our stance on such issues as whether abortion and/or euthanasia enhance or negate the widely accepted tenet of the absolute value of human life. At what point do such acts become the killing of a human mind, spirit, soul, as well as of a human body, or are they inseparable?

Object Relations assumptions of personhood suggest that without the possibility of meaning or relationship, life is hardly worth living (although, equally, that does not automatically make life *not* worth living). If no joy can be felt at the light of a spring day, no love at the sight of a cherished face, no anger at an insensitive touch, no internal sense of conflict or harmony, but only a dim neutrality, capacities which we see as essentially human are not there, and the life is not a human life. Conversely, the life of a person, however tortured, who is capable of experiencing love or a sense of meaning alongside intense suffering is infinitely precious in an Object Relations perspective.

The pragmatism of the view that a life without meaning is a less than human life will not appeal to everyone; it is arguable that the worth of any life is subjective and thus by definition unassessable by another. Finite emotional and material resources can tilt social philosophy towards a relative devaluing of less conscious existence. However, the centrality of the capacity for external and internal relationship constitutes a general late twentieth-century Western consensus of human status.

This consensus implies that we lapse from our full human capacity insofar as we blot meaning out with pleasure through using things, fantasies or people as commodities. We reach for a more complete humanity to the extent that we also acknowledge otherness in our lives or suffer from experiencing the absence of the meaning that otherness brings.

As existential-bodily beings, these polarities are part of a human condition which the Western world has never wholly accepted. Neither pure body nor pure spirit, we both yearn for and are shut out of our fantasy of the perfect realisation of either. Minute by minute we shift our allegiance between gratification and contact, pleasure and meaning, evasion and authenticity. Unsatisfaction and conflict are guaranteed by the inexorable division between the Western body and mind.

Good and Evil

Freud and Klein saw love and destructiveness as arising from separate sources in a constant state of partial, shifting fusion. Later theorists moved towards the assumption of a single source from which we reach towards contact with another and react when contact is breached. Attempts to demonstrate an underlying unity have often led to difficulty, whether in Winnicott's erotic and aggressive roots, Guntrip's regressed ego or Fairbairn's full infantile dependence. Our relapses into destructiveness reflect the limitations of our self-centred vision. Freudian theory sees these relapses as a rising drive for a type of gratification before which otherness and meaning disappear, leading towards the ultimate gratification of death and total non-meaning. Winnicott's and Balint's dual-strand views imply that in the imperative to seek satisfaction in sensation, the subjectivity of the other person is an irrelevance. Fairbairn suggests that the pressure to relieve internal conflict by externalisation, or by displacing relationship with pleasure as an immediate aim, similarly blocks out of perception the other's existential reality. They all see the potential for destructiveness in a part of our nature which does not seek full relationship.

Destructiveness is thus explained as an intrinsic pull towards death, as a consequence of our jigsaw puzzle nature or as the unfortunate outcome of the impact of an imperfect environment. The universality of inner conflict puts a question mark over Fairbairn's utopian vision of theoretical normality, and the dual strands of instinct and relationship join uneasily. How then can we evolve an account which does justice to the reality of conflict and destructiveness without a supposed death instinct? It is a concept which evidently is not easily made redundant. We can tentatively propose that destructiveness arises from a limitation of our perception in which what is outside ourselves disappears: but is this through accident or design?

Difficulties arise from the categorical distinction between love and anger, which in Western thought is easily mapped on to the difference between good and evil. This distinction has not been fully thought through after Freud laid down the initial terms, in a theoretical edifice which may have been underpinned by the impact of war on the one hand, and the slow and painful progress of his cancer on the other.

The early Object Relations theorists lived through two world wars, as children and then as adults, and many worked directly with traumatised soldiers or civilians. Given the savagery of twentieth-century warfare, the horrifying discovery of the concentration camps, the brutal treatment of prisoners in the Far East, the dropping of nuclear bombs at Hiroshima and Nagasaki, human destructiveness must have seemed an ungovernable force. Surely it could have little in common with the love of the 'ordinary devoted mother' for her child. These realities may have continually and subliminally driven the wedge further between love and destructiveness, preventing the finding of an adequate common root despite efforts to do so.

Martha Nussbaum grapples with many such issues in her call for philosophy to be brought out of academia into everyday life (1994). In a sparkling journey through Greek and Roman philosophical conceptions of emotion and desire, she concludes that love and destructiveness are a single phenomenon.

Feelings and emotions are grounded in assessments, judgements, interpretations, at conscious and unconscious levels. Wanting something means judging it important to our own well-being. We experience this judgement as appetite, anticipation or desire when the good we want from outside ourselves seems available to us; as anxiety or fear when it seems threatened; as anger when threatened by someone else's actions. In loving a person, or transitionally an abstraction such as music or philosophy, we add to that judgement a belief that the person or entity is important in its own right, over and above our own interests. This double valuation opens us to the possibility of relational emotion: love when the person we desire seems potentially responsive to our love; grief when his love is lost; jealousy when another threatens to deprive us of his love.

All emotions thus have a common root in the judgement or phantasy that this object or person is of positive or negative value to us. This does not imply that cognition is prior to emotion, but rather that cognition, emotion and sensation are a single event which appears in different forms and from which different elements can be secondarily separated out. A wider vision transforms connection with a thing into a human relationship, sometimes in the special form Winnicott articulated as the transitional area. The difference between emotions thus lies not in separate capacities, but in the way the light falls from the world outside: a world which reaches into us and which is also reached by us.

Desire and rage both spill into destructiveness. Like Hitler, whose passionate valuing of what he saw as purity led him to destroy what he saw as contaminating elements, we also destroy in our minds and in our actions the objects which sully our preferred image of the world. In the blindness of our search for justice, truth and beauty, we also attack those parts which spoil our preferred image of what or whom we love. Yet never to do this is to live less fully. If we do not really hate, we will not really love, because we will not value highly what is outside our own control.

What can partially hold us back from destructiveness is the double valuation through which we see the other person as valuable in himself, apart from our own self-interest. Our appreciation of the other's separateness and subjectivity takes him forever beyond our possessive control, yet we only discern the otherness that we honour through our own inviolate subjectivity. Seeing a person as a thing, however, does not require the double valuing of what is outside the self. We are back to the thing-self as a simpler and narrower view than the self-as-process.

While we may aspire to tilt the balance away from the limitations of gratification towards the larger view, any aspiration to overcome self-centredness must be doomed to failure. Seeing beyond the self, retaining the knowledge that the other continues to have value regardless of our own deprivation, does not do away with the smaller conception of the self as finite. We use the term 'sainthood' for the inhumanity of one for whom the larger conception takes all the space. It is more ordinarily human to have mere glimpses of that vista where self and other are not reduced to commodities. Thus at least in Western thought human beings aspire to more than can be reached; we cannot obliterate our nature, and to try to do so acts out upon ourselves the destructiveness we fear. In wanting pleasure and loving meaning, putting ourselves first but also valuing others for themselves, the struggle of our dual nature is human living.

Desire for a thing is thus both like and different from mature relationship. To see oneself and others as thing, object, possession, rather than subjective stream of consciousness and unconsciousness, is to be tied to sensation without meaning. As thing-self, we may be satisfied with possession rather than relationship, but in our wider vision we grow to want not just the other person's services but his soul. 'Man does not desire an object. Man desires the object's desire', said Hegel (1807, quoted in Grotstein and Rinsley 1994: 141), whose writing Fairbairn knew from his study of philosophy. Desiring what can only be given freely involves the painful recognition and always fragile acceptance of the fact that what we most value about the other lies in what is forever beyond our reach. We experience this as love, longing and pain. We protest against this knowledge in anger.

In seeking the physical, we recognise the bodily self as an entity and look no further than sensation; in seeking the social, we recognise our dependence on others who are accessible to us only in their inaccessibility. Mind and body, good and evil, drive and relationship have led us to the thought that the more we allow ourselves to perceive, the more human we can be in all our capacities and all our limitations. While purity will be beyond us, richness of experience will not. We do not have a more adequate language for the humanity we can only see as split.

*   *   *

New ideas are only of value to the extent that we can change them. The challenge is always to find out what matters supremely to us. No two understandings will be the same, and each of us will despair as what we grasped yesterday disintegrates today, even as we promise not to grab at it. Our thoughts will be as fraught with contradiction and inadequacy as those of the theorists we have met. The dividing lines between mind and body, love and hate, individual and group, technique and relationship, disappear and yet become ever more sharply fixed. The cultural heritage of our conceptual structures and tools both limits and enhances our vision, bestowing a blessing and a curse on our striving to see clearly that which we can never be outside.

It is through our actions that our beliefs speak loudest. Our practice will reveal to us the world view on which we rest our weight. We are likely to be as horrified as relieved to discover this, finding it as comforting, and as unbearably restricting, as any homecoming.

BIBLIOGRAPHY

This bibliography includes publications referred to in the text and also other publications which the reader might find useful.

Abraham, K. (1927) *Selected Papers on Psycho-Analysis*. London: Hogarth; Karnac (1979).

Ainsworth, M., Blehar, M., Waters, E. and Wall, S. (1978) *Patterns of Attachment: Assessed in the Strange Situation and at Home*. Hillsdale, NJ: Erlbaum.

Alexander, F. (1954) 'Some Quantitative Aspects of Psychoanalytic Technique', *Journal of the American Psychoanalytic Society* 2: 685–701.

American Psychiatric Association (1995) *Diagnostic and Statistical Manual of Mental Disorders*. Washington, DC: American Psychiatric Association.

Balint, A. (1939) 'Love of the Mother and Mother Love', in M. Balint, *Primary Love and Psychoanalytic Technique*. London: Hogarth (1952); New York: Liveright (1965).

Balint, M. (1935) 'The Pregenital Organisation of the Libido', in *The Basic Fault: Therapeutic Aspects of Regression*. London: Tavistock (1968).

Balint, M. (1936) 'Eros and Aphrodite', in *Primary Love and Psychoanalytic Technique*.

Balint, M. (1947) 'On Genital Love', in *Primary Love and Psychoanalytic Technique*.

Balint, M. (1949) 'Changing Therapeutical Aims and Techniques in Psycho-analysis', in *Primary Love and Psychoanalytic Technique*.

Balint, M. (1951) 'On Love and Hate', in *Primary Love and Psychoanalytic Technique*.

Balint, M. (1952) *Primary Love and Psychoanalytic Technique*. London: Hogarth; New York: Liveright (1965).

Balint, M. (1957a) *The Doctor, His Patient and the Illness*. London: Pitman; New York: International Universities Press.

Balint, M. (1957b) 'Criticism of Fairbairn's Generalisation about Object-Relations', in E. Fairbairn Birtles and D. Scharff, eds, *From Instinct to Self: Selected Papers of W.R.D. Fairbairn. Volume I: Clinical and Theoretical Papers*. London and Northvale, NJ: Jason Aronson (1994).

Balint, M. (1959) *Thrills and Regressions*. London: Hogarth.

Balint, M. (1968) *The Basic Fault: Therapeutic Aspects of Regression*. London: Tavistock.

Berne, E. (1961) *Games People Play*. New York: Grove; Harmondsworth: Penguin (1964).

Bettelheim, B. (1982) *Freud and Man's Soul*. London: Hogarth; New York: Alfred Knopf; London: Penguin (1991).

Bion, W. (1962a) *Learning From Experience*. London: Heinemann; Karnac (1984).

Bion, W. (1962b) 'A Theory of Thinking', *International Journal of Psycho-Analysis* 43: 110–19. Reprinted in W. Bion, *Second Thoughts*. London: Heinemann; New York: Jason Aronson (1967).

Bowlby, J. (1944) 'Forty-four Juvenile Thieves: Their Characters and Home Life', *International Journal of Psycho-Analysis* 25: 1–57, 207–8.

Bowlby, J. (1953) *Child Care and the Growth of Love*. Harmondsworth: Penguin; enlarged edition, 1965.

Bowlby, J. (1969) *Attachment and Loss. Volume I: Attachment*. London: Hogarth; New York: Basic Books; Harmondsworth: Penguin (1971).

Bowlby, J. (1973) *Attachment and Loss. Volume II: Separation: Anxiety and Anger*. London: Hogarth; New York: Basic Books; Harmondsworth: Penguin (1975).

Bowlby, J. (1980) *Attachment and Loss. Volume III: Loss: Sadness and Depression*. London: Hogarth; New York: Basic Books; Harmondsworth: Penguin (1981).

Bowlby, J. (1988) *A Secure Base: Clinical Applications of Attachment Theory*. London: Routledge.

Bowlby, J. (1990) *Charles Darwin: A New Biography*. London: Hutchinson.

Breuer, J. and Freud, S. (1895) 'Studies on Hysteria', in James Strachey ed., *The Standard Edition of the Complete Works of Sigmund Freud*, 24 vols, London: Hogarth, 1953–73, Volume 2; *Pelican Freud Library* Volume 3. Harmondsworth: Penguin.

Casement, P. (1985) *On Learning From the Patient*. London: Tavistock.

Chodorow, N. (1989) *Feminism and Psychoanalytic Theory*. New Haven, CT: Yale University Press; Cambridge: Polity Press.

Chodorow, N. (1994) *Femininities, Masculinities, Sexualities: Freud and Beyond*. London: Free Association Books; Lexington, KT: University of Kentucky Press.

Crews, F. (1993) 'The Unknown Freud', *New York Review*, November 1993.

d'Ardenne, P. and Mahtani, A. (1989) *Transcultural Counselling in Action*. London: Sage.

Davis, M. and Wallbridge, D. (1981) *Boundary and Space: An Introduction to the Work of D.W. Winnicott*. London: Karnac.

Eagle, M. (1984) *Recent Developments in Psychoanalysis: A Critical Evaluation*. Cambridge, MA: Harvard University Press.

Eichenbaum, L. and Orbach, S. (1982) *Outside In ... Inside Out. Women's Psychology: A Feminist Psychoanalytic Approach*. Harmondsworth: Penguin.

Ellis, M.L. (1994) 'Lesbians, Gay Men and Psychoanalytic Training', *Free Associations*, vol. 4. 4, no. 32 (1994): 501–17.

Erikson, E. (1950) *Childhood and Society*. New York: Norton; Harmondsworth: Penguin (1965) .

Fairbairn, R. (1940) 'Schizoid Factors in the Personality', in R. Fairbairn, *Psycho-Analytic Studies of the Personality*. London: Routledge and Kegan Paul (1952).

Fairbairn, R. (1941) 'A Revised Psychopathology of the Psychoses and Psychoneuroses', in *Psycho-Analytic Studies of the Personality*.

Fairbairn, R. (1943) 'The Repression and Return of Bad Objects (with Special Reference to the "War Neuroses")', in *Psycho-Analytic Studies of the Personality*.

Fairbairn, R. (1944) 'Endopsychic Structure Considered in terms of Object-Relationships', in *Psycho-Analytic Studies of the Personality*.

Fairbairn, R. (1946) 'Object Relations and Dynamic Structure', in *Psycho-Analytic Studies of the Personality*.

Fairbairn, R. (1952) *Psycho-Analytic Studies of the Personality*. London: Routledge and Kegan Paul. Also published as *An Object Relations Theory of the Personality*. New York: Basic Books.

Fairbairn, R. (1955) 'Observations in Defence of the Object-Relations Theory of Personality', in E. Fairbairn Birtles and D. Scharff, eds, *From Instinct to Self: Selected Papers of W.R.D. Fairbairn, Volume I: Clinical and Theoretical Papers*.

Fairbairn, R. (1994a) Fairbairn Birtles, E. and Scharff, D., eds, *From Instinct to Self: Selected Papers of W.R.D. Fairbairn, Volume I: Clinical and Theoretical Papers*. London and Northvale, NJ: Jason Aronson.

Fairbairn, R. (1994b) Fairbairn Birtles, E. and Scharff, D., eds. *From Instinct to Self: Selected Papers of W.R.D. Fairbairn, Volume II: Applications and Early Contributions*. London and Northvale, NJ: Jason Aronson.

Ferenczi, S. (1932) 'Confusion of Tongues between the Adults (Plural) and the Child (Singular)', in *Final Contributions to the Problems and Methods of Psycho-Analysis*. London: Hogarth (1955).

Freud, A. (1927) 'Four Lectures on Child Analysis', in *Introduction to Psychoanalysis*. London: Hogarth (1974).

Freud, S. (1905a) 'Fragment of an Analysis of a Case of Hysteria', *S.E.* Volume 7. London: Hogarth. *Pelican Freud Library* Volume 8. Harmondsworth: Penguin.

Freud, S. (1905b) 'Three Essays on the Theory of Sexuality', *S.E.* Volume 7. *Pelican Freud Library* Volume 7.

Freud, S. (1914) 'On Narcissism: An Introduction', *S.E.* Volume 14. *Pelican Freud Library* Volume 11.

Freud, S. (1916–17) 'The Path to Symptom Formation', *Introductory Lectures on Psychoanalysis, S.E.* Volume 15. *Pelican Freud Library* Volume 1.

Freud, S. (1920) 'Beyond the Pleasure Principle', *S.E.* Volume 18. *Pelican Freud Library* Volume 11.

Freud, S. (1923) 'The Ego and the Id', *S.E.* Volume 19. *Pelican Freud Library* Volume 11.

Freud, S. (1930) 'Civilisation and its Discontents', *S.E.* Volume 21. *Pelican Freud Library* Volume 12.

Freud, S. (1933a) 'Dissection of the Personality', *New Introductory Lectures, S.E.* Volume 22. *Pelican Freud Library* Volume 2.

Freud, S. (1933b) 'Anxiety and Instinctual Life', *New Introductory Lectures, S.E.* Volume 22. *Pelican Freud Library* Volume 2.

Freud, S. (1938a) 'An Outline of Psychoanalysis', *S.E.* Volume 23. *Pelican Freud Library* Volume 15.

Freud, S. (1938b) 'Splitting of the Ego in the Service of Defence', *S.E.* Volume 23. *Pelican Freud Library* Volume 11.

Fromm, E. (1942) *The Fear of Freedom*. London: Routledge and Kegan Paul.

Gay, P. (1988) *Freud: A Life For Our Time*. London: Dent.

Goldman D. (1993) *In Search of the Real: The Origins and Originality of D.W. Winnicott*. Northvale, NJ: Jason Aronson.

Greenberg, J. and Mitchell, S. (1983) *Object Relations in Psychoanalytic Theory*. Cambridge, MA: Harvard University Press.

Groddeck, G. (1949) *The Book of the It*. London: Vision Press. First published as *Das Buch vom Es* (1923).

Grof, S. (1975) *Realms of the Human Unconscious: Observations from LSD Research*. New York: Viking.

Grolnick, S. (1990) *The Work and Play of Winnicott*. Northvale, NJ: Jason Aronson.

Grosskurth, P. (1986) *Melanie Klein: Her World and Her Work*. London: Hodder and Stoughton; Cambridge, MA: Harvard University Press.

Grotstein, J. and Rinsley, D., eds (1994) *Fairbairn and the Origins of Object Relations*. London: Free Association Books.

Guntrip, H. (1961) *Personality Structure and Human Interaction: The Developing Synthesis of Psychodynamic Theory*. London: Hogarth; New York: International Universities Press.

Guntrip, H. (1968) *Schizoid Phenomena, Object Relations and the Self*. London: Hogarth; New York: International Universities Press (1969).

Guntrip, H. (1971) *Psychoanalytic Theory, Therapy and the Self*. New York: Basic Books; London: Karnac (1977).

Guntrip, H. (1975) 'Analysis with Fairbairn and Winnicott: (How Complete a Result does Psycho-Analytic Therapy Achieve?)', *International Review of Psychoanalysis* 2: 145–56. Reprinted in J. Hazell, ed., *Personal Relations Therapy: The Collected Papers of H.J.S. Guntrip*. Northvale, NJ: Jason Aronson (1994).

Harlow, H. and Zimmerman, R. (1959) 'Affectional Responses in the Infant Monkey', *Science* 130: 421.

Haynal, A. (1988) *The Technique at Issue: Controversies in Psychoanalysis from Freud and Ferenczi to Michael Balint*. London: Karnac.

Hazell, J. (1991) 'Reflections on my Experience of Psychoanalysis with Guntrip', *Contemporary Psychoanalysis* 27 (1): 148–66.

Hazell, J., ed. (1994) *Personal Relations Therapy: The Collected Papers of H.J.S. Guntrip*. Northvale, NJ: Jason Aronson.

Hazell, J. (1996) *H.J.S. Guntrip: A Psychoanalytic Biography*. London and New York: Free Association Books.

Hegel, G. (1807) *The Phenomenology of Spirit*. Translated by A. Miller. London: Oxford University Press (1977).

Hinshelwood, R. (1989) *A Dictionary of Kleinian Thought*. London: Free Association Books.

Hinshelwood, R. (1994) *Clinical Klein*. London: Free Association Books.

Holmes, J., ed. (1991) *Textbook of Psychotherapy in Psychiatric Practice*. Edinburgh: Churchill Livingstone.

Holmes, J. (1993) *John Bowlby and Attachment Theory*. London and New York: Routledge.

Horney, K. (1945) *Our Inner Conflicts: A Constructive Theory of Neurosis*. New York: Norton; London: Kegan Paul (1946).

Hughes, J. (1989) *Reshaping the Psychoanalytic Domain: The Work of Melanie Klein, W.R.D. Fairbairn and D.W. Winnicott*. Berkeley, CA: University of California Press.

Isaacs, S. (1943) 'The Nature and Function of Phantasy', *International Journal of Psycho-Analysis* 29: 73–97; reprinted in M. Klein, P.

Heimann, S. Isaacs and J. Rivière, *Developments in Psycho-analysis.* London: Hogarth (1952).

Jacobs, M. (1986) *The Presenting Past: An Introduction to Practical Psychodynamic Counselling.* Milton Keynes: Open University Press.

Jacobs, M. (1995) *Key Figures in Counselling and Psychotherapy: D.W. Winnicott.* London: Sage.

Jones, E. (1957) *The Life and Work of Sigmund Freud.* London: Hogarth; New York: Basic Books.

Journal of the Balint Society.

Keleman, S. (1985) *Emotional Anatomy: The Structure of Experience.* Berkeley, CA: Center Press.

Kernberg, O. (1975) *Borderline Conditions and Pathological Narcissism.* New York: Jason Aronson.

King, P. and Steiner, R., eds (1991) *The Freud–Klein Controversies 1941–45.* London: Routledge.

Klein, J. (1987) *Our Need for Others and its Roots in Infancy.* London and New York: Tavistock.

Klein, M. (1928) 'Early Stages of the Oedipus Complex', in M. Klein, *Love, Guilt and Reparation.* London: Hogarth (1975); London: Virago (1988).

Klein, M. (1935) 'A Contribution to the Psychogenesis of Manic-Depressive States', in *Love, Guilt and Reparation.*

Klein, M. (1940) 'Mourning and its Relations to Manic-Depressive States', in *Love, Guilt and Reparation.*

Klein, M. (1945) 'The Oedipus Complex in the Light of Early Anxieties', in *Love, Guilt and Reparation.*

Klein, M. (1946) 'Notes on Some Schizoid Mechanisms', in M. Klein, *Envy and Gratitude and Other Works.* London: Hogarth (1975); London: Virago (1988).

Klein, M. (1952) 'Some Theoretical Conclusions Regarding the Emotional Life of the Infant', in *Envy and Gratitude and Other Works.*

Klein, M. (1955) 'The Psycho-Analytic Play Technique, its History and Significance', in *Envy and Gratitude and Other Works.*

Klein, M. (1957) 'Envy and Gratitude', in *Envy and Gratitude and Other Works.*

Klein, M. (1959) 'Our Adult World and its Roots in Infancy', in *Envy and Gratitude and Other Works.*

Kohut, H. (1977) *The Restoration of the Self.* New York: International Universities Press.

Kohut, H. and Wolf, E. (1978) 'The Disorders of the Self and Their Treatment: An Outline', *International Journal of Psycho-Analysis* 59: 413–24.

Kovel, J. (1988) *White Racism: A Psychohistory.* London: Free Association Books.

Laing, R. (1960) *The Divided Self: A Study of Sanity and Madness.* London: Tavistock; New York: Pantheon; Harmondsworth: Penguin (1965).

Laing, R. and Cooper, D. (1964) *Reason and Violence.* London: Tavistock.

Lake, F. (1966) *Clinical Theology.* London: Darton, Longman and Todd.

Little, M. (1990) *Psychotic Anxieties and Containment: A Personal Record of an Analysis with Winnicott.* Northvale, NJ: Jason Aronson.

Lomas, P. (1987) *The Limits of Interpretation: What's Wrong With Psychoanalysis?* Harmondsworth: Penguin.

Lorenz, K. (1952) *King Solomon's Ring: New Light on Animal Ways.* London: Methuen.

Lowen, A. (1975) *Bioenergetics.* New York: Coward, McCann and Geoghegan; Harmondsworth: Penguin.

Macmurray, J. (1961) *Persons in Relation.* London: Faber.

Mahler, M., Pine, F. and Bergman, A. (1975) *The Psychological Birth of the Human Infant: Symbiosis and Individuation.* London: Hutchinson; New York: Basic Books.

Milner, M. (1969) *The Hands of the Living God: An Account of a Psychoanalytic Treatment.* London: Hogarth.

Mitchell, J. (1974) *Psychoanalysis and Feminism.* London: Allen Lane; Harmondsworth: Penguin (1975).

Mott, F. (1964) *The Universal Design of Creation.* Edenbridge: Mark Beech.

Nussbaum, M. (1994) *The Therapy of Desire.* Princeton, NJ: Princeton University Press.

O'Connor, N. and Ryan, J. (1993) *Wild Desires and Mistaken Identities: Lesbianism and Psychoanalysis.* London: Virago.

Ogden, T. (1989) *The Primitive Edge of Experience.* Northvale, NJ: Jason Aronson; London: Karnac (1992).

Rayner, E. (1991) *The Independent Mind in British Psychoanalysis.* London: Free Association Books.

Rey, H. (1994) *Universals of Psychoanalysis in the Treatment of Psychotic and Borderline States.* London: Free Association Books.

Robertson, J. (1952) *A Two-Year-Old Goes to Hospital* (video). London: Robertson Centre; Ipswich: Concord Video and Film Council.

Robertson, J. and Robertson, J. (1976) *John, aged 17 months, for 9 Days in a Residential Nursery* (video). *Young Children in Brief Separation:*

Five Films. London: Robertson Centre; Ipswich: Concord Video and Film Council.

Rodman, F., ed. (1987) *The Spontaneous Gesture: Selected Letters of D.W. Winnicott.* Cambridge, MA and London: Harvard University Press.

Roland, A. (1988) *In Search of Self in India and Japan: Towards a Cross-Cultural Psychology.* Princeton, NJ and Oxford: Princeton University Press.

Rosenfeld, H. (1964) 'On the Psychopathology of Narcissism: a Clinical Approach', in *Psychotic States.* London: Hogarth.

Rosenfeld, H. (1971) 'A Clinical Approach to the Psycho-Analytic Theories of the Life and Death Instincts: an Investigation into the Aggressive Aspects of Narcissism', *International Journal of Psycho-Analysis* 51: 169–78. Reprinted in E. Bott Spillius, ed., *Melanie Klein Today. Volume I: Mainly Theory.* London: Routledge (1988).

Rustin, M. (1991) *The Good Society and the Inner World: Psychoanalysis, Politics and Culture.* London: Verso.

Salzberger-Wittenberg, I. (1970) *Psycho-Analytic Insight and Relationships: A Kleinian Approach.* London: Routledge & Kegan Paul.

Sartre, J-P. (1938) *La Nausée.* Paris: Gallimard.

Savege Scharff, J. and Scharff, D. (1992) *Scharff Notes: A Primer of Object Relations Therapy.* London: Jason Aronson.

Sayers, J. (1991) *Mothering Psychoanalysis.* London: Hamish Hamilton; London: Penguin (1992).

Schoenhals, H., ed. (1994) 'Contemporary Kleinian Psychoanalysis', *Psychoanalytic Inquiry* Volume 14 no. 3.

Schorske, C. (1961) *Fin-de-Siècle Vienna: Politics and Culture.* Cambridge: Cambridge University Press; New York: Alfred Knopf.

Searles, H. (1960) *The Nonhuman Environment in Normal Development and in Schizophrenia.* New York: International Universities Press.

Segal, H. (1957) 'Notes on Symbol Formation', *International Journal of Psycho-Analysis* 38: 391–7. Reprinted in E. Bott Spillius, ed., *Melanie Klein Today. Volume I: Mainly Theory.*

Segal, H. (1973) *Introduction to the Work of Melanie Klein.* London, Hogarth; New York: Basic Books.

Senf, M. (1995) 'The Revaluation of the Feminine in Psychoanalytic Theory and Practice'. Unpublished dissertation.

Sinason, V. (1992) *New Approaches from the Tavistock: Mental Handicap and the Human Condition.* London: Free Association Books.

Skynner, R. and Cleese, J. (1983) *Families and How to Survive Them.* London: Methuen.

Spillius, E. Bott. ed. (1988a) *Melanie Klein Today: Developments in Theory and Practice. Volume I: Mainly Theory*. London: Routledge.

Spillius, E. Bott, ed. (1988b) *Melanie Klein Today: Developments in Theory and Practice. Volume II: Mainly Practice*. London: Routledge.

Steiner, C. (1974) *Scripts People Live By*. New York: Grove.

Steiner, J. (1993) *Psychic Retreats: Pathological Organisations in Psychotic, Neurotic and Borderline Patients*. London: Routledge.

Stern, D. (1985) *The Interpersonal World of the Infant: A View from Psychoanalysis and Developmental Psychology*. New York: Basic Books.

Stoller, R. (1968) *Sex and Gender*. London: Hogarth; New York: Science House.

Stoller, R. (1985) *Presentations of Gender*. London and New Haven, CT: Yale University Press.

Stubrin, J. (1994) *Sexualities and Homosexualities*. London: Karnac.

Sullivan, H. (1953) *The Interpersonal Theory of Psychiatry*. New York: Norton; London: Tavistock (1955).

Sulloway, F.J. (1979) *Freud: Biologist of the Mind. Beyond the Psychoanalytic Legend*. New York: Basic Books; London: Fontana (1980).

Sutherland, J. (1971) 'Obituary: Michael Balint', *International Journal of Psycho-Analysis* 52: 331.

Sutherland, J. (1989) *Fairbairn's Journey into the Interior*. London: Free Association Books.

Taylor, A. (1948) *The Habsburg Monarchy*. London: Hamish Hamilton; London: Penguin (1990).

Taylor, C. (1989) *Sources of the Self: The Making of the Modern Identity*. Cambridge: Cambridge University Press.

Tustin, F. (1972) *Autism and Childhood Psychosis*. London: Hogarth.

Whyte L.. (1962) *The Unconscious Before Freud*. London: Tavistock.

Winnicott Studies: the Journal of the Squiggle Foundation.

Winnicott, C. (1983) 'Clare Winnicott talks to Michael Neve', *Free Associations*, Vol. 3. 2, no. 26 (1992): 167–84.

Winnicott, C. (1989) 'D.W.W: A Reflection', in C. Winnicott, R. Shepherd and M. Davis, eds, *Psycho-Analytic Explorations*. London, Karnac; Cambridge, MA: Harvard University Press (1989).

Winnicott, D. (1947) 'Hate in the Countertransference', *Collected Papers: Through Paediatrics to Psycho-Analysis*. London: Hogarth; New York: Basic Books (1975); London: Karnac (1992).

Winnicott, D. (1949a) 'Mind and its Relation to the Psyche-Soma', in *Collected Papers: Through Paediatrics to Psycho-Analysis*.

Winnicott, D. (1949b) 'Leucotomy', *Psycho-Analytic Explorations*.

Winnicott, D. (1950–55) 'Aggression in Relation to Emotional Development', *Collected Papers: Through Paediatrics to Psycho-Analysis.*

Winnicott, D. (1952a) 'Anxiety Associated with Insecurity', *Collected Papers: Through Paediatrics to Psycho-Analysis.*

Winnicott, D. (1952b) 'Psychoses and Child Care', *Collected Papers: Through Paediatrics to Psycho-Analysis.*

Winnicott, D. (1955) 'A Case Managed at Home', *Collected Papers: Through Paediatrics to Psycho-Analysis.*

Winnicott, D. (1956) 'The Anti-social Tendency', *Collected Papers: Through Paediatrics to Psycho-Analysis.*

Winnicott, D. (1958) 'The Capacity to be Alone', D. Winnicott, *The Maturational Processes and the Facilitating Environment.* London: Hogarth (1965).

Winnicott, D. (1959–64) 'Classification: Is There a Psycho-Analytic Contribution to Psychiatric Classification?', *The Maturational Processes and the Facilitating Environment.*

Winnicott, D. (1960a) 'String: a Technique of Communication', *The Maturational Processes and the Facilitating Environment.*

Winnicott, D. (1960b) 'Ego Distortion in Terms of the True and False Self', *The Maturational Processes and the Facilitating Environment.*

Winnicott, D. (1960c) 'Countertransference', *The Maturational Processes and the Facilitating Environment.*

Winnicott, D. (1960d) 'The Theory of the Parent–Infant Relationship', *The Maturational Processes and the Facilitating Environment.*

Winnicott, D. (1962a) 'A Personal View of the Kleinian contribution', *The Maturational Processes and the Facilitating Environment.*

Winnicott, D. (1962b) 'Ego Integration in Child Development', *The Maturational Processes and the Facilitating Environment.*

Winnicott, D. (1963a) 'Two Notes on the Use of Silence', *Psycho-Analytic Explorations.*

Winnicott, D. (1963b) 'Communicating and Not Communicating Leading to a Study of Certain Opposites', *The Maturational Processes and the Facilitating Environment.*

Winnicott, D. (1963c) 'From Dependence towards Independence in the Development of the Individual', *The Maturational Processes and the Facilitating Environment.*

Winnicott, D. (1963d) 'The Development of the Capacity for Concern', in *The Maturational Processes and the Facilitating Environment.*

Winnicott, D. (1963e) 'Fear of Breakdown', *Psycho-Analytic Explorations.*

Winnicott, D. (1963f) 'Psychotherapy of Character Disorders', *The Maturational Processes and the Facilitating Environment.*

Winnicott, D. (1964–68) 'The Squiggle Game', *Psycho-Analytic Explorations*.

Winnicott, D. (1965) Acknowledgements, *The Maturational Processes and the Facilitating Environment*.

Winnicott, D. (1965) *The Maturational Processes and the Facilitating Environment*. London: Hogarth; Karnac (1990).

Winnicott, D. (1967a) 'The Concept of Clinical Regression Compared with that of Defence Organisation', *Psycho-Analytic Explorations*.

Winnicott, D. (1967b) 'D.W.W. on D.W.W.', *Psycho-Analytic Explorations*.

Winnicott, D. (1968) 'On "The Use of an Object", Part II', *Psycho-Analytic Explorations*.

Winnicott, D. (1971) 'Transitional Objects and Transitional Phenomena', D. Winnocott, *Playing and Reality*. London: Tavistock (1971).

Winnicott, D. (1977) *The Piggle: An Account of the Psychoanalytic Treatment of a Little Girl*. London: Hogarth.

Winnicott, D. (1984) C. Winnicott, R. Shepherd and M. Davis, eds, *Deprivation and Delinquency*. London: Tavistock.

Winnicott, D. (1989) C. Winnicott, R. Shepherd and M. Davis, eds, *Psycho-Analytic Explorations*. London: Karnac; Cambridge, MA: Harvard University Press.

Winnicott, D. and Khan, M. (1953) 'Review of Psychoanalytic Studies of the Personality by W.R.D. Fairbairn', *International Journal of Psycho-Analysis* 34: 329–33. Reprinted in *Psycho-Analytic Explorations*.

INDEX

Index compiled by Judith Lavender